D1261905

# THE
# EPIC

BLOOM'S LITERARY CRITICISM 20TH ANNIVERSARY COLLECTION

## BLOOM'S LITERARY CRITICISM 20TH ANNIVERSARY COLLECTION

Dramatists and Dramas
The Epic
Essayists and Prophets
Novelists and Novels
Poets and Poems
Short Story Writers and Short Stories

BLOOM'S LITERARY CRITICISM 20TH ANNIVERSARY COLLECTION

# THE
# EPIC

Harold Bloom
Sterling Professor of the Humanities
Yale University

CHELSEA HOUSE
PUBLISHERS
A Haights Cross Communications ✦ Company ®

Philadelphia

©2005 by Chelsea House Publishers, a subsidiary of
Haights Cross Communications.

A Haights Cross Communications ⚊ Company ®

www.chelseahouse.com

Introduction © 2005 by Harold Bloom.

Printed and bound in the United States of America.

10  9  8  7  6  5  4  3  2  1

Library of Congress Cataloging-in-Publication Data

Bloom, Harold.
  The epic / Harold Bloom.
     p. cm. -- (Bloom's 20th anniversary collection)
  ISBN 0-7910-8229-6 HC  ISBN 0-7910-8368-3 PB
  1. Epic literature--History and criticism.  I. Title.
  PN56.E65B66 2005
  809'.93358--dc22
                                       2005005379

Cover designed by Takeshi Takahashi
Cover illustration by David Levine
Layout by EJB Publishing Services

# Table of Contents

50.55

# Preface

**Harold Bloom**

I BEGAN EDITING ANTHOLOGIES OF LITERARY CRITICISM FOR CHELSEA House in early 1984, but the first volume, *Edgar Allan Poe: Modern Critical Views*, was published in January, 1985, so this is the twentieth anniversary of a somewhat Quixotic venture. If asked how many separate books have been issued in this project, I no longer have a precise answer, since in so long a span many volumes go out of print, and even whole series have been discontinued. A rough guess would be more than a thousand individual anthologies, a perhaps insane panoply to have been collected and introduced by a single critic.

Some of these books have surfaced in unlikely places: hotel rooms in Bologna and Valencia, Coimbra and Oslo; used-book stalls in Frankfurt and Nice; on the shelves of writers wherever I have gone. A batch were sent by me in answer to a request from a university library in Macedonia, and I have donated some of them, also by request, to a number of prisoners serving life sentences in American jails. A thousand books across a score of years can touch many shores and many lives, and at seventy-four I am a little bewildered at the strangeness of the endeavor, particularly now that it has leaped between centuries.

It cannot be said that I have endorsed every critical essay reprinted, as my editor's notes have made clear. Yet the books have to be reasonably reflective of current critical modes and educational fashions, not all of them provoking my own enthusiasm. But then I am a dinosaur, cheerfully naming myself as "Bloom Brontosaurus Bardolator." I accept only three criteria for greatness in imaginative literature: aesthetic splendor, cognitive power, wisdom. What is now called "relevance" will be in the dustbins in

less than a generation, as our society (somewhat tardily) reforms prejudices
and inequities. The fashionable in literature and criticism always ebbs away
into Period Pieces. Old, well-made furniture survives as valuable antiques,
which is not the destiny of badly constructed imaginings and ideological
exhortings.

Time, which decays and then destroys us, is even more merciless in
obliterating weak novels, poems, dramas, and stories, however virtuous
these may be. Wander into a library and regard the masterpieces of thirty
years ago: a handful of forgotten books have value, but the iniquity of
oblivion has rendered most bestsellers instances of time's revenges. The
other day a friend and former student told me that the first of the Poets
Laureate of twentieth-century America had been Joseph Auslander, concerning whom even my still retentive memory is vacant. These days, Mrs.
Felecia Hemans is studied and taught by a number of feminist Romantic
scholars. Of the poems of that courageous wisdom, who wrote to support
her brood, I remember only the opening line of "Casabianca" but only
because Mark Twain added one of his very own to form a couplet:

> The boy stood on the burning deck
> *Eating peanuts by the peck.*

Nevertheless, I do not seek to affirm the social inutility of literature,
though I admire Oscar Wilde's grand declaration: "All art is perfectly useless." Shakespeare may well stand here for the largest benign effect of the
highest literature: properly appreciated, it can heal part of the violence that
is built into every society whatsoever. In my own judgment, Walt
Whitman is the central writer yet brought forth by the Americas—North,
Central, South, Caribbean—whether in English, Spanish, Portuguese,
French, Yiddish or other tongues. And Walt Whitman is a healer, a poet-
prophet who discovered his pragmatic vocation by serving as a volunteer,
unpaid wound-dresser and nurse in the Civil War hospitals of Washington,
D.C. To read and properly understand Whitman can be an education in
self-reliance and in the cure of your own consciousness.

The function of literary criticism, as I conceive it in my gathering old
age, is primarily appreciation, in Walter Pater's sense, which fuses analysis
and evaluation. When Pater spoke of "art for art's sake' he included in
the undersong of his declaration what D.H. Lawrence meant by "art for
life's sake," Lawrence, the most provocative of post-Whitmanian vitalists,
has now suffered a total eclipse in the higher education of the English-
speaking nations. Feminists have outlawed him with their accusations of

misogyny, and they describe him as desiring women to renounce sexual pleasure. On this supposed basis, students lose the experience of reading one of the major authors of the twentieth century, at once an unique novelist, storyteller, poet, critic, and prophet.

An enterprise as vast as Chelsea House Literary Criticism doubtless reflects both the flaws and the virtues of its editor. Comprehensiveness has been a goal throughout, and I have (for the most part) attempted to set aside many of my own literary opinions. I sorrow when the market keeps an important volume out of print, though I am solaced by the example of my idol, Dr. Samuel Johnson, in his *Lives of the Poets*. The booksellers (who were both publishers and retailers) chose the poets, and Johnson was able to say exactly what he thought of each. Who remembers such worthies as Yalden, Sprat, Roscommon, and Stepney? It would be invidious for me to name the contemporary equivalents, but their name is legion.

I have been more fully educated by this quest for comprehensivness, which taught me how to write for a larger audience. Literary criticism is both an individual and communal mode. It has its titans: Johnson, Coleridge, Lessing, Goethe, Hazlitt, Sainte-Beuve, Pater, Curtius, Valèry, Frye, Empson, Kenneth Burke are among them. But most of those I reprint cannot be of that eminence: one makes a heap of all that can be found. Over a lifetime in reading and teaching one learns so much from so many that no one can be certain of her or his intellectual debts. Hundreds of those I have reprinted I never will meet, but they have helped enlighten me, insofar as I have been capable of learning from a host of other minds.

# Introduction

**Harold Bloom**

THERE NO LONGER IS A CLEAR GENRE WE CAN CALL "THE EPIC", IN THE sense that Homer, Virgil, and Milton composed epics. In the course of a long career as a critic, I have written commentaries upon a number of "heroic poems" not included here. Among them, are Shelley's *Prometheus Unbound*, Keats's two *Hyperion* fragments, Tennyson's *Idylls of the King*, and the three visionary "brief epics" of William Blake: *The Four Zoas, Milton,* and *Jerusalem*.

I find though that this volume has its own implicit design, starting as it does with the great Hebrew prose epic of the Yahwist or J Writer, which we know as the earliest layer of the palimpsest now called Genesis, Exodus, and Numbers, and going on to five great panoramic prose epics: *Moby-Dick, War and Peace, In Search of Lost Time, The Magic Mountain,* and *Ulysses*. After these five titanic books come the two modern American brief epics, *The Waste Land* and *The Bridge*.

In the earlier periods, the works surveyed are extraordinarily diverse: *Beowulf, The Tale of Genji, The Divine Comedy, The Canterbury Tales, The Faerie Queene, The Prelude, The Rime of the Ancient Mariner, Song of Myself.* There are nineteen "epics" in this book, and they cover three thousand years from the J Writer to Hart Crane. Are any common features to be located in them, particularly in the *praxis* of the critic who meditates upon them?

As I interpret the Yahwist, she (or he) is the most sophisticated ironist here, a startling judgment when Chaucer and Thomas Mann also are discussed in these pages, not to mention Lady Murasaki and Marcel Proust. However broadly you take the term "epic", irony initially seems to be a curious tonality to invoke. Do heroic vision and saga say one thing while always meaning another? Hamlet, a hero of consciousness but not of epic, almost never says what he means and only rarely means what he says. Jacob who becomes Israel is an ironist, even when heroically he wrestles all the night, holding off the angel of death, to win the blessing of more life into a time without boundaries.

What defines epic, ancient and modern, for me is heroism, which transcends irony. The heroism of Dante the Pilgrim, of Milton in *Paradise Lost's* four great invocations, of Ahab and Walt Whitman as American questers, can be defined as persistence. Call it the persistence of vision, in which everything beheld is intensified by a spiritual aura. I never understood why Captain Ahab, Promethean defier of the tyranny of nature, is regarded by so many as a Macbeth-like villain, though he indeed echoes Macbeth. The epic hero is *contra naturam*: his quest is antithetical, from Jacob's refusal of dying through the violence of Achilles, who kills because he is not immortal, or to Hart Crane the Pilgrim, making his song one Bridge of Fire in defiance of America's failure to fulfill the prophecies of Walt Whitman.

Proust and Joyce, as creators, are more heroic than their protagonists, but so was Tolstoy, until he found an ultimate hero in the Chechen Hadji Murad, in a late short novel that, for me, is the culmination of heroic tradition. Even the confused amorist, Murasaki's Genji, is heroic in his persistent longing. A longing for sustained vision may be the authentic mark of achieved epic.

# Genesis and Exodus

To my best knowledge, it was the Harvard historian of religion George Foot Moore who first called the religion of the rabbis of the second century of the Common Era "normative Judaism." Let me simplify by centering on one of those rabbis, surely the grandest: normative Judaism is the religion of Akiba. That vigorous scholar, patriot, and martyr may be regarded as the standard by which any other Jewish religious figure must be judged. If your faith and praxis share enough with Akiba's, then you too are a representative of normative Judaism. If not, then probably not. There is a charming legend in which Moses attends Akiba's seminar, and goes away baffled by the sage's interpretation—of Moses! But the deepest implication of the legend, as I read it, is that Akiba's strong misreading of Moses was in no way weakened by the Mosaic bafflement.

The Great Original of the literary and oral traditions that merged into normative Judaism was the writer scholarly convention rather wonderfully chose to call "J." Since Kafka is the most legitimate descendant of one aspect of the antithetical J (Tolstoy and the early, pre-Coleridgean Wordsworth are the most authentic descendants of J's other side), I find it useful to adopt the formula "from J to K," in order to describe the uncanny or antithetical elements in J's narratives. The J who could have written *Hadji Murad* or *The Tale of Margaret* was the inevitable fountainhead of what eventually became normative Judaism. But this first, strongest, and still somehow most Jewish of all our writers also could have written "The Hunter Gracchus" or even "Josephine the Singer and the Mouse Folk." Indeed he wrote uncannier stories than Kafka lived to write. How those stories ever could have been acceptable or even comprehensible to the P authors or the Deuteronomist, to the Academy of Ezra or the Pharisees, let alone to Akiba and his colleagues, is a mystery that I have been trying to

1

clarify by developing a critical concept of what I call "facticity," a kind of brute contingency by which an author's strength blinds and incarcerates a tradition of belated readership. But here I primarily want to describe the uncanniness of J's work, so as to break out of facticity, insofar as I am able to do so.

By "the uncanny" I mean Freud's concept, since that appears to be the authentic modern version of what once was called the Sublime. Freud defines "the uncanny" as being "in reality nothing new or foreign, but something familiar and old-established in the mind that has been estranged only by the process of repression." Since I myself, as a critic, am obsessed with the Sublime or Freud's "uncanny," I realize that my reading of any Sublime work or fragment is always dependent upon an estrangement, in which the repressed returns upon me to end that estrangement, but only momentarily. The uncanniness of the Yahwist exceeds that of all other writers, because in him both the estrangement and the return achieve maximum force.

Of course J himself is considered to be a fiction, variously referred to by scholars as a school, a tradition, a document, and a hypothesis. Well, Homer is perhaps a fiction too, and these days the slaves of critical fashion do not weary of proclaiming the death of the author, or at least the reduction of every author to the status of a Nietzschean fiction. But J is pragmatically the author-of-authors, in that his authority and originality constitute a difference that has made a difference. The teller of the tales of Jacob and of Joseph, of Moses and the Exodus, is a writer more inescapable than Shakespeare and more pervasive in our consciousness than Freud. J's only cultural rival would be an unlikely compound of Homer and Plato. Plato's contest with Homer seems to me to mark one of the largest differences between the ancient Greeks and the Hebrews. The agon for the mind of Athens found no equivalent in Jerusalem, and so the Yahwist still remains the mind of Jerusalem, everywhere that Jerusalem happens to be.

I do not believe that J was a fiction, and indeed J troubles me because his uncanniness calls into question my own conviction that every writer is belated, and so is always an inter-poet. J's freedom from belatedness rivals Shakespeare's, which is to say that J's originality is as intense as Shakespeare's. But J wrote twenty-five hundred years before Shakespeare, and that time-span bewilders comparison. I am going to sketch J's possible circumstances and purposes, in order to hazard a description of J's tone or of the uncanniness of his stance as a writer. Not much in my sketch will flout received scholarship, but necessarily I will have to go beyond the present state of biblical scholarship, since it cannot even decide precisely which texts are J's, or even revised by others from J. My attempt at transcending scholarship is simply a literary critic's final reliance upon her or his own sense of a text, or what I have called the necessity of misreading. No critic, whatever her or his moldiness or skepticism, can evade a Nietzschean will to power over a text, because interpretation is at last nothing else. The text, even if it was written that morning, and shown by its poet to the critic at high noon, is already lost in time, as lost as the Yahwist. Time says, "It was," and authentic criticism, as Nietzsche implied, is necessarily pervaded by a will for revenge against time's "it was." No interpreter can suspend the will to relational knowledge for more than an isolated moment, and since all narrative and all poetry are also interpretation, all writing manifests such a will.

Solomon the King, nowhere of course overtly mentioned by J, is the dominant contemporary force in the context of J's writing. I would go further, and as a pious Stevensian would say that Solomon is J's motive for metaphor. The reign of Solomon ended in the year 922 before the Common Era, and J quite possibly wrote either in Solomon's last years, or—more likely, I think—shortly thereafter. One can venture that Solomon was to J what Elizabeth was to Shakespeare, an idea of order, as crucial in J's Jerusalem as it was in Shakespeare's London. The Imperial Theme is J's countersong, though J's main burden is a heroic and agonistic past represented by David the King, while his implied judgment upon the imperial present is at best skeptical, since he implies also an agonistic future. J's vision of agon centers his uncanny stance, accounting for his nearly unique mode of irony.

How much of J's actual text we have lost to the replacement tactics of redactors we cannot know, but biblical scholarship has not persuaded me that either the so-called Elohistic or the Priestly redactors provide fully coherent visions of their own, except perhaps for the Priestly first chapter of Genesis, which is so startling a contrast to J's account of how we all got started. But let me sketch the main contours of J's narrative, as we appear to have it. Yahweh begins his Creation in the first harsh Judean spring, before the first rain comes down. Water wells up from the earth, and Yahweh molds Adam out of the red clay, breathing into the earthling's nostrils a breath of the divine life. Then come the stories we think we know: Eve, the serpent, Cain and Abel, Seth, Noah and the Flood, the tower of Babel, and something utterly new with Abraham. From Abraham on, the main sequence again belongs to J: the Covenant, Ishmael, Yahweh at Mamre and on the road to Sodom, Lot, Isaac and the Akedah, Rebecca, Esau and Jacob, the tales of Jacob, Tamar, the story of Joseph and his brothers, and then the Mosaic account. Moses, so far as I can tell, meant much less to J than he did to the normative redactors, and

so the J strand in Exodus and Numbers is even more laconic than J tend-
ed to be earlier.

In J's Exodus we find the oppression of the Jews, the birth of Moses,
his escape to Midian, the burning bush and the instruction, the weird mur-
derous attack by Yahweh upon Moses, the audiences with Pharaoh, the
plagues, and the departure, flight, and crossing. Matters become sparser
with Israel in the wilderness, at the Sinai covenant, and then with the dis-
sensions and the battles in Numbers. J flares up finally on a grand scale in
the seriocomic Balaam and Balak episode, but that is not the end of J's
work, even as we have it. The Deuteronomist memorably incorporates J in
his chapters 31 and 34 dealing with the death of Moses. I give here in
sequence the opening and the closing of what we hear J's Yahweh speaking
aloud, first to Adam and last to Moses: "Of every tree in the garden you
are free to eat; but as for the tree of knowledge of good and bad, you must
not eat of it; for as soon as you eat of it, you shall die." "This is the land of
which I swore to Abraham, Isaac, and Jacob, 'I will give it to your offspring.' I have let you see it with your own eyes, but you shall not cross
there." Rhetorically, the two speeches share the same cruel pattern of
power: "Here it is; it is yours and yet it is not yours." Akin to J's counter-
pointing of Yahweh's first and last speeches is his counterparting of
Yahweh's first and last actions: "Yahweh formed man from the dust of the
earth," and "Yahweh buried him, Moses, in the valley in the land of Moab,
near Beth-peor; and no one knows his burial place to this day." From
Adam to Moses is from earth to earth; Yahweh molds us and he buries us,
and both actions are done with his own hands. As it was with Adam and
Moses, so it was with David and with Solomon, and with those who come
and will come after Solomon. J is the harshest and most monitory of writers, and his Yahweh is an uncanny god, who takes away much of what he
gives, and who is beyond any standard of measurement. And yet what I
have said about J so far is not even part of the truth; isolated, all by itself,
it is not true at all, for J is a writer who exalts man, and who has most peculiar relations with God. Gorky once said of Tolstoy that Tolstoy's relation
to God reminded him of the Russian proverb "Two bears in one den." J's
relation to his uncanny Yahweh frequently reminds me of my favorite
Yiddish apothegm: "Sleep faster, we need the pillows." J barely can keep up
with Yahweh, though J's Jacob almost can, while J's Moses cannot keep up
at all. Since what is most problematic about J's writing is Yahweh, I suggest
we take a closer look at J's Yahweh than the entire normative and modern
scholarly tradition has been willing or able to take. Homer and Dante,
Shakespeare and Milton, hardly lacked audacity in representing what may
be beyond representation, but J was both bolder and shrewder than any

other writer at inventing speeches and actions for God Himself. Only J convinces us that he knows precisely how and when Yahweh speaks; Isaiah compares poorly to J in this, while the Milton of *Paradise Lost*, book 3, hardly rates even as an involuntary parodist of J.

I am moved to ask a question which the normative tradition—Judaic, Christian, and even secular—cannot ask: What is J's stance toward Yahweh? I can begin an answer by listing all that it is not: creating Yahweh, J's primary emotions do not include awe, fear, wonder, much surprise, or even love. J *sounds* rather matter-of-fact, but that is part of J's unique mode of irony. By turns, J's stance toward Yahweh is appreciative, wryly apprehensive, intensely interested, and above all attentive and alert. Toward Yahweh, J is perhaps a touch wary; J is always *prepared to be surprised*. What J knows is that Yahweh is Sublime or "uncanny," incommensurate yet rather agonistic, curious and lively, humorous yet irascible, and all too capable of suddenly violent action. But J's Yahweh is rather *heimlich* also; he sensibly avoids walking about in the Near Eastern heat, preferring the cool of the evening, and he likes to sit under the terebinths at Mamre, devouring roast calf and curds. J would have laughed at his normative descendants—Christian, Jewish, secular, scholarly—who go on calling his representations of Yahweh "anthropomorphic," when they should be calling his representations of Jacob "theomorphic."

"The anthropomorphic" always has been a misleading concept, and probably was the largest single element affecting the long history of the redaction of J that evolved into normative Judaism. Most modern scholars, Jewish and Gentile alike, cannot seem to accept the fact that there was no Jewish theology before Philo. "Jewish theology," despite its long history from Philo to Franz Rosenzweig, is therefore an oxymoron, particularly when applied to Biblical texts, and most particularly when applied to J. J's Yahweh is an uncanny personality, and not at all a concept. Yahweh sometimes *seems* to behave like us, but because Yahweh and his sculpted creature, Adam, are incommensurate, this remains a mere seeming. Sometimes, and always within limits, we behave like Yahweh, and not necessarily because we will to do so. There is a true sense in which John Calvin was as strong a reader of J as he more clearly was of Job, a sense displayed in the paradox of the Protestant Yahweh who entraps his believers by an impossible double injunction, which might be phrased: "Be like me, but don't you dare to be too like me!" In J, the paradox emerges only gradually, and does not reach its climax until the theophany on Sinai. Until Sinai, J's Yahweh addresses himself only to a handful, to his elite: Adam, Noah, Abraham, Jacob, Joseph, and, by profound implication, David. But at Sinai, we encounter the crisis of J's writing, as we will see.

What is theomorphic about Adam, Noah, Abraham, Jacob, Joseph? I think the question should be rephrased: What is Davidic about them? About Joseph, everything, and indeed J's Joseph I read as a fictive representation of David, rather in the way Virgil's Divine Child represents Augustus, except that J is working on a grand scale with Joseph, bringing to perfection what may have been an old mode of romance.

I have called Solomon J's motive for metaphor, but that calling resounds with Nietzsche's motive for all trope: the desire to be different, the desire to be elsewhere. For J, the difference, the elsewhere, is David. J's agonistic elitism, the struggle for the blessing, is represented by Abraham, above all by Jacob, and by Tamar also. But the bearer of the blessing is David, and I have ventured the surmise that J's Joseph is a portrait of David. Though this surmise is, I think, original, the centering of J's humanism upon the implied figure of David is not, of course, original with me. It is a fundamental postulate of the school of Gerhard von Rad, worked out in detail by theologians like Hans Walter Wolff and Walter Brueggemann. Still, a phrase like Wolff's "the Kerygma of the Yahwist" makes me rather uneasy, since J is no more a theologian than he is a priest or prophet. Freud, like St. Paul, has a message, but J, like Shakespeare, does not. J *is* literature and not "confession," which of course is not true of his redactors. They were on the road to Akiba, but J, always in excess of the normative, was no quester.

I find no traces of cult in J, and I am puzzled that so many read as kerygmatic Yahweh's words to Abram in Gen. 12:3: "So, then, all the families of the earth can gain a blessing in you." The blessing, in J, simply does not mean what it came to mean in his redactors and in the subsequent normative tradition. To gain a blessing, particularly through the blessing that becomes Abraham's, is in J to join oneself to that elitest agon which culminated in the figure of the agonistic hero, David. To be blessed means ultimately that one's name will not be scattered, and the remembered name will retain life into a time without boundaries. The blessing then is temporal, and not spatial, as it was in Homer and in the Greeks after him, who like his heroes struggled for the foremost place. And a temporal blessing, like the kingdom in Shakespeare, finds its problematic aspect in the vicissitudes of descendants.

Jacob is J's central man, whose fruition, deferred in the beloved Joseph, because given to Judah, has come just before J's time in the triumph of David. I think that Brueggemann is imaginatively accurate in his hypothesis that David represented, for J, a new kind of man, almost a new Adam, the man whom Yahweh (in 2 Sam. 7) had decided to trust. Doubtless we cannot exclude from our considerations the Messianic tradition that the normative, Jewish and Christian, were to draw out from those two great contemporary writers, J and the author of 2 Samuel. But J does not have any such Messianic consciousness about David. Quite the reverse: for him, we can surmise, David had been and was the elite image; not a harbinger of a greater vision to come, but a fully human being who already had exhausted the full range and vitality of man's possibilities. If, as Brueggemann speculates, J's tropes of exile (Gen. 3:24, 4:12, 11:8) represent the true images of the Solomonic present, then I would find J's prime Davidic trope in Jacob's return to Canaan, marked by the all-night, all-in wrestling match that concentrates Jacob's name forever as Israel. The Davidic glory then is felt most strongly in Jacob's theomorphic triumph, rendered so much the more poignant by his permanent crippling: "The sun rose upon him as he passed Penuel, limping on his hip."

If Jacob is Israel as the father, then David, through the trope of Joseph, is Jacob's or Israel's truest son. What then is Davidic about J's Jacob? I like the late E.A. Speiser's surmise that J personally knew his great contemporary, the writer who gave us, in 2 Samuel, the history of David and his immediate successors. J's Joseph reads to me like a lovingly ironic parody of the David of the court historian. What matters most about David, as that model narrative presents him, is not only his charismatic intensity, but the marvelous gratuity of Yahweh's *hesed*, his Election-love for this most heroic of his favorites. To no one in J's text does Yahweh speak so undialectically as he does through Nathan to David in 2 Samuel 7:12–16:

> When your days are done and you lie with your fathers, I will raise up your offspring after you, one of your own issue, and I will establish his kingship. He shall build a house for My name, and I will establish his royal throne forever. I will be a father to him, and he shall be a son to Me. When he does wrong, I will chastise him with the rod of men and the affliction of mortals; but I will never withdraw My favor from him as I withdrew it from Saul, whom I removed to make room for you. Your house and your kingship shall ever be secure before you; your throne shall be established forever.

The blessing in J, as I have written elsewhere, is always agonistic, and Jacob is J's supreme agonist. But J makes a single exception for Joseph, and clearly with the reader's eye centered upon David. From the womb on to the ford of the Jabbok, Jacob is an agonist, and until that night encounter at Penuel by no means a heroic one. His agon, as I've said, is for the temporal blessing that will prevail into a time without boundaries; and so it never resembles the Homeric or the Athenian contest for the foremost place, a kind of topological or spatial blessing. In J, the struggle is for the uncanny gift of life, for the breath of Yahweh that transforms *adamah* into Adam. True, David struggles, and suffers, but J's Joseph serenely voyages through all vicissitudes, as though J were intimating that David's agon had been of a new kind, one in which the obligation was wholly and voluntarily on Yahweh's side in the Covenant. Jacob the father wrestles lifelong, and is permanently crippled by the climactic match with a nameless one among the Elohim whom I interpret as the baffled angel of death, who learns that Israel lives, and always will survive. Joseph the son charms reality, even as David seems to have charmed Yahweh.

But Jacob, I surmise, was J's signature, and while the portrait of the Davidic Joseph manifests J's wistfulness, the representation of Jacob may well be J's self-portrait as the great writer of Israel. My earlier question would then become: What is Davidic about J himself, not as a person perhaps, but certainly as an author? My first observation here would have to be this apparent paradox: J is anything but a religious writer, unlike all his revisionists and interpreters, and David is anything but a religious personality, despite having become the paradigm for all Messianic speculation, both Jewish and Christian. Again I am in the wake of von Rad and his school, but with this crucial Bloomian swerve: J and David are not religious, just as Freud, for all his avowedly antireligious polemic, is finally nothing but religious. Freud's overdetermination of meaning, his emphasis upon primal repression or a flight from representation—before, indeed, there was anything to represent—establishes Freud as normatively Jewish despite himself. Turn it and turn it, for everything is in it, the sage ben Bag Bag said of Torah, and Freud says the same of the psyche. If there is sense in everything, then everything that is going to happen has happened already, and so reality is already in the past and there never can be anything new. Freud's stance toward psychic history is the normative rabbinical stance toward Jewish history, and if Akiba is the paradigm for what it is to be religious, then the professedly scientistic Freud is as religious as Akiba, if we are speaking of the Jewish religion. But J, like the court historian's David of 2 Samuel, is quite Jewish without being at all religious, in the belated normative sense. For the uncanny J, and for the path-breaking David, everything that matters most is perpetually new.

But this is true of J's Jacob also, as it is of Abraham, even Isaac, and certainly Tamar—all live at the edge of life rushing onwards, never in a static present but always in the dynamism of J's Yahweh, whose incessant temporality generates anxious expectations in nearly every fresh sentence of certain passages. This is again the Kafkan aspect of J, though it is offset by J's strong sense of human freedom, a sense surpassing its Homeric parallels. What becomes theodicy in J's revisionists down to Milton is for J not at all a perplexity. Since J has no concept of Yahweh but rather a sense of Yahweh's peculiar personality, the interventions of Yahweh in primal family history do not impinge upon his elite's individual freedom. So we have the memorable and grimly funny argument between Yahweh and Abraham as they walk together down the road to Sodom. Abraham wears Yahweh down until Yahweh quite properly begins to get exasperated. The shrewd courage and humanity of Abraham convince me that in the Akedah the redactors simply eliminated J's text almost completely. As I read the Hebrew, there is an extraordinary gap between the Elohistic language and the sublime invention of the story. J's Abraham would have argued far more tenaciously with Yahweh for his son's life than he did in defense of the inhabitants of the sinful cities of the plain, and here the revisionists may have defrauded us of J's uncanny greatness at its height.

But how much they *have* left us which the normative tradition has been incapable of assimilating! I think the best way of seeing this is to juxtapose with J the Pharisaic Book of Jubilees, oddly called also "the Little Genesis," though it is prolix and redundant in every tiresome way. Written about one hundred years before the Common Era, Jubilees is a normative travesty of Genesis, far more severely, say, than Chronicles is a normative reduction of 2 Samuel. But though he writes so boringly, what is wonderfully illuminating about the author of Jubilees is that he totally eradicates J's text. Had he set out deliberately to remove everything idiosyncratic about J's share in Torah, he could have done no more thorough a job. Gone altogether is J's creation story of Yahweh molding the red clay into Adam and then breathing life into his own image. Gone as well is Yahweh at Mamre, where only angels now appear to Abraham and Sarah, and there is no dispute on the road to Sodom. And the Satanic prince of angels, Mastema, instigates Yahweh's trial of Abraham in the Akedah. Jacob and Esau do not wrestle in the womb, and Abraham prefers Jacob, though even the author of Jubilees does not go so far as to deny Isaac's greater love for Esau. Gone, alas totally gone, is J's sublime invention of the night wrestling at Penuel. Joseph lacks all charm and mischief, necessarily, and the agony of Jacob, and the subsequent grandeur of the reunion, are vanished away. Most revealingly, the uncanniest moment in J, Yahweh's attempt to murder Moses en route to Egypt, becomes Mastema's act. And wholly absent is J's most enigmatic vision, the Sinai theophany, which is replaced by the safe removal of J's too-lively Yahweh back to a sedate dwelling in the high heavens.

J's originality was too radical to be absorbed, and yet abides even now as the originality of a Yahweh who will not dwindle down into the normative Godhead of the Jews, Christians, and Muslims. Because J cared more for personality than for morality, and cared not at all for cult, his legacy is a disturbing sense that, as Blake phrased it, forms of worship have been chosen from poetic tales. J was no theologian and yet not a maker of saga or epic, and again not a historian, and not even a storyteller as such. We have no description of J that will fit, just as we have no idea of God that will contain his irrepressible Yahweh. I want to test these observations by a careful account of J's Sinai theophany, where his Yahweh is more problematic than scholarship has been willing to perceive.

Despite the truncation, indeed the possible mutilation of J's account of the Sinai theophany, more than enough remains to mark it as the crisis or crossing-point of his work. For the first time, his Yahweh is overwhelmingly self-contradictory, rather than dialectical, ironic, or even crafty. The moment of crisis turns upon Yahweh's confrontation with the Israelite host. Is he to allow himself to be seen by them? How direct is his self-representation to be? Mamre and the road to Sodom suddenly seem estranged, or as though they never were. It is not that here Yahweh is presented less anthropomorphically, but that J's Moses (let alone those he leads) is far less theomorphic or Davidic than J's Abraham and J's Jacob, and certainly less theomorphic or Davidic than J's Joseph. Confronting his agonistic and theomorphic elite, from Abraham to the implied presence of David, Yahweh is both canny and uncanny. But Moses is neither theomorphic nor agonistic. J's Sinai theophany marks the moment of the blessings transition from the elite to the entire Israelite host, and in that transition a true anxiety of representation breaks forth in J's work for the first time.

I follow Martin Noth's lead, in the main, as to those passages in Exodus 19 and 24 that are clearly J's, though my ear accepts as likely certain moments he considers only probable or at least quite possible. Here are Exod. 19:9–15, 18, 20–25, literally rendered:

> Yahweh said to Moses: "I will come to you in a thick cloud, that the people may hear that I speak with you and that they may trust you forever afterwards." Moses then reported the people's words to Yahweh, and Yahweh said to Moses: "Go to the people and warn them to be continent today and tomorrow. Let them wash their clothes. Let them be prepared for the third day, for on the third day Yahweh will descend upon Mount Sinai, in the sight of all the people. You shall set limits for the people all around, saying: 'Beware of climbing the mountain or

touching the border of it. Whoever touches the mountain shall be put to death; no hand shall touch him, but either he shall be stoned or shot; whether beast or man, he shall not live.' When there is a loud blast of the ram's horn, then they may ascend the mountain."

Moses came down from the mountain unto the people and warned them to remain pure, and they washed their clothes. And Moses said to the people: "Prepare for the third day; do not approach a woman."

Yahweh will come at first in a thick cloud, that the people may hear yet presumably not see him; nevertheless, on the third day he will come down upon Sinai "in the sight of all the people." Sinai will be taboo, but is this only a taboo of touch? What about seeing Yahweh? I suspect that an ellipsis, wholly characteristic of J's rhetorical strength, then intervened, again characteristically filled in by the E redactors as verses 16 and 17, and again as verse 19; but in verse 18 clearly we hear J's grand tone:

Now Mount Sinai was all in smoke, for the Lord had come down upon it in fire; the smoke rose like the smoke of a kiln, and all the people trembled violently.

Whether people or mountain tremble hardly matters in this great trope of immanent power. Yahweh, as we know, is neither the fire nor in the fire, for the ultimate trope is the *makom*: Yahweh is the place of the world, but the world is not his place, and so Yahweh is also the place of the fire, but the fire is not his place. And so J touches the heights of his own Sublime, though himself troubled by an anxiety of representation previously unknown to him, an anxiety of touch and, for the first time, of sight:

Yahweh came down upon Mount Sinai, on the mountain top, and Yahweh called Moses to the mountain top, and Moses went up. Yahweh said to Moses: "Go down, warn the people not to break through to gaze at Yahweh, lest many of them die. And the priests who come near Yahweh must purify themselves, lest Yahweh break forth against them." But Moses said to Yahweh: "The people cannot come up to Mount Sinai, for You warned us when You said: 'Set limits about the mountain and render it holy.'" So Yahweh said to Moses: "Go down and come back with Aaron, but do not allow the priests or the people to break through to come up to Yahweh, lest Yahweh break out against them." And Moses descended to the people and spoke to them.

However much we have grown accustomed to J, he has not prepared us for this. Never before has Yahweh, bent upon Covenant, been a potential catastrophe as well as a potential blessing. But then, certainly the difference is in the movement from an elite to a whole people. If, as I suspect, the pragmatic covenant for J was the Davidic or humanistic or theomorphic covenant, then the most salient poetic meaning here was contemporary, whether Solomonic or just after. The true covenant, without anxiety or the problematic of representation, was agonistic: with Abraham, with Jacob, with Joseph, with David, but neither with Moses nor with Solomon, and so never with the mass of the people, whether at Sinai or at J's own moment of writing. J is as elitist as Shakespeare, or as Freud; none of the three was exactly a writer on the left. Yahweh himself, in J's vision, becomes dangerously confused in the anxious expectations of at once favoring and threatening the host of the people, rather than the individuals, that he has chosen. When Moses reminds Yahweh that Sinai is off limits anyway, Yahweh evidently is too preoccupied and too little taken with Moses even to listen, and merely repeats his warning that he may be uncontrollable, even by himself.

As our text now stands, the revisionists take over, and the Commandments are promulgated. I surmise that in J's original text the Commandments, however phrased, came *after* some fragments of J that we still have in what is now Exodus 24:

> Then Yahweh said to Moses: "Come up to Yahweh, with Aaron, Nadab and Abihu, and seventy elders of Israel, and bow low but from afar. And only Moses shall come near Yahweh. The others shall not come near, and the people shall not come up with him at all.

Then Moses and Aaron, Nadab and Abihu, and seventy elders of Israel went up, and they saw the God of Israel; under His feet there was the likeness of a pavement of sapphire, like the very sky for purity. Yet He did not raise His hand against the leaders of the Israelites; they beheld God, and they ate and drank.

This is again J at his uncanniest, the true Western Sublime, and so the truest challenge to a belated Longinian critic like myself. We are at Mamre again, in a sense, except that here the seventy-four who constitute an elite (of sorts) eat and drink, as did the Elohim and Yahweh at Mamre, while now Yahweh watches enigmatically, and (rather wonderfully) is watched. And again, J is proudly self-contradictory, or perhaps even dialectical, his irony being beyond my interpretive ken, whereas his Yahweh is so outrageously self-contradictory that I do not know where precisely to begin in reading the phases of this difference. But rather than entering that labyrinth—of who may or may not see Yahweh, or how, or when—I choose instead to test the one marvelous visual detail against the Second Commandment. Alas, we evidently do not have J's phrasing here, but there is a strength in the diction that may reflect an origin in J:

> You shall not make for yourself a sculptured image, or any likeness of what is in the heavens above, or on the earth below, or in the waters under the earth.

Surely we are to remember J's Yahweh, who formed the *adam* from the dust of the *adamah* and blew into his sculptured image's nostrils the breath of life. The *zelem* is forbidden to us, as our creation. But had it been forbidden to J, at least until now? And even now, does not J make for himself, and so also for us, a likeness of what is in the heavens above? The seventy-four eaters and drinkers saw with their own eyes the God of Israel, and they saw another likeness also: "under His feet there was the likeness of a pavement of sapphire, like the very sky for purity." Why precisely this visual image, from this greatest of writers who gives us so very few visual images, as compared to images that are auditory, dynamic, motor urgencies? I take it that J, and not the Hebrew language, inaugurated the extraordinary process of describing any object primarily by telling us not how it looked, but how it was *made*, wonderfully and fearfully made. But here J describes what is seen, not indeed Yahweh in whole or in part, but what we may call Yahweh's chosen stance.

Stance in writing is also tone, and the tone of this passage is crucial but perhaps beyond our determination. Martin Buber, as an eloquent rhetorician, described it with great vividness but with rather too much interpretive confidence in his book, *Moses*. The seventy-four representatives of Israel are personalized by this theorist of dialogical personalism:

> They have presumably wandered through clinging, hanging mist before dawn; and at the very moment they reach their goal, the swaying darkness tears asunder (as I myself happened to witness once) and dissolves except for one cloud already transparent with the hue of the still unrisen sun. The sapphire

proximity of the heavens overwhelms the aged shepherds of the Delta, who have never before tasted, who have never been given the slightest idea, of what is shown in the play of early light over the summits of the mountains. And this precisely is perceived by the representatives of the liberated tribes as that which lies under the feet of their enthroned *Melek*.

Always ingenious and here refreshingly naturalistic, Buber nevertheless neglects what he sometimes recognized: J's uncanniness. Buber's motive, as he says, is to combat two opposed yet equally reductive views of Biblical theophanies: that they are either supernatural miracles or else impressive fantasies. But had J wanted us to believe that the seventy-four elders of Israel saw only a natural radiance, he would have written rather differently. The commentary of Brevard Childs is very precise: "The text is remarkable for its bluntness: 'They saw the God of Israel.'" Childs adds that from the Septuagint on to Maimonides there is a consistent toning down of the statement's directness. Surely the directness is realized yet more acutely if we recall that this is Yahweh's only appearance in the Hebrew Bible where he says absolutely nothing. J's emphasis is clear: the seventy-four are on Sinai to eat and drink in Yahweh's presence, while they stare at him, and he presumably stares right back. But that confronts us with the one visual detail J provides: "under His feet there was the likeness of a pavement of sapphire, like the very sky for purity." J gives us a great trope, which all commentary down to the scholarly present weakly misreads by literalization. J, himself a strong misreader of tradition, demands strong misreadings, and so I venture one here. Let us forget all such notions as Yahweh standing so high up that he seems to stand on the sky, or the old fellows never having seen early light in the mountains before. J is elliptical always; that is crucial to his rhetorical stance. He is too wily to say what you would see, if you sat there in awe, eating and drinking while you saw Yahweh. Indeed, we must assume that Yahweh is sitting, but nothing whatsoever is said about a throne, and J after all is not Isaiah or Micaiah ben Imlah or Ezekiel or John Milton. As at Mamre, Yahweh sits upon the ground, and yet it is as though the sky were beneath his feet. May not this drastic reversal of perspective represent a vertigo of vision on the part of the seventy-four? To see the God of Israel is to see as though the world had been turned upside down. And that indeed Yahweh *is* seen, *contra* Buber, we can know through J's monitory comment: "Yet He did not raise His hand against the leaders of the Israelites; they beheld God, and they ate and drank." The sublimity is balanced *not* by a Covenant meal, as all the scholars solemnly assert, but by a picnic on Sinai.

That this uncanny festivity contradicts Yahweh's earlier warnings is not J's confusion, nor something produced by his redactors, but is a dramatic confusion that J's Yahweh had to manifest if his blessing was to be extended from elite individuals to an entire people. Being incommensurate, Yahweh cannot be said to have thus touched his limits, but in the little more that J wrote Yahweh is rather less lively than he had been. His heart, as J hints, was not with Moses but with David, who was to come. J's heart, I venture as I close, was also not with Moses, nor even with Joseph, as David's surrogate, and not really with Yahweh either. It was with Jacob at the Jabbok, obdurately confronting death in the shape of a time-obsessed nameless one from among the Elohim. Wrestling heroically to win the temporal blessing of a new name, Israel—that is uniquely J's own agon.

II

Martin Noth termed the Covenant meal—what I have called a picnic on Sinai—not only the most original element of the Sinai narrative, but also noted that the silent bystanders who appear alongside of Moses in the E version seem to be competitors of Moses, since they are representatives of the host, and not of the elite. But that introduces the largest irony in the relation of J to the normative tradition. Nahum M. Sarna rightly emphasizes the Israelite innovation that marks the Sinai Covenant: there is no analogy in ancient Near Eastern history to the idea "that God and an entire people become parties to the Covenant." If my reading of J is imaginatively accurate, then J himself resisted what is central to his people's vision of itself. I think that returns one to the puzzle of J's Moses, who so clearly is not Davidic or theomorphic, unlike J's grand sequence of Abraham, Jacob, and Joseph.

Though J is, to me, no theologian, I agree with Noth's emphasis when he remarks that "the entire weight of the theology of J rests upon the beginning of his narrative." No writer, fittingly, ever has valued origins as highly as J. For him, to tell how the people were formed is to tell also what they are and what they will be. It is an oddity that J's Moses is a latecomer, while J's implied David, in Joseph, returns to the theomorphic origins. I think that accounts for why Pharaoh, in the J sequence, is so much more formidable in regard to Moses than he is in the received tradition, where he is essentially a stiff-necked despot who at last is compelled to give in. Brevard S. Childs, in his commentary on Exodus, shrewdly notes the difference in the much more imaginative J writer:

But to J belongs the picture of Pharaoh who slyly spars with Moses, who passionately confesses his wrong, but with equal speed relents once the pressure has been removed. He can be violent (10:28) and sarcastic (10:10), almost to the extent of getting the best of the argument (10:11). He even seems to know Jewish law! Then when all is lost, the portrayal is not one of tragic despair, but of a sly fox still trying to salvage what he can (12:32).

J's Pharaoh is augmented (and entertainingly so) only because J's Moses is so deliberately less than overwhelming. If we are able to recover that scaled-down Moses, what would the consequences be, not just for how we read what we now call Exodus, but for how we regard what is now called Judaism? I take it that J keenly cared about the Yahweh of Abraham, Jacob, and Joseph (and through Joseph, of David), but that he felt a certain disinterest in the Yahweh of Moses. What if we were to emulate J? To ask such a question is not to devalue Exodus, or even to back away from Moses. What the question does involve is our freedom, as contemporary Jewish intellectuals, to return to the Yahwist's elitist concerns. Is there a way back to a vision of Yahweh that would set aside the Moses of the Priestly authors, and the Deuteronomist? That Moses surged on, to become the Moses of the normative sages of the Second Century of the Common Era. Is their Judaism the only authentic Judaism that ever will be available to us?

All that is constitutive of authentic Jewish belief must be the Hebrew Bible itself, but what precisely is the Bible? Genesis, Exodus, and Numbers are, for me, the J writer, and not the composite text in which the redactors have had the last word, a word they never earned. Unlike J, the other strands are vitiated for me not just because they are tendentious, but because their authors, unlike J, simply were not strong enough writers, not what (following Nietzsche) I would call "strong poets." To adopt Richard Rorty's post-philosophical and pragmatic formulation, they sought to achieve universality by the transcendence of J's contingency, whereas J, with Shakespeare and Homer the strongest of poets, achieved self-creation by the recognition of contingency. J created his own mind by creating his own language, whereas the redactors neither could nor would emulate J, their great original.

It is difficult to read J as J because of the deep nostalgia we feel for the normative tradition. But an awareness of J's strength gradually leads one to the realization that normative Judaism is an extremely strong mis-reading of the Hebrew Bible that was concluded eighteen centuries ago in order to meet the needs of the Jewish people in a Palestine under Roman occupation. Does it bind us forever as the proper version of the Covenant?

The more deeply I read in J, the more I have the same experience that I have when I read in Shakespeare, which is the revelation of radical originality. The history of J's revisionists is a long march away from J, and so becomes an endless distancing from J's Yahweh. It is a dark paradox that the Yahwist's Yahweh is not the God of normative Judaism, or of historical Christianity, or of Islam. And it is Western culture's largest irony, in our very late time, approaching the year 2000 of the Common Era, that we still need to recover the vision of God that was seen so vividly by the uncanny writer, J, who was our origin.

# Homer

## (c. 8th cen. B.C.E)

*The Iliad*

Hektor in his ecstasy of power
is mad for battle, confident in Zeus,
deferring to neither men nor gods. Pure frenzy
fills him, and he prays for the bright dawn
when he will shear our stern-post beaks away
and fire all our ships, while in the shipways
amid that holocaust he carries death
among our men, driven out by smoke. All this
I gravely fear; I fear the gods will make
good his threatenings, and our fate will be
to die here, far from the pastureland of Argos.
Rouse yourself, if even at this hour
you'll pitch in for the Akhaians and deliver them
from Trojan havoc. In the years to come
this day will be remembered pain for you
if you do not.
*Iliad*, Fitzgerald translation, bk. 9, ll. 237–50

For the divisions of Reuben there were great thoughts of heart.
  Why abidest thou among the sheepfolds, to hear the bleatings of the
    flocks?
For the divisions of Reuben there were great searchings of heart.
  Gilead abode beyond Jordan: and why did Dan remain in ships?
Asher continued on the sea shore, and abode in his breaches.
  Zebulun and Naphtali were a people that jeoparded their lives unto

the death in the high places of the field.
    Judges 5:15–18

SIMONE WEIL LOVED BOTH THE *ILIAD* AND THE GOSPELS, AND RATHER ODDLY
associated them, as though Jesus had been a Greek and not a Jew:

> The Gospels are the last marvelous expression of the Greek
> genius, as the *Iliad* is the first … with the Hebrews, misfortune
> was a sure indication of sin and hence a legitimate object of
> contempt; to them a vanquished enemy was abhorrent to God
> himself and condemned to expiate all sorts of crimes—this is a
> view that makes cruelty permissible and indeed indispensable.
> And no text of the *Old Testament* strikes a note comparable to
> the note heard in the Greek epic, unless it be certain parts of
> the book of Job. Throughout twenty centuries of Christianity,
> the Romans and the Hebrews have been admired, read, imitat-
> ed, both in deed and word; their masterpieces have yielded an
> appropriate quotation every time anybody had a crime he
> wanted to justify.

Though vicious in regard to the Hebrew Bible, this is also merely
banal, being another in that weary procession of instances of Jewish self-
hatred, and even of Christian anti-Semitism. What is interesting in it however is Weil's strong misreading of the *Iliad* as "the poem of force," as when
she said: "Its bitterness is the only justifiable bitterness, for it springs from
the subjections of the human spirit to force, that is, in the last analysis, to
matter." Of what "human spirit" did Weil speak? That sense of the spirit
is of course Hebraic, and not at all Greek, and is totally alien to the text of
the *Iliad*. Cast in Homer's terms, her sentence should have ascribed justifiable bitterness, the bitterness of Achilles and Hector, to "the subjections of
the human force to the gods' force and to fate's force." For that is how
Homer sees men; they are not spirits imprisoned in matter but forces or
drives that live, perceive, and feel. I adopt here Bruno Snell's famous
account of "Homer's view of man," in which Achilles, Hector and all the
other heroes, even Odysseus, "consider themselves a battleground of arbitrary forces and uncanny powers." Abraham, Jacob, Joseph and Moses
clearly do not view themselves as a site where arbitrary forces clash in battle, and neither of course does David or his possible descendant, Jesus. The
*Iliad* is as certainly the poem of force as *Genesis, Exodus, Numbers* is the
poem of the will of Yahweh, who has his arbitrary and uncanny aspects but
whose force is justice and whose power is also canny.

II

The poet of the *Iliad* seems to me to have only one ancient rival, the prime and original author of much of *Genesis, Exodus, Numbers*, known as the Yahwist or J writer to scholars. Homer and J have absolutely nothing in common except their uncanny sublimity, and they are sublime in very different modes. In a profound sense, they are agonists, though neither ever heard of the other, or listened to the other's texts. They compete for the consciousness of Western nations, and their belated strife may be the largest single factor that makes for a divided sensibility in the literature and life of the West. For what marks the West is its troubled sense that its cognition goes one way, and its spiritual life goes in quite another. We have no ways of thinking that are not Greek, and yet our morality and religion—outer and inner—find their ultimate source in the Hebrew Bible.

The burden of the word of the Lord, as delivered by Zechariah (9:12–13) has been prophetic of the cultural civil war that, for us, can never end:

> Turn you to the stronghold, ye prisoners of hope: even today
> do I declare that I will render double unto thee;
>    When I have bent Judah for me, filled the bow of Ephraim,
> and raised up thy sons, O Zion, against thy sons, O Greece, and
> made thee as the sword of a mighty man.

Like the Hebrew Bible, Homer is both scripture and book of general knowledge, and these are necessarily still the prime educational texts, with only Shakespeare making a third, a third who evidences most deeply the split between Greek cognition and Hebraic spirituality. To read the *Iliad* in particular without distorting it is now perhaps impossible, and for reasons that transcend the differences between Homer's language and implicit socioeconomic structure, and our own. The true difference, whether we are Gentile or Jew, believer or skeptic, Hegelian or Freudian, is between Yahweh, and the tangled company of Zeus and the Olympians, fate and the daemonic world. Christian, Moslem, Jew or their mixed descendants, we are children of Abraham and not of Achilles. Homer is perhaps most powerful when he represents the strife of men and gods. The Yahwist or J is as powerful when he shows us Jacob wrestling a nameless one among the Elohim to a standstill, but the instance is unique, and Jacob struggles, not to overcome the nameless one, but to delay him. And Jacob is no Heracles; he wrestles out of character, as it were, so as to give us a giant trope for Israel's persistence in its endless quest for a time without boundaries.

The *Iliad*, except for the Yahwist, Dante, and Shakespeare, is the most extraordinary writing yet to come out of the West, but how much of it is spiritually acceptable to us, or would be, if we pondered it closely? Achilles and Hector are hardly the same figure, since we cannot visualize Achilles living a day-to-day life in a city, but they are equally glorifiers of battle. Defensive warfare is no more an ideal (for most of us) than is aggression, but in the *Iliad* both are very near to the highest good, which is victory. What other ultimate value is imaginable in a world where the ordinary reality is battle? It is true that the narrator, and his personages, are haunted by similes of peace, but, as James M. Redfield observes, the rhetorical purpose of these similes "is not to describe the world of peace but to make vivid the world of war." Indeed, the world of peace, in the *Iliad*, is essentially a war between humans and nature, in which farmers rip out the grain and fruit as so many spoils of battle. This helps explain why the *Iliad* need not bother to praise war, since reality is a constant contest anyway, in which nothing of value can be attained without despoiling or ruining someone or something else.

To compete for the foremost place was the Homeric ideal, which is not exactly the biblical ideal of honoring your father and your mother. I find it difficult to read the *Iliad* as "the tragedy of Hector," as Redfield and others do. Hector is stripped of tragic dignity, indeed very nearly of all dignity, before he dies. The epic is the tragedy of Achilles, ironically enough, because he retains the foremost place, yet cannot overcome the bitterness of his sense of his own mortality. To be only half a god appears to be Homer's implicit definition of what makes a hero tragic. But this is not tragedy in the biblical sense, where the dilemma of Abraham arguing with Yahweh on the road to Sodom, or of Jacob wrestling with the angel of death, is the need to act as if one were everything in oneself while knowing also that, compared to Yahweh, one is nothing in oneself. Achilles can neither act as if he were everything in himself, nor can he believe that, compared even to Zeus, he is nothing in himself. Abraham and Jacob therefore, and not Achilles, are the cultural ancestors of Hamlet and the other Shakespearean heroes.

What after all is it to be the "best of the Achaeans," Achilles, as contrasted to the comparable figure, David (who in Yahweh's eyes is clearly the best among the children of Abraham)? It is certainly not to be the most complete man among them. That, as James Joyce rightly concluded, is certainly Odysseus. The best of the Achaeans is the one who can kill Hector, which is to say that Achilles, in an American heroic context, would have been the fastest gun in the West. Perhaps David would have been that also, and certainly David mourns Jonathan as Achilles mourns Patroklos, which reminds us that David and Achilles both are poets. But Achilles, sulking in his tent, is palpably a child, with a wavering vision of himself, inevitable since his vitality, his perception, and his affective life are all divided from one another, as Bruno Snell demonstrated. David, even as a child, is a mature and autonomous ego, with his sense of life, his vision of other selves, and his emotional nature all integrated into a new kind of man, the hero whom Yahweh had decided not only to love, but to make immortal through his descendants, who would never lose Yahweh's favor. Jesus, *contra* Simone Weil, can only be the descendant of David, and not of Achilles. Or to put it most simply, Achilles is the son of a goddess, but David is a Son of God.

III

The single "modern" author who compels comparison with the poet of the *Iliad* and the writer of the J text is Tolstoy, whether in *War and Peace* or in the short novel which is the masterpiece of his old age, *Hadji Murad*. Rachel Bespaloff, in her essay *On the Iliad* (rightly commended by the superb Homeric translator, Robert Fitzgerald, as conveying how distant, how refined the art of Homer was) seems to have fallen into the error of believing that the Bible and Homer, since both resemble Tolstoy, must also resemble one another. Homer and Tolstoy share the extraordinary balance between the individual in action and groups in action that alone permits the epic accurately to represent battle. The Yahwist and Tolstoy share an uncanny mode of irony that turns upon the incongruities of incommensurable entities, Yahweh or universal history, and man, meeting in violent confrontation or juxtaposition. But the Yahwist has little interest in groups; he turns away in some disdain when the blessing, on Sinai, is transferred from an elite to the mass of the people. And the clash of gods and men, or of fate and the hero, remains in Homer a conflict between forces not wholly incommensurable, though the hero must die, whether in or beyond the poem.

The crucial difference between the Yahwist and Homer, aside from their representations of the self, necessarily is the indescribable difference between Yahweh and Zeus. Both are personalities, but such an assertion becomes an absurdity directly they are juxtaposed. Erich Auerbach, comparing the poet of the *Odyssey* and the Elohist, the Yahwist's revisionist, traced the mimetic difference between the *Odyssey's* emphasis upon "foregrounding" and the Bible's reliance upon the authority of an implied "backgrounding." There is something to that distinction, but it tends to fade out when we move from the *Odyssey* to the *Iliad* and from the Elohist to the Yahwist. The *Iliad* may not demand interpretation as much as the Yahwist does, but it hardly can be apprehended without any reader's considerable labor of aesthetic contextualization. Its man, unlike the Yahwist's, has little in common with the "psychological man" of Freud.

Joseph, who may have been the Yahwist's portrait of King David, provides a fascinating post-Oedipal contrast to his father Jacob, but Achilles seems never to have approached any relation whatever to his father Peleus, who is simply a type of ignoble old age wasting towards the wrong kind of death. Surely the most striking contrast between the *Iliad* and the J text is that between the mourning of Priam and the grief of Jacob when he believes Joseph to be dead. Old men in Homer are good mostly for grieving, but in the Yahwist they represent the wisdom and the virtue of the fathers. Yahweh is the God of Abraham, the God of Isaac, the God of Jacob, even as He will be the God of Moses, the God of David, the God of Jesus. But Zeus is nobody's god, as it were, and Achilles might as well not have had a father at all.

Priam's dignity is partly redeemed when his mourning for Hector is joined to that of Achilles for Patroklos, but the aged Jacob is dignity itself, as his grandfather Abraham was before him. Nietzsche's characterization is just. A people whose ideal is the agon for the foremost place must fall behind in honoring their parents, while a people who exalt fatherhood and motherhood will transfer the agon to the temporal realm, to struggle there not for being the best at one time, but rather for inheriting the blessing, which promises more life in a time without boundaries.

Yahweh is the source of the blessing, and Yahweh, though frequently enigmatic in J, is never an indifferent onlooker. No Hebrew writer could conceive of a Yahweh who is essentially an audience, whether indifferent or engrossed. Homer's gods are human—all-too-human—particularly in their abominable capacity to observe suffering almost as a kind of sport. The Yahweh of Amos and the prophets after him could not be further from Homer's Olympian Zeus.

It can be argued that the spectatorship of the gods gives Homer an immense aesthetic advantage over the writers of the Hebrew Bible. The sense of a divine audience constantly in attendance both provides a fascinating interplay with Homer's human auditors, and guarantees that Achilles and Hector will perform in front of a sublimity greater even than their own. To have the gods as one's audience enhances and honors the heroes who are Homer's prime actors. Yahweh frequently hides Himself, and will not be there when you cry out for Him, or He may call out your name unexpectedly, to which you can only respond: "Here I am." Zeus is capricious and is finally limited by fate. Yahweh surprises you, and has no limitation. He will not lend you dignity by serving as your audience, and yet He is anything but indifferent to you. He fashioned you out of the moistened red clay, and then blew his own breath into your nostrils, so as to make you a living being. You grieve Him or you please Him, but fundamentally He is your longing for the father, as Freud insisted. Zeus is not your longing for anyone, and he will not save you even if you are Heracles, his own son.

IV

In Homer, you fight to be the best, to take away the women of the enemy, and to survive as long as possible, short of aging into ignoble decrepitude. That is not why you fight in the Hebrew Bible. There you fight the wars of Yahweh, which so appalled that harsh saint, Simone Weil. I want to close this introduction by comparing two great battle odes, the war song of Deborah and Barak, in Judges 5, and the astonishing passage in book 18 of the *Iliad* when Achilles reenters the scene of battle, in order to recover his arms, his armor, and the body of Patroklos:

> At this,
> Iris left him, running downwind. Akhilleus,
> whom Zeus loved, now rose. Around his shoulders
> Athena hung her shield, like a thunderhead
> with trailing fringe. Goddess of goddesses,
> she bound his head with golden cloud, and made
> his very body blaze with fiery light.
> Imagine how the pyre of a burning town
> will tower to heaven and be seen for miles
> from the island under attack, while all day long
> outside their town, in brutal combat, pikemen
> suffer the wargod's winnowing; at sundown
> flare on flare is lit, the signal fires
> shoot up for other islanders to see,
> that some relieving force in ships may come:
> just so the baleful radiance from Akhilleus
> lit the sky. Moving from parapet
> to moat, without a nod for the Akhaians,
> keeping clear, in deference to his mother,
> he halted and gave tongue. Not far from him
> Athena shrieked. The great sound shocked the Trojans
> into tumult, as a trumpet blown

by a savage foe shocks an encircled town,
so harsh and clarion was Akhilleus' cry.
The hearts of men quailed, hearing that brazen voice.
Teams, foreknowing danger, turned their cars
and charioteers blanched, seeing unearthly fire,
kindled by the grey-eyed goddess Athena,
brilliant over Akhilleus. Three great cries
he gave above the moat. Three times they shuddered,
whirling backward, Trojans and allies,
and twelve good men took mortal hurt
from cars and weapons in the rank behind.
Now the Akhaians leapt at the chance
to bear Patroklos' body out of range.
They placed it on his bed,
and old companions there with brimming eyes
surrounded him. Into their midst Akhilleus
came then, and he wept hot tears to see
his faithful friend, torn by the sharp spearhead,
lying cold upon his cot. Alas,
the man he sent to war with team and chariot
he could not welcome back alive.

Exalted and burning with Athena's divine fire, the unarmed Achilles
is more terrible even than the armed hero would be. It is his angry shouts
that panic the Trojans, yet the answering shout of the goddess adds to their
panic, since they realize that they face preternatural powers. When
Yahweh roars, in the prophets Isaiah and Joel, the effect is very different,
though He too cries out "like a man of war." The difference is in Homer's
magnificent antiphony between man and goddess, Achilles and Athena.
Isaiah would not have had the king and Yahweh exchanging battle shouts
in mutual support, because of the shocking incommensurateness which
does not apply to Achilles and Athena.

I began this introduction by juxtaposing two epigraphs, Odysseus
shrewdly warning Achilles that "this day," on which Hector may burn the
Achaean ships, "will be remembered pain for you," if Achilles does not
return to the battle, and a superb passage from Deborah's war song in
Judges 5. Hector's "ecstasy of power" would produce "remembered pain"
for Achilles, as power must come at the expense of someone else's pain, and
ecstasy results from the victory of inflicting *memorable* suffering. Memory
depends upon pain, which was Nietzsche's fiercely Homeric analysis of all
significant memory. But that is not the memory exalted in the Hebrew

Bible. Deborah, with a bitter irony, laughs triumphantly at the tribes of Israel that did not assemble for the battle against Sisera, and most of all at Reuben, with its scruples, doubts, hesitations: "great searchings of heart." She scorns those who kept to business as usual, Dan who remained in ships, and Asher who continued on the sea shore. Then suddenly, with piercing intensity and moral force, she utters a great paean of praise and triumph, for the tribes that risked everything on behalf of their covenant with Yahweh, for those who transcended "great thoughts" and "great searchings of heart":

> Zebulun and Naphtali were a people that jeoparded their lives
> unto the death in the high places of the field.

The high places are both descriptive and honorific; they are where the terms of the covenant were kept. Zebulun and Naphtali fight, not to be the foremost among the tribes of Israel, and not to possess Sisera's women, but to fulfill the terms of the covenant, to demonstrate *emunah*, which is trust in Yahweh. Everyone in Homer knows better than to trust in Zeus. The aesthetic supremacy of the *Iliad* again must be granted. Homer is the best of the poets, and always will keep the foremost place. What he lacks, even aesthetically, is a quality of trust in the transcendent memory of a covenant fulfilled, a lack of the sublime hope that moves the Hebrew poet Deborah:

> They fought from heaven; the stars in their courses fought
> against Sisera.
>    The river of Kishon swept them away, that ancient river, the
> river Kishon. O my soul, thou hast trodden down strength.

### The Odyssey

The *Odyssey*, though a clear sequel to the *Iliad*, is an immensely different poem in the experience of all readers. If one author wrote both, then the change from the *Iliad* to the *Odyssey* is as great as the difference between *War and Peace* and *Anna Karenina*, or between *Paradise Lost* and *Paradise Regained*. Such comparisons suggest a darkening of vision in Homer, as in Tolstoy or Milton, but of course the movement from *Iliad* to *Odyssey* is from tragic to comic, from epic to romance, from the rage of Achilles against mortality to the prudence of Odysseus in recovering wife, son, father, home, and kingdom. The *Iliad*, in fierce agon with the Bible, has set our standards for sublimity, but the *Odyssey* has been the more fecund

work, particularly in modern literature. Joyce did not write a novel called
*Achilles*, nor did Pound and Stevens devote poems to the hero of the *Iliad*.
Like Dante and Tennyson before them, they became obsessed with
Ulysses, whose quest for home contrasts oddly with the role of anti-Aeneas
assigned to him by Dante and, more uneasily, by Tennyson.

A permanent mystery of the contrast between *Iliad* and *Odyssey* is that
the *Iliad* seems much farther away from us, though it has less of the fantastic or the fabulous than the *Odyssey*. Achilles is a remote Sublime, whereas Odysseus is the complete man of Joyce's vision, coping with the everyday. Realistic description of marvels is the romance formula of the *Odyssey*
and seems very different from the tragic world in which Achilles and
Hector strive to be the best. A literary critic who is not a classicist, and with
indifferent Greek, nevertheless takes away from both epics an overwhelming sense of the unity of very separate designs in the immense consciousness of a comprehensive poet coming very late in a tradition. Samuel
Johnson, my critical hero, darkly judged every Western poet coming after
Homer to be belated. It is a productive irony that Johnson seems to me
correct as to the *Iliad*, but that the *Odyssey* overwhelmingly strikes me as
the epic of belatedness, the song of things-in-their-farewell.

We cannot envision Achilles existing in the day-to-day world of the
*Odyssey*, which cannot accommodate so single-minded a hero. You go west,
to the Islands of the Dead, to find the great Achilles or the frustrated spirit
of Ajax, doomed always to be the second best. The Odysseus of Homer,
superbly unlike the anti-Aeneas of Dante and Tennyson, is the true prototype of Aeneas, but Virgil's priggish moralist is an involuntary travesty of the
hero of the Odyssey. Poor Aeneas actually must carry the emperor Augustus
on his back, while Odysseus is free of ideology, unless the desire to reclaim
what was once your own is to be considered a politics of the spirit.

Achilles, as critics note, is somewhat childlike, but Odysseus has had
to put away childish things and lives in a world where you can freeze to
death, as well as be devoured by one-eyed monsters. Self-control, a virtue
alien to Achilles, is hardly a poetic quality as such and in Odysseus seems
unallied to any system of morality. Americans justly find in Homer's later
hero the first pragmatist, unimpressed by differences that do not make a
difference. Existence, for the necessarily cunning Odysseus, is a vast obsta-
cle course that has kept you away from home for a full decade and that will
exercise you for a second decade as you voyage back. When you get there,
your largest ordeal begins, since a slaughter in your own home, even with
yourself as shrewd slaughterer, is an altogether more daunting prospect
than even the most ferocious battling upon the windy plain of Troy.

Joyce's Ulysses, the humane though masochistic Poldy, is the most amiable personage in all literature, despite the absurd moralizings against him of Modernist critics. Homer's Odysseus is a very dangerous figure, whom we admire and respect but do not love. He is a great survivor, the one man who will stay afloat when all his shipmates drown. You would not want to be in one boat with him then, but there is no one you would rather read or hear about, because survival is the best of all stories. Stories exist to defer death, and Odysseus is a grand evader of mortality, unlike the tragic Achilles, who rages against being only half a god, yet who is pragmatically doom-eager. The agon of Achilles, the best of the Achaeans, is thus of a different order than the sensible ecstasy of Odysseus, who fights only when he must and always for sharply delineated ends. The desire for the foremost place recedes, and the will to live another day takes on its own aura of heroism.

The enmity of Poseidon is so great a burden for an island-king who needs to voyage back that Odysseus has only the two choices: heroic endurance or death, unless he wishes to forget household and hearth and yield to one of the manifold temptations that are made available to him. He is not exactly a yielder, and consequently he has provided a model for every striver since. The model, as Dante and even Tennyson show, is a dangerous one, since it encourages the development of the ability to deceive others. But if the cosmos of water and wind is against you and you cannot stay on the mainland, then you must choose the remaining element and speak out of the fire, as Dante's Ulysses does. Fire, which in the *Iliad* is associated with death in battle, becomes in the *Odyssey* a trope for survival, the light not of flashing arms and armor but of the hearth where Penelope holds court, delaying the suitors while waiting for the pragmatic or belated hero to return to her, never forgetting him that kept coming so close:

> Now from his breast into his eyes the ache
> of longing mounted, and he wept at last,
> his dear wife, clear and faithful, in his arms,
> longed for as the sunwarmed earth is longed for by a swimmer
> spent in rough water where his ship went down
> under Poseidon's blows, gale winds and tons of sea.
> Few men can keep alive through a big surf
> to crawl, clotted with brine, on kindly beaches
> in joy, in joy, knowing the abyss behind:
> and so she too rejoiced, her gaze upon her husband,
> her white arms round him pressed as though forever.
> (Translated by Robert Fitzgerald)

# Virgil

## (C. 84–54 B.C.E)

When Aeneas is sent by Virgil to the shades, he meets Dido the Queen of Carthage, whom his perfidy had hurried to the grave; he accosts her with tenderness and excuses; but the lady turns away like Ajax in mute disdain. She turns away like Ajax, but she resembles him in none of those qualities which give either dignity or propriety to silence. She might, without any departure from the tenour of her conduct, have burst out like other injured women into clamour, reproach, and denunciation; but Virgil had his imagination full of Ajax, and therefore could not prevail on himself to teach Dido any other mode of resentment.
—DR. SAMUEL JOHNSON, *The Rambler*, no. 121

TO BE EMPLOYED AS THE KEY INSTANCE OF "THE DANGERS OF IMITATION" by the greatest Western literary critic is the saddest of all Virgil's melancholy-ridden posthumous vicissitudes. It is unhappy enough that the excessively noble Aeneas should be considered by many readers to be a prig, a Trojan version of George Eliot's Daniel Deronda, as it were. But to read Virgil while keeping Homer too steadily in mind is clearly to impose upon the strongest Latin poet a burden that only a few Western writers could sustain. Virgil is not Dante or Shakespeare, Tolstoy or Joyce. He has his affinities with Tennyson, and with other poets in the elegiac mode, down to Matthew Arnold and T.S. Eliot, both of whom celebrated Virgil as a beautiful "inadequacy" (Arnold) and a mature "poet of unique destiny" (Eliot), two apparently antithetical judgments that actually say much the same thing, which is not much. Like Arnold and Eliot, poor Virgil has become the poet of professors, many of whom praise Virgil as a splendid revisionist of Homer, a very different view from Dr. Johnson's.

Other classicists have given us a more Tennysonian Virgil, a knowing latecomer infatuated "with twilight moods, with blurred images, with haunted, half-enacted interviews and confrontations that disintegrate before our eyes just as we begin to perceive them." I quote from *Darkness Visible* by W.R. Johnson, the best study of Virgil that I have read, and hasten to add that Johnson is eloquently summing up the judgment of other critics, rather than stating his own, which seems to me more persuasive. W.R. Johnson's Virgil is marked by a "vast Epicurean sensitivity to pain and suffering," and is not concerned so much "about winning battles but about losing them and learning how to lose them." This Virgil has the "imagination of darkness" and has "discovered and revealed the perennial shape of what truly destroys us."

In some sense, W.R. Johnson moves the fantastic and menacing figure of Virgil's Juno to the center of the epic, which is certainly a useful corrective to many previous readings of Virgil. Juno is Virgil's most ambiguous achievement, and doubtless is one of the major Western representations of what contemporary feminist critics like to call the projection of male hysteria. I would prefer to name Virgil's Juno as the male dread that origin and end will turn out to be one. We do not judge Nietzsche to be hysterical when he warns us, in his *Geneology of Morals*, that origin and end, for the sake of life, must be kept apart. Despite his all-too-frequently deconstructed dislike of women (so amiable, compared to his master Schopenhauer's), Nietzsche is hardly to be dismissed as what feminists like to call a "patriarchal critic" (are there any? could there be?). What Nietzsche suggests, as Freud does after him, is that all Western images are either origin or end, except for the trope of the father.

It is frightening that the only Western image that is neither origin nor end is, in Virgil, reduced to the pathetic figure of Anchises, who has to be carried out of burning Troy upon the shoulders of his pious son, the drearily heroic Aeneas. The image of the mother in the poem is somehow not that of the merely actual mother, Venus, but rather the hardly maternal Juno, who is truly one of the great nightmare images in Western literary tradition. Virgil is rightly wary of her, and if we read closely, so are we:

> O hateful race, and fate of the Phrygians
> Pitted against my own. Could they be killed
> On the Sigean battlefield? When beaten,
> Could they be beaten? Troy on fire, did Troy
> Consume her men? Amid the spears, amid
> The flames, they found a way. I must, for my part,
> Think my powers by this time tired out,
> Supine, or sleeping, surfeited on hate?

Well, when they were ejected from their country
I had the temerity as their enemy
To dog them, fight them, over the whole sea,
These refugees. The strength of sea and sky
Has been poured out against these Teucrians.
What were the Syretës worth to me, or Scylla,
What was huge Charybdis worth? By Tiber's
Longed-for bed they now lay out their town,
Unworried by deep water or by me.
Mars had the power to kill the giant race
Of Lapiths, and the Father of Gods himself
Gave up old Cálydon to Diana's wrath.
And what great sin brought Cálydon or Lapiths
Justice so rough? How differently with me,
The great consort of Jove, who nerved myself
To leave no risk unventured, lent myself
To every indignity. I am defeated
And by Aeneas. Well, if my powers fall short,
I need not falter over asking help
Wherever help may lie. If I can sway
No heavenly hearts I'll rouse the world below.
It will not be permitted me—so be it—
To keep the man from rule in Italy;
By changeless fate Lavinia waits, his bride.
And yet to drag it out, to pile delay
Upon delay in these great matters—that
I can do: to destroy both countries' people,
That I can do. Let father and son-in-law
Unite at that cost to their own! In blood,
Trojan and Latin, comes your dowry, girl;
Bridesmaid Bellona waits now to attend you.
Hecuba's not the only one who carried
A burning brand within her and bore a son
Whose marriage fired a city. So it is
With Venus' child, a Paris once again,
A funeral torch again for Troy reborn!
(VII. 295–326, Fitzgerald translation)

There is certainly a dark sense in which Juno is Virgil's pragmatic Muse, as it were, the driving force of his poem. She represents, in this passage, Virgil's authentic if repressed aggressivity towards his daunting father, Homer. As the inspiration of an agonistic intensity, she necessarily speaks for Virgil himself when he confronts the Iliad and the *Odyssey*:

> Well, if my powers fall short,
> I need not falter over asking help
> Wherever help may lie. If I can sway
> No heavenly hearts I'll rouse the world below.

Is not that Virgil's actual achievement as compared to Homer's? Juno, though she is a nightmare, is Virgil's own nightmare, his dark creation, a "darkness visible" in the great Miltonic phrase that W.R. Johnson chose as title for his study of the *Aeneid*. What Virgil most powerfully and originally gives us might be called the creatures of Juno: Allecto and the Dira (though technically the Dira is sent by Jupiter). Virgilian invention, though deprecated by Dr. Samuel Johnson, is marked by a negative exuberance that cannot have pleased the author of *Rasselas*, who rightly had his positive imagination full of Homer, and necessarily feared his own dark side.

## II

It is no fresh oddity for a poet to become the official representative of the sensibility and ideology of an age, while actually producing work of morbid splendor and equivocal pathology. Virgil's double fate is precisely prophetic of Tennyson's and T.S. Eliot's. Walt Whitman, belatedly accepted as our national bard, would be a parallel figure if his poetry had received wide contemporary acceptance in post–Civil War America, as would Hart Crane, had he been acclaimed in the days of the Depression.

This phenomenon is now over, since our era is overtly paranoid in its sensibility. The best writers in contemporary America—John Ashbery, Thomas Pynchon, James Merrill—are truly representative of the dumb-foundering abyss between the private, aesthetic sensibility and the public sphere of Ronald Reagan. The abyss was as great between Virgil and the Emperor Augustus, but both chose to believe and act otherwise. A vision of President Reagan placing Thomas Pynchon under his patronage is not without its charm.

Virgil, as Dante's precursor, became for Western literary tradition a kind of proto-Christian poet. He can hardly be blamed for this, though perhaps Aeneas can, since Aeneas unfortunately is sometimes prophetic of that civic ideal, the Victorian Christian gentleman, Gladstone say, rather than the exotic Christian Jew, Disraeli. However, Aeneas (though replete with noble sentiments) actually behaves like a cad towards Dido, and finally like a brute towards Turnus. Though no Achilles, Aeneas pragmatically is quite frightening, and really about as benign as the Emperor Augustus, his contemporary model. Machiavelli is more in the line of Aeneas than of Virgil. Perhaps the greatest strength and lasting puzzle of the poem is Virgil's relation to his own hero. Does Virgil, like most of us, prefer Turnus to Aeneas? He was not writing the *Turneid*, but would he have been happier doing so?

The violent nature of Turnus, at once neurotic and attractive, has about it the aura of a Latin Hotspur, though Turnus lacks Hotspur's antic wit. But then Hotspur exists in a cosmos ultimately centered, not upon Bolingbroke the usurper and Prince Hal, but upon Falstaff, legitimate monarch of wit. Virgil is not exactly a humorous writer, and I suspect that, if he was in love with any of his own characters in the poem, it was with Turnus, rather than Dido, let alone Aeneas. The dreadful death of Turnus, which causes the poem to break off, in some sense is also the death of Virgil, or at least of Virgil's poetry:

The man brought down, brought low, lifted his eyes
And held his right hand out to make his plea:

> "Clearly I have earned this, and I ask no quarter.
> Make the most of your good fortune here.
> If you can feel a father's grief—and you, too,
> Had such a father in Anchises—then
> Let me bespeak your mercy for old age
> In Daunus, and return me, or my body,
> Stripped, if you will, of life, to my own kin.
> You have defeated me. The Ausonians
> Have seen me in defeat, spreading my hands.
> Lavinia is your bride. But go no further
> Out of hatred."

>               Fierce under arms, Aeneas
> Looked to and fro, and towered, and stayed his hand
> Upon the sword-hilt. Moment by moment now
> What Turnus said began to bring him round
> From indecision. Then to his glance appeared
> The accurst swordbelt surmounting Turnus' shoulder,
> Shining with its familiar studs—the strap
> Young Pallas wore when Turnus wounded him
> And left him dead upon the field; now Turnus
> Bore that enemy token on his shoulder—

Enemy still. For when the sight came home to him,
Aeneas raged at the relic of his anguish
Worn by this man as trophy. Blazing up
And terrible in his anger, he called out:

"You in your plunder, tom from one of mine,
Shall I be robbed of you? This wound will come
From Pallas: Pallas makes this offering
And from your criminal blood exacts his due."

He sank his blade in fury in Turnus' chest.
Then all the body slackened in death's chill,
And with a groan for that indignity
His spirit fled into the gloom below.
(XII. 930–952, Fitzgerald translation)

The death of Turnus indeed is a terrible indignity, heroic neither for
him nor for Aeneas. Turnus is truly slaughtered by Jove, who has been able
to impose his will upon Juno, and then takes on something of her spirit
when she yields. The Dira, manifesting as a gruesome carrion bird, sickens
poor Turnus, numbing his giant force until he does not know himself. In a
waking nightmare, unable to speak, standing defenseless, Turnus becomes
merely an object into which Aeneas hurls a spear. Aeneas furiously stab-
bing to death a man already ruined by the Dira is hardly an Achilles or a
Roland, and it is very good that the poem abruptly ends there. Could we
forgive an Aeneas who exulted in such a triumph? Why does Virgil end his
poem with so gratuitous a slaughter? Can he have intended to give us a
Jupiter so contaminated by Juno? Such a Jupiter is more like a Gnostic
Archon than in any way an Epicurean vision of the divine.

All we can be certain of is that Virgil deliberately wounds himself
even as he wounds us. All of Book XII is an effective horror, an epiphany
of lacerations and self-destroyings. I do not pretend to understand the
scene in which Jupiter and Juno are reconciled to one another, and she
agrees to give up her vendetta against the Trojans. Perhaps Virgil did not
understand it either. If he was a convinced Epicurean, then he must have
turned against his own rationality in his final vision of Jove, who is certainly not indifferent but positively malevolent, and pragmatically as sadistic as Juno. A passionately intense Valentinian Gnostic could have ended
on no darker vision of the demonic, masquerading as the fury of God.

Against Book XII, every reader rightly sets the poignance of Book
VI, and yet Book VI does not culminate the poem. It is well to remember

that Book V ends with the elegiac words of Aeneas to the memory of the lost helmsman, Palinurus:

> For counting
> Overmuch on a calm world, Palinurus,
> You must lie naked on some unknown shore.

Book VI concludes with the passage of Aeneas and the Sibyl out of the world below by the Ivory Gate, and yet Book VII is Juno's book, and Allecto's, "with her lust for war, / For angers, ambushes, and crippling crimes." W.R. Johnson finds the poem's center, for him, in Book XII, lines 665–669, where Turnus makes a great recovery:

> Stunned and confused
> By one and another image of disaster,
> Turnus held stock-still with a silent stare.
> In that one heart great shame boiled up, and madness
> Mixed with grief, and love goaded by fury,
> Courage inwardly known. When by and by
> The darkness shadowing him broke and light
> Came to his mind again, wildly he turned
> His burning eyes townward and from his car
> Gazed at the city.

That is magnificent, but each reader of the *Aeneid* chooses his or her own center. Mine is Book VI, lines 303–314, always admired by readers through the generations:

> Here a whole crowd came streaming to the banks,
> Mothers and men, the forms of life all spent
> Of heroes great in valor, boys and girls
> Unmarried, and young sons laid on the pyre
> Before their parents' eyes—as many souls
> As leaves that yield their hold on boughs and fall
> Through forests in the early frost of autumn,
> Or as migrating birds from the open sea
> That darken heaven when the cold season comes
> And drives them overseas to sunlit lands.
> There all stood begging to be first across
> And reached out longing hands to the far shore.

Homer's fiction of the leaves as the human generations is transumed here with an inventiveness that has inspired poets from Dante to Spenser, Milton and Shelley, and on to Whitman and Wallace Stevens. What is, to me, peculiarly Virgilian and surpassingly beautiful is the movement from the tropes of the autumnal leaves and the migrating birds to the terrible pathos of the "pauper souls, the souls of "the unburied," who must flutter and roam the wrong side of the black waters for a century. To stretch out one's longing hands to the farther shore, when that shore is oblivion, is a purely Virgilian figure, not Homeric, and has about it the uniquely Virgilian plangency. The *Aeneid* is a poem that attempts to compel itself to the grandeur of Augustan vistas, but its genius has little to do with Augustus, and at last little to do even with Aeneas. Of all the greater Western poems, it reaches out most longingly to the farther shore.

### The Aeneid

W.R. Johnson, one of Virgil's most acute critics, submits that the poet of the *Aeneid* persuades us of his compassion for others by "the nakedness, the purity of his initial pity for himself." Johnson strongly reminds us that Virgil was an Epicurean both by temperament and by spiritual and philosophical conviction. Epicurus and his Roman disciple, the poet Lucretius, saw the human being as too flawed to will either personal happiness or a just political order. The Epicurean-Lucretian elitism preaches release from ignorance as the only salvation for a rational few; empire cannot save anyone, for it is founded upon the illusion of civic virtue. Going within the self is the Epicurean path to the only truth that matters: personal, individual, disillusioned, denying transcendence. The two dominant poetic influences upon Virgil were Homer and Lucretius; the spiritual influence that mattered was wholly Epicurean. Nothing could have been more mistaken than the Christian misreading of Virgil, which Dante made permanent among us. Virgil has no hope, and his only belief is the faithless faith of the Epicureans, who accepted human suffering as inevitable, except for that rational remnant that could abandon all illusion.

Virgil's greatest originality, which redeems the *Aeneid* from its confusions, is his powerfully negative imagination. The one figure who does not embody all of this imagination is Aeneas, whom many readers will regard as a prig or a stick, who comes to life only when he is being a cad in regard to Dido or a brute in regard to Turnus. It cannot be said that Aeneas always shares his creator's extraordinary sensitivity to suffering and to pain. True to his undoubted model, Virgil's patron the emperor Augustus, Aeneas keeps his mind upon the foundation of Rome and its future greatness. Since Aeneas is anything but an Epicurean hero (if there could be such an oddity), we have the puzzle, as we read the *Aeneid*, as to whether we are to trust the song or the singer. The singer, despite his Augustan allegiances, maintains a powerful and desperate undersong that is at variance with the poem's overt and official purposes. Who after all is the Muse of the *Aeneid*? Lucretius celebrated an Epicurean Venus, but Virgil's poem is dominated by the sinister queen of Heaven, the vindictive Juno, who wishes to destroy Aeneas, the rather unlikely son of Venus. Juno is a great nightmare, inspirited by the full vivacity of Virgil's negative imagination, including doubtless his fear of women. Her stormy wrath makes her the Goddess of Resentment, an inward brooder whose inflamed heart memorializes every possible grudge. Poor Dido, when abandoned, becomes the authentic high priestess of Juno, particularly by the act of self-immolation.

Since Aeneas eventually triumphs, Juno presumably does not, but actually she does, since her compact with Jupiter rather subtly involves his taking on much of her dark spirit, once she has given in. What are we to make of Virgil's Jupiter, who is anything but an Epicurean god? The gods of Epicurus and of Lucretius serenely dwell apart, being sublimely indifferent to human fate. Virgil is celebrated for always seeing two sides to everything, but Jupiter is simply not that dialectical. It is because of Jupiter that the poem's two most attractive persons are destroyed so dreadfully, punished for being so full of life. Dido and Turnus only can be themselves, which for Jupiter is unforgivable. Aeneas the exile, pious but drab when compared to Turnus and to Dido, is therefore acceptable to the high god. Either there is a Virgilian irony in this, or more likely it is the revenge of the poet's Epicureanism upon his patriotic Augustanism. Aeneas wins, but at the cost of an extraordinary self-abnegation.

Virgil weeps not so much the tears of a universal nature but of a poetry that must reconcile itself to the power and purposes of the state. Dying at fifty-one, Virgil requested that the *Aeneid* be burned rather than published, a plea that Augustus refused. The supposed reason for Virgil's Dido-like desire was that the poem had not been completed. Perhaps there were other sentiments that also governed the dying Virgil. He cannot have been altogether happy with his poem's overt celebration of empire and order. The elegiac voice, as Adam Parry demonstrated, is always the undersong in this Augustan epic. Aeneas is a strange hero since, as Parry observes, he serves a purely impersonal power. Finally the *Aeneid* seems the most elegiac of epics, and yet Epicurus refused to grant any significance to human suffering. If we care for Aeneas at all, it is because of the quality of his grief, his perpetual suffering as he remembers the fall of Troy. Virgil's

*Aeneid* achieves greatness because it is a great poem of defeat, but also of the heroism (if it is that) of sustaining defeat. Divided in his own deepest self, Virgil may have doubted whether his poem deserved to survive. Posterity would appear to have resolved any such doubt.

# Anonymous

## (written c. 700–750)

*Beowulf*

WHETHER ANY PARTICULAR POEM CAN BE TERMED "CHRISTIAN" OR EVEN "religious" is a much more problematical question than we tend to recognize. *Beowulf* is generally judged to be a Christian poem on a Germanic hero. I myself would deny that even *Paradise Lost* is a Christian poem, because John Milton was a Protestant sect of one, and his epic reflects his highly individual spiritual stance. More crucially, the distinction between a sacred and a secular poem never seems to me a *poetic* distinction. You can regard all strong poetry as being religious, or all strong poetry as being secular, but to judge one authentic poem as being more religious or more secular than another seems to me a societal or political matter rather than an aesthetic finding.

Why then care whether or not *Beowulf* is a Christian, as well as being a heroic poem? The answer is partly historical, partly imaginative or poetic. During the first half of the fifth century the Angles, Saxons, and Jutes overran Roman Britain. By the end of the seventh century these Germans, and the Celts they ruled, mostly had been converted to Christianity. *Beowulf* is assigned by some scholars to the first half of the eighth century, and its nameless author undoubtedly was a Christian, at least nominally. But if *Beowulf* is to be considered a Christian poem, we must ask, Can there be Christianity without the figure of Jesus Christ, and without the presence of the New Testament? Every biblical allusion in *Beowulf*, all scholars agree, is to what Christians call the Old Testament. E. Talbot Donaldson, distinguished scholar-critic of medieval English literature, expresses this oddity with his usual laconic good sense:

Yet there is no reference to the New Testament—to Christ and His Sacrifice which are the real bases of Christianity in any intelligible sense of the term. Furthermore, readers may well feel that the poem achieves rather little of its emotional power through invocation of Christian values or of values that are consonant with Christian doctrine as we know it....

... One must, indeed, draw the conclusion from the poem itself that while Christian is a correct term for the religion of the poet and of his audience, it was a Christianity that had not yet by any means succeeded in obliterating an older pagan tradition, which still called forth powerful responses from men's hearts, despite the fact that many aspects of this tradition must be abhorrent to a sophisticated Christian.

I first read *Beowulf* thirty-five years ago, as a graduate student, and have just reread it, cheerfully using Donaldson's splendid prose translation to eke out my faded command of the text. Certainly Donaldson describes what I have read: a heroic poem celebrating the same values that Tacitus discerned in the Germans of his day. Courage is the prime virtue exalted in *Beowulf*. No one reading the poem would find Beowulf to be a particularly Christian hero. His glory has little to do with worship, unless it be justified self-worship, and he fights primarily for glory, to increase his fame, to show that he occupies the foremost place among all Germanic heroes. It is true that Grendel and his even more monstrous mother are portrayed for us as descendants of Cain, but neither they nor the fatal dragon at the poem's end can be said to fight against Christ, or the things that are Christ's. When Beowulf goes forth to battle, he is in quest of reputation and treasure, but not of Christ or God or the truth.

The subtlest defense of a Christian reading of *Beowulf* is by Fred C. Robinson, who finds in the poem an appositive style that balances Dark Age heroism and Christian regret, and that enables the poet to "communicate his Christian vision of pagan heroic life." The dominant tone of *Beowulf*, according to Robinson, is one of "combined admiration and regret" for heroic paganism, as it were. The Christian present confronts the Germanic past, admires its heroism, and supposedly regrets its paganism. In much the most sophisticated critical reading yet afforded the poem, Robinson sets out to correct the view of Tolkien, who somehow could give us Hrothgar as Christian surrounded by pagan companions:

Because Hrothgar advises Beowulf against overweening pride, avarice, and irascible violence, some scholars have wanted to see this as a Christian homily on the Seven Deadly Sins, and many parallels in Scripture and commentary have been adduced. But there is nothing in the speech that is not equally accordant with Germanic pre-Christian piety.

For Robinson, the entire poem manifests a double perspective of a remarkable kind:

> Reading *Beowulf* is, in a way, like reading the centos of Proba, Luxorius and Pomponius, who composed entire poems on Christian subjects by rearranging the verses of Virgil, Horace, and Ovid in order to make them convey Christian meanings. Students of these curious works hold two contexts in mind at the same time, for their pleasure is in following the Christian level of the narrative while remaining aware of the source of the poetic language. Just as in reading the centos we think simultaneously of Aeneas and Christ, so in reading *Beowulf* we should hear distant echoes of Thunor and Woden when the men of old appeal to their "mihtig dryhten" and "fæder alwalda." We know to whom these words refer in the Christian present, but we also know that they once referred to other, darker beings.

A polysemous theological diction thus dominates *Beowulf*, just as it does *Paradise Lost*, if Robinson is wholly correct. Holding Christian and pagan terms in patterns of apposition, the *Beowulf* poet is able to imply Christian values without repudiating ancestral virtues, and yet, in Robinson's judgment, the poem ends upon a kind of modified repudiation, with the statement that Beowulf was *lofgeornost*, translated by Donaldson as "most eager for fame." To say with your last word that the hero, above all men, desired to be praised, wanted a glory bestowed by his fellows, is to insinuate that the hero is wanting, by Christian standards. To maintain his case, Robinson is compelled to this reading, which seems to me to possess a fine desperation:

> The people of Christian England can never reenter the severe, benighted world of the men of old, nor would they. All the poetry of *Beowulf* can do is bring the two together in a brief, loving, and faintly disquieting apposition.

But here is the conclusion of *Beowulf*, in Donaldson's translation:

Then the people of the Weather-Geats built a mound on the promontory, one that was high and broad, wide-seen by seafarers, and in ten days completed a monument for the bold in battle, surrounded the remains of the fire with a wall, the most splendid that men most skilled might devise. In the barrow they placed rings and jewels, all such ornaments as troubled men had earlier taken from the hoard. They let the earth hold the wealth of earls, gold in the ground, where now it still dwells, as useless to men as it was before. Then the brave in battle rode round the mound, children of nobles, twelve in all, would bewail their sorrow and mourn their king, recite dirges and speak of the man. They praised his great deeds and his acts of courage, judged well of his prowess. So it is fitting that man honor his liege lord with words, love him in heart when he must be led forth from the body. Thus the people of the Geats, his hearth-companions, lamented the death of their lord. They said that he was of world-kings the mildest of men and the gentlest, kindest to his people, and most eager for fame.

Does this indeed end with a disquieting apposition? Do we feel that the mildness, gentleness, and kindness of Beowulf (to *his* people, not to monsters, enemies, traitors, or whatever) is in apposition to his lust for renown? Heroic poetry can do little with the virtues of the New Testament Christ, though considerably more with certain epic qualities of the Old Testament. The *Beowulf* poet may have felt no personal nostalgia for the beliefs of his Germanic ancestors, but after all he had chosen to write a heroic poem rather than a work on the finding of the True Cross. Is a poem Christian only because it undoubtedly was written by a Christian? There is nothing about God's grace in *Beowulf*, though something about God's glory as a creator. And there is much tribute to Fate, hardly a Christian category, and rarely is Fate set in apposition with the will of God, as Robinson's pattern might lead us to expect.

Rereading *Beowulf* gives one a fierce and somber sense of heroic loss, in a grim world, not wholly unlike the cosmos of Virgil's *Aeneid*. In spirit, the poem does seem to me more Virgilian than Christian. Though addressed to a Christian audience, it seems not to be addressed to them as Christians but as descendants of heroic warriors. Beowulf does not die so as to advance the truth but so as to maintain his own glory, the fame of a man who could slay a monster with only his own bare hands to do the heroic work. The bareness of those unfaltering hands counts for much more than does the monster's descent from the wicked line of the accursed Cain.

# Lady Murasaki

## (978–1014)

And when I play my *koto* rather badly to myself in the cool breeze of the evening, I worry lest someone might hear me and recognize how I am just "adding to the sadness of it all"; how vain and sad of me. So now both my instruments, the one with thirteen strings and the one with six, stand in a miserable, sooty little closet still ready-strung. Through neglect—I forgot, for example, to ask that the bridges be removed on rainy days—they have accumulated dust and lean between the cupboard and a pillar.

Here is also a pair of larger cupboards crammed to bursting point. One is full of old poems and tales that have become the home for countless insects which scatter in such an unpleasant manner that no one cares to look at them any more; the other is full of Chinese books that have lain unattended ever since he who carefully collected them passed away. Whenever my loneliness threatens to overwhelm me, I take out one or two of them to look at; but my women gather together behind my back. "It's because she goes on like this that she is so miserable. What kind of lady is it who reads Chinese books?" they whisper. "In the past it was not even the done thing to read sutras!" "Yes," I feel like replying, "but I've never met anyone who lived longer just because they believed in superstitions!" But that would be thoughtless of me. There is some truth in what they say.
(translated by Richard Bowring)

LADY MURASAKI, IN HER *DIARY* AS IN *THE TALE OF GENJI*, CONDUCTS AN almost Proustian search for lost time, which is appropriate in a writer who truly was the genius of longing. The splendid Genji paradoxically is destroyed by his own incessant longing for the renewed experience of falling in love. When the significantly named Murasaki, the authentic love of his life, wastes away as an involuntary reaction to having been replaced, Genji does nor survive her for more than a decent interval.

*The Tale of Genji* is eons away from Proust, yet I wonder whether Lady Murasaki's incessant longing is not a valid analogue for Proust's search. In Proust, love dies but jealousy is eternal; the narrator still quests for every possible detail of Albertine's lesbian attachments even though his memories of his dead beloved have become very tenuous. Jealousy is subdued in Lady Murasaki, as exclusive female possession of the male is not possible.

I would hesitate to affirm that the perspective of *The Tale of Genji* is entirely female, so firmly does Lady Murasaki identify herself with "the shining Genji." And yet the exaltation of longing over fulfillment throughout the novel may be an indication that the male vision of sexual love is essentially secondary.

Lady Murasaki's own splendor, like Proust's, is her gathering wisdom, in which a mingled spiritual and aesthetic nostalgia takes the place of a waning social order. To be a genius of longing, you must excel in narrative patience, and it is astonishing how well she varies her stories.

Lady Murasaki's vast romance narrative has been part of literary culture in English since Arthur Waley completed his version in 1933. I read Wiley's *Genji* a half-century ago, and retained vivid impressions of it, but have only now read Edward G. Seidensticker's very different translation, though it has been available since 1976. Rereading Waley alongside Seidensticker is instructive: *Genji* is so nuanced and splendid a work that one hopes for many more versions. The German translation by Oscar Bent (1966) provides yet another reflection of Murasaki's immense tale, and enriches a reader who knows neither medieval nor modern Japanese. One gathers that Murasaki's language, in relation to our Japanese contemporaries, is somewhere between Old English and Middle English in regard to us. She is not as distant as *Beowulf*, nor so close as Chaucer; modern Japanese translations therefore are essential for current readers.

Doubtless *The Tale of Genji* is more culturally remote from us than Waley, Seidensticker, and Bent make it seem, but literary genius is uniquely capable of universality, and I have the strong illusion, as I read, that Lady Murasaki is as available to my understanding as Jane Austen is, or Marcel Proust, or Virginia Woolf. Austen is a secular novelist, and so is Murasaki: her romance, as it develops, seems more and more a novel, except that it has a bewildering plethora of protagonists. There are almost fifty principal characters, and keeping clear who has been married and when, or had a sexual relationship, or is secretly someone's father or daughter, can be rather difficult. In reading through Seidensticker's version of nearly eleven hundred pages (it is more faithful and less condensed than Waley's), one never loses interest, but it is difficult not to get lost. Genji, an imperial prince sent into internal exile as a commoner, is an exuberantly passionate personage, whose longings are perpetual, mutable, and impatient when thwarted. It may be more accurate to speak of "longing" than "longings." He *is* a state of longing, and evidently irresistible to the extraordinary (and extraordinarily varied) women of the court and of the provinces.

We are not to consider Genji to be a Don Juan, though he certainly manifests what Lord Byron called "mobility." Lady Murasaki herself, through her narrator, clearly finds Genji more than sympathetic; he is a figure who radiates light, and who ought to be emperor. Eros, in Murasaki and her major contemporary woman writers, is not exactly what we think we mean by "romantic love," but in obsessiveness, self-destructiveness, and overdetermination or apparent inevitability there is little pragmatic difference. Though everyone in *The Tale of Genji* is a Buddhist, and so warned by doctrine against desire, just about all of them are very susceptible indeed, Genji most of all. Renunciation, that "piercing virtue," as Emily Dickinson termed it, is resorted to only after disaster by each lady in turn, and only after many turns by the perpetually passionate Genji.

Genji, who will never be emperor, is particularly liable to sudden (and then lasting) attachments to ladies not of the first tank, thus repeating his imperial father's passion for Genji's mother, forced out of the court by the malice of more aristocratic consorts. Broken by the experience, Genji's mother dies while he is still a baby, and his eagerness for intimacy clearly has a link to this early loss. But Lady Murasaki, who, before her *Tale* is done, will have anticipated Cervantes as the first novelist, is also an accomplished ironist. Her delicious second chapter, "The Broom Tree," gives us a pragmatic symposium on love conducted by Genji and three other courtiers:

> At this point two young courtiers, a guards officer and a functionary in the ministry of rites, appeared on the scene, to attend the emperor in his retreat. Both were devotees of the way of love and both were good talkers. To no Chujo, as if he had been waiting for them, invited their views on the question that had just been asked. The discussion progressed, and included a number of rather unconvincing points.
>
> "Those who have just arrived at high position," said one of

the newcomers, "do not attract the same sort of notice as those who were born to it. And those who were born to the highest rank but somehow do not have the right backing—in spirit they may be as proud and noble as ever, but they cannot hide their deficiencies. And so I think that they should both be put in your middle rank.

"There are those whose families are not quite of the highest rank but who go off and work hard in the provinces. They have their place in the world, though there are all sorts of little differences among them. Some of them would belong on anyone's list. So it is these days. Myself, I would take a woman from a middling family over one who has rank and nothing else. Let us say someone whose father is almost but not quite a councillor. Someone who has a decent enough reputation and comes from a decent enough family and can live in some luxury. Such people can be very pleasant. There is nothing wrong with the household arrangements, and indeed a daughter can sometimes be set out in a way that dazzles vote. l can think of several such women it would he hard to find fault with. When they go into court service, they are the ones the unexpected favors have a way of falling on. I have seen cases enough of it, I can tell you."

Lady Murasaki's irony makes us wonder as to just which are the "rather unconvincing points." In what may he the *Tale*'s ultimate irony. Genji encounters the major relationship of his life in a ten-year-old girl he calls Murasaki, whom he adopts and brings up. Her name (and the author's) refers to the aromatic lavender plant, and Genji's relationship to her is outrageous from the start:

> She thought little of her father. They had lived apart and she scarcely knew him. She was by now extremely fond of her new father. She would be the first to run out and greet him when he came home, and she would climb on his lap, and they would talk happily together, without the least constraint or embarrassment. He was delighted with her. A clever and watchful woman can create all manner of difficulties. A man must always be on his guard, and jealousy can have the most unwelcome consequences. Murasaki was the perfect companion, a toy for him to play with. He could not hove been so free and uninhibited with a daughter of his own. There are restraints upon paternal intimacy. Yes, he had come upon a remarkable little treasure.

Again we are given an ironic pathos, which seems to me Lady Murasaki's most characteristic tonality. She herself came from the second level of court aristocrats, her family having fallen gradually from much higher rank. When we first meet the child who will he renamed Murasaki by the infatuated Genji, her nurse is called Shonagon, which seems to me an irony aimed at Sei Shonagon, whose *The Pillow Book of Sei Shonagon* is the chief rival to *The Tale of Genji*, and who is deprecated in Lady Murasaki's *Diary* as being "dreadfully conceited" in her supposed display of false erudition in the use of Chinese characters, almost as if she were the Ezra Pound of her day.

Lady Murasaki, more than nine hundred years before Freud, understood that all erotic transferences were substitute-formations for earlier attachments. Plato, even earlier, thought the same, though for him the archetypal relationship was to the Idea, rather than to the parental image. When the child Murasaki is fourteen, Genji takes her:

> It was a tedious time. He no longer had any enthusiasm for the careless night wanderings that had once kept him busy. Murasaki was much on his mind. She seemed peerless, the nearest he could imagine to his ideal. Thinking that she was no longer too young for marriage, he had occasionally made amorous overtures; but she had not seemed to understand. They had passed their time in games of Go and *hentsugi*. She was clever and she had many delicate ways of pleasing him in the most trivial diversions. He had not seriously thought of her as a wife. Now he could not restrain himself. It would be a shock, of course.
>
> What had happened? Her women had no way of knowing when the line had been crossed. One morning Genji was up early and Murasaki stayed on and on in bed. It was not at all like her to sleep so late. Might she be unwell? As he left for his own rooms, Genji pushed an inkstone inside her bed curtains.
>
> At length, when no one else was near, she raised herself from her pillow and saw beside it a tightly folded bit of paper. Listlessly she opened it. There was only this verse, in a casual hand:
>
> "Many have been the nights we have spent together Purposelessly, these coverlets between us."

As her foster father, Genji has brought a figurative stigma of incest to Murasaki, and she herself will never become a mother. The narrator, as always, makes no judgments, and the violated fourteen-year-old makes the transition into a phase of happiness with Genji, but such a phase is purely ironic. Genji, perpetually questing for what is not to be found, goes on to other consorts, while holding Murasaki in place. But she is a remarkable consciousness, who will not abide with him, and she turns to Buddhist devotion as the path back to herself, and to her own childhood. Since Genji will not permit her to become a Buddhist nun, she arranges a ceremony in honor of the Lotus Sutra, which allows women their part in salvation. And after that, she lapses into a long day's dying to ease her pain, as John Milton might have termed it. With her beauty as a child returned to her, she dies, leaving Genji properly bereft.

Lady Murasaki no more blames Genji than she would chide one season for replacing another. And yet, after this, he is on the path that must lead finally to life's triumph over him. After another year, he begins to make ready to depart, and dies between chapters 41 and 42, as though Lady Murasaki herself were too attached to her creation to represent his dying. Chapter 42 begins, "The shining Genji was dead, and there was no one quite like him." The novel will go on for another three hundred and fifty pages, and the genius of an ironic pathos continues to manifest itself, but it becomes another tale.

The book became, and still is, a kind of secular Bible for Japanese culture. What *Don Quixote* almost uniquely was to Miguel de Unamuno, *The Tale of Genji* has been for a myriad of Japanese men and women of aesthetic sensibility. As a secular scripture, Lady Murasaki's huge romance-novel takes on a very ambiguous status, because it is almost impossible to define the book's relationship to Buddhism. Desire, the longing for another person, is almost the primal fault in most versions of Buddhism. Longing destroys Genji, and the best among his women. But it is the essence of Genji, and as readers we are captured by him, and by the answering passion that he evokes. The best book I have found on Lady Murasaki's masterwork, by Norma Field, accurately and eloquently is titled *The Splendor of Longing in the "Tale of Genji"* (1987). And there, I think, is where Murasaki's genius must be located, in that oxymoronic "splendor of longing." A longing is a yearning that never can be fulfilled, a desire never to be appeased. After reading Lady Murasaki, you never feel the same again about loving, or falling in love. She is the genius of longing, and we are her students even before we come to her.

# Dante Alighieri

## (1265-1321)

THE LIFE OF DANTE ALIGHIERI ITSELF CAN SEEM A TURBULENT POEM, closer to his *Inferno* than to his *Purgatorio*, quite aside from his *Paradiso*. Biographies so far are mostly inadequate to Dante's genius, with the major exception of the very first, Giovanni Boccaccio's, aptly described by Giuseppe Mazzotta as a "self-conscious fictional work akin to Dante's own *Vita Nuova* (*The New Life*) which responds imaginatively to Dante's steady self-dramatization in his works." This need not surprise anyone; Dante, like Shakespeare, is so large a form of thought and imagination that individual biographers, scholars, and critics tend to see only aspects of an extraordinary panoply. I always recommend to my students, in preference to all biographies of Shakespeare, the late Anthony Burgess's *Nothing Like the Sun*, a rather Joycean novel narrated by Shakespeare in the first person.

The exalted Dante regarded himself as a prophet, at least the equal of Isaiah or Jeremiah. Shakespeare, we can assume, had no such self-estimate; the creator of Hamlet, Falstaff, and Lear has much in common with Geoffrey Chaucer, the maker of the Pardoner and the Wife of Bath, and Chaucer subtly mocks Dante. One has to be of Chaucer's eminence, if Dante is to be treated ironically, and even Chaucer clearly admires far more intensely than he dissents.

One cannot discuss genius in all the world's history without centering upon Dante, since only Shakespeare, of all geniuses of language, is richer. Shakespeare to a considerable extent remade English: about eighteen hundred words of the twenty-one thousand he employed were his own coinage, and I cannot pick up a newspaper without finding Shakespearean turns of phrase scattered through it, frequently without intention. Yet Shakespeare's English was inherited by him, from Chaucer and from William Tyndale, the principal translator of the Protestant Bible. Had Shakespeare written nothing, the English language, pretty much as we know it, would have prevailed, but Dante's Tuscan dialect became the Italian language largely because of Dante. He is the national poet, as Shakespeare is wherever English is spoken, and Goethe wherever German dominates. No single French poet, not even Racine or Victor Hugo, is so unchallenged in eminence, and no Spanish-language poet is so central s Cervantes. And yet Dante, though he essentially founded literary Italian, hardly thought of himself as Tuscan, let alone Italian. He was a Florentine, obsessively so, exiled from his city in the last nineteen of his fifty-six years.

A few dates are crucial for the reader of Dante, starting with the death of Beatrice, his beloved ideal or idealized beloved, on June 8, 1290, when the poet was twenty-five. By his own account, Dante's devotion to Beatrice was what we call platonic, though nothing concerning Dante ever can be termed anything but Dantesque, including his Catholicism. He set Easter 1300 as the fictive date of the journey he undertakes in the *Divine Comedy*, and he completed the *Inferno*, its first and most notorious part, in 1314. In the seven years remaining to him, he had the sublime fortune of composing both the *Purgatorio* and the *Paradiso*, so that his magnificent poem was fully composed by almost a year before his death.

Shakespeare died as he turned fifty-two, but we lost nothing by it, because he had stopped writing some three years before. Dante, one feels, would have gone on to other literary achievements, had he lived the quarter-century more that he expected in order to reach the "perfect" age of eighty-one, nine nines in a numerological vision of his own, which cannot altogether be deciphered.

Here is Dante in the *Convivio* (book 4, 24) telling us that age ends at the seventieth year, but that there can be sublimity, if we live on:

> Whence we have it of Plato—whom (both in the strength of his own nature, and because of the physiognomiscope which Socrates cast for him when first he saw him) we may believe to have had the most excellent nature—that he lives eighty-one years, as testifies Tully in that *Of Old Age*. And I believe that if Christ had not been crucified and had lived out the space which his life had power to cover according to its nature, he would have been changed at the eighty-first year from mortal body to eternal.

What change did Dante expect at the eighty-first year? Would Beatrice, the Lady Nine, have appeared to him again, in this life? George Santayana found in Beatrice a Platonizing of Christianity; E.R. Curtius saw her as the center of Dante's personal and poetic gnosis. She has some crucial relation to the transfiguration that Christ would have undergone at eighty-one, since her own death, according to her lover's *Vita Nuova*, is dated by him through a process in which the perfect number nine is completed nine times. At twenty-five she changed from mortal to eternal body. Dante, implicitly and explicitly, tells us throughout the *Comedy* that he, Dante, is the truth. The Sufi martyr Hallaj died for proclaiming that he was the truth, though in the American Religion (in its various forms) such an affirmation is almost commonplace. I talk to dissident Mormons, Baptist sectaries, and many Pentecostals who candidly assure me that they are the truth. Neither Augustine nor Aquinas would have said that he was the truth. The *Commedia* would not work if Beatrice were not the truth, and yet, without Dante, none of us would have heard of Beatrice. I think that too much cannot be made of this, and I never quite understand why Dante, who now defines Catholicism for so many intellectuals, overcame the possibility that his personal myth of Beatrice was as much a heresy as the Gnostic myths of a Sophia, or female principle, in the Godhead. Simon Magus found his Helena in a whorehouse in Tyre, and proclaimed her to be both Helen of Troy and the fallen Sophia, or Wisdom of God. The Samaritan Simon, always denounced by Christians, was the first Faustus, audacious and imaginative, but now is universally regarded as a charlatan. Dante found his unfallen Wisdom of God in a Florentine young woman, and raised her to the heavenly hierarchy. Simon the magician, like Jesus the magician, belongs to oral tradition, while Dante—except for Shakespeare—is the supreme poet of all Western history and culture. And yet Dante was not less arbitrary than Simon, as we ought not to forget. Though he says otherwise, Dante usurps poetic authority and establishes himself as central to Western culture.

How different Dante's centrality is from Shakespeare's! Dante imposes his personality upon us; Shakespeare, even in the Sonnets, evades us, because of his uncanny detachment. In the *Vita Nuova*, Dante immerses us in the story of his extraordinary love for a young woman whom he scarcely knew. They first meet as nine-year-olds, though that "nine" is a warning against any literalization of this story. Nine years after the poet first saw Beatrice, she spoke to him, a formal greeting in the street. Another greeting or two, a snub after he poetically professed love for another lady as a "screen" defense, and one gathering where Beatrice may have joined in a gentle mockery of her smitten admirer: this seems to have been their entire relationship. The best commentary on this mere actuality is that of the Argentine fabulist Jorge Luis Borges, who speaks of "our certainty of an unhappy and superstitious love," unreciprocated by Beatrice.

We can speak of Shakespeare's "unhappy and superstitious love" for the fair young nobleman of the Sonnets, but some other phrase would have to be found for Shakespeare's descent into the Hell of the Dark Lady of the same sequence. To call Dante's love for Beatrice Neoplatonic would be insufficient, but how can we define that love? A passion for one's own genius, for a muse of one's own creation, could seem a dark idolatry of self in almost anyone else, but not in the central man. The myth or figure of Beatrice is fused with Dante's lifework; in a crucial sense she is the *Commedia*, and cannot be understood if you stand outside the poem. And yet Dante presents her as the truth, though not to be mistaken for the Christ, who is the way, the truth, the light.

Dante scholarship, vastly useful for mastering the complexities of the *Commedia*, nevertheless does not much help me in apprehending Beatrice. She is more Christological in the *Vita Nuova* than in the *Commedia*, though sometimes there she reminds me of what the Gnostics called "the Angel Christ," since she breaks down the distinction between the human and the angelic. A fusion between the divine and the mortal may or may not be heretical, depending upon how it is presented. Dante's vision does not impress me as Augustinian or Thomistic, but though hermetic, it is not Hermetist, as it were. Rather than identifying with theology, Dante strives to identify it with himself. The presence of the human in the divine is not the same as God's presence in a person, and in Beatrice in particular.

That sounds perhaps odd, since Dante was not William Blake, who urged us to worship only what he called the Human Form Divine. Yet Dante early on wrote that Beatrice was a miracle. This miracle was for all Florence, and not for Dante alone, though he was its sole celebrant. His best friend and poetic mentor, Guido Cavalcanti, is later condemned by Dante for not joining the celebration, but Dante has the same relation to Cavalcanti that the young Shakespeare had to Christopher Marlowe, a shadow of influence-anxiety. Are we to believe Dante when he implies that Cavalcanti would have been saved if he had acknowledged Beatrice? Is a shared originality still original?

As readers, we can abandon Dante's supposed theology to his exegetes, but you cannot read Dante without coming to terms with his Beatrice. For Dante, she is certainly an Incarnation, which he declines to see as a being in competition with the Incarnation. She is, he insists, whatever happiness he has had, and without her he would not have found his way to salvation. But Dante is not a Faust, to be damned or saved, or a Hamlet, who dies of the truth. Dante is bent upon triumph, total vindication, a prophecy fulfilled. His "fathers," Brunetto Latini and Vergil, are transcended, with love, but still firmly set aside. His poetic "brothers" are acknowledged (rather darkly, in Cavalcanti's case) but are not his companions on the way. Does he persuade us, in the *Commedia*, that Beatrice is something more than his individual genius? He is both inside and outside his poem, as Beatrice was in the *Vita Nuova*. Has she a reality that might enable her to be invoked by others?

Shakespeare's grandest characters can walk out of their plays and live in our consciousness of them. Can Beatrice? Dante's personality is so large that it allows room for no one else; the Pilgrim of Eternity takes up all the space. This is hardly a poetic fault, as it would be in any other poet whatsoever. In Dante it is poetic strength, energized by absolute originality, a newness that cannot be staled by endless rereadings, and that cannot be assimilated to its sources, literary or theological.

Augustine, opposing the great Neoplatonists, Plotinus and Porphyry, insisted that self-confidence and pride were not sufficient for the ascent to God. Guidance and assistance were necessary, and could come only from God. Is there a fiercer pride or a more resolute self-confidence than Dante's? He portrays himself as a pilgrim, reliant upon guidance, comfort, and assistance, but as a poet he is more a prophet being called than he is a Christian undergoing conversion. Does he bother truly to persuade us of his humility? His heroism—spiritual, metaphysical, imaginative—makes Dante the poet pragmatically as much a miracle as was his Beatrice.

Fortunately, he presents himself as a personality, not as a miracle. We know him so well, in essence rather than in outline, that we can accept his hard-won changes as he develops, throughout the *Commedia*. Indeed, only he can change in the *Commedia*, as everyone else has reached finality, though there is a process of refining that dwellers in the *Purgatorio* must undergo. Outrageously vivid as everyone is in the *Commedia*, they are past altering, in kind. They will not change because of what Dante has them say or do. This makes total revelation possible: Dante gives us the last word upon them, beyond dispute, and always provoking wonder. Whether you can have personality after a last judgment has been passed upon you, is a very pretty question.

Beatrice, as Dante's creation, possesses little enough personality, because she clearly has had an angelic preexistence before her birth into Florence. Dante shows us, in the *Vita Nuova*, only that she is of unearthly beauty, and is capable of severity, a stance towards him that augments in the *Commedia*, though it is merely rhetorical. There is rather a leap from her relative unawareness of her idealizing lover, in life, and her cosmological concern for his salvation, after her death. So clearly is she Dante's good genius or better angel that the transmutation is easily acceptable. Laertes rather wistfully says that the rejected Ophelia will be a ministering angel after her death, presumably one of those flights of angels that Horatio invokes at the close, to one's surprise, when we brood about it. Dante, long preparing his own apotheosis, has had his Beatrice in training for quite some time.

No other writer ever is nearly as formidable as Dante, not even John Milton or Leo Tolstoy. Shakespeare, a miracle of elusiveness, is everyone and no one, as Borges said. Dante is Dante. No one is going to explain Dante away by historicizing him, or by emulating his own audacious self-theologizing: Cavalcanti, had he lived, would doubtless have written even more powerful lyrics than earlier, but he is not likely to have composed a Third Testament which is precisely what the *Divine Comedy* appears to be. The question of Shakespeare's genius is forever beyond us, yet Dante's genius is an answer not a question. With the exception of Shakespeare, who came three centuries later, the strongest poet of the Western world completed its single greatest work of literary art by the close of the second decade of the fourteenth century. To equal the *Commedia*, and in some ways surpass it, you would have to regard the two dozen most remarkable of Shakespeare's thirty-nine plays as somehow a single entity. But Dante and Shakespeare are very difficult to take in sequence: try to read *King Lear* after the *Purgatorio*, or *Macbeth* after the *Inferno*: a curious disturbance is felt. These two most central of poets are violently incompatible, at least in my experience: Dante would have wanted his reader to judge that Beatrice was Christ in Dante's soul; many of us may be uncomfortable with that, for various reasons, but how startled we would be if Shakespeare, in the Sonnets, were to intimate that the fair young lord (Southampton or whomever) was a type of Christ for the poet who would go on to compose *Hamlet* and *King Lear*.

To the common reader who can absorb the *Commedia* in the original, Beatrice is scarcely a puzzle, since Italian critics are very unlike Anglo-American scholars in their approach to Dante, and their more worldly sense of him has filtered down. I treasure the observation of Giambattista Vico that even Homer would have yielded to Dante had the Tuscan been less erudite in theology. Dante, like Freud (and the mystics), thought that erotic sublimation was possible, differing in this from his friend Cavalcanti, who regarded love as an illness that had to be lived through. Dante, who has Francesca and her Paolo down in Hell for adultery, was widely noted for his venery, in regard to women very different (in his view) from the sacred Beatrice. About the only place where Dante and Shakespeare meet is in their mutual supremacy at rendering erotic suffering, of others and their own:

Yet shall the streams turn back and climb the hills
Before Love's flame in this damp wood and green
Burns, as it burns within a youthful lady,
For my sake, who would sleep away in stone
My life, or feed like beasts upon the grass,
Only to see her garments cast a shade.

That is from Dante Gabriel Rossetti's version of the "stony" sestina "To
the dim Light," one of the "stony rhymes" passionately addressed by
Dante to one Pietra. Beatrice is not very Shakespearean; Pietra is, and
would have done well as the Dark Lady of the Sonnets:

Th'expense of spirit in a waste of shame
Is lust in action; and, till action, lust
Is perjured, murd'rous, bloody, full of blame,
Savage, extreme, rude, cruel, not to trust;
Enjoyed no sooner but despised straight ...

Pious reactions to Dante are not so clearly useless as attempts to
Christianize the tragedies of Hamlet and of Lear, but they do the
*Commedia* more harm than feminist resentment, which tends to mistrust
the idealization of Beatrice. Dante's praise of Beatrice is immensely
poignant; his exaltation of an unrequited love is more problematic, unless
we think back to the profound visions of early childhood, when we fell in
love with someone we scarcely knew, and perhaps never saw again. T.S.
Eliot shrewdly surmised that Dante's experience of first loving Beatrice
must have come before he was nine, and the numerological paradigm
indeed could have induced Dante to set the experience two or three years
later than it took place. Not being Dante, most of us can do little with so
early an epiphany, and part of Dante's achievement is that he could found
greatness upon it.

If Beatrice is universal in her origins, she becomes in the *Commedia*
an esoteric figure, the center of Dante's own gnosis, since it is by and
through her that Dante asserts knowledge rather less traditional than most
of his exegetes will grant. The permanent notoriety of the *Inferno* has not
obscured the dramatic eloquence of the Purgatorio, which retains a reasonably wide leadership. It is the *Paradiso* which is immensely difficult, and
yet that difficulty represents Dante's genius at its most indisputable, breaking beyond the limits of imaginative literature. There is nothing else that
resembles the *Paradiso*, unless it be certain sequences in the *Meccan
Revelations* of the Andalusian Sufi Ibn Arabi (1165–1240), who had

encountered *his* Beatrice in Mecca. Nizam, the Sophia of Mecca, like Beatrice of Florence, was the center of a theophany and converted Ibn Arabi to an idealized, sublimated love.

At seventy-one, I am perhaps not yet ready for the *Paradiso* (where, being of the Jewish persuasion, I am not going to end anyway), and I have begun to recoil from the *Inferno*, an authentically terrifying if sublime work. I do keep going back to the *Purgatorio*, for reasons wonderfully phrased by W.S. Merwin in the foreword to his admirable translation of the middle canticle of the *Commedia*.

Of the three sections of the poem, only *Purgatorio* happens *on* the earth, as our lives do, with our feet on the ground, crossing a beach, climbing a mountain ... To the very top of the mountain hope is mixed with pain, which brings it still closer to the living present. (xiii).

My friends all differ upon which canto of the *Purgatorio* is their personal favorite; I choose the vision of Matilda gathering flowers, in the Earthly Paradise of canto 28. The first fifty-one lines, beautifully rendered by Merwin, I give here in Percy Bysshe Shelley's ecstatic version, his only extended translation from the *Commedia*:

> And earnest to explore within—around—
> The divine wood, whose thick green living woof
> Tempered the young day to the sight—I wound
>
> Up the green slope, beneath the forest's roof,
> With slow, soft steps leaving the mountain's steep,
> And sought those inmost labyrinths, motion-proof
>
> Against the air, that in that stillness deep
> And solemn, struck upon my forehead bare,
> The slow, soft, stroke of a continuous ...
>
> In which the leaves tremblingly were
> All bent towards that part where earliest
> The sacred hill obscures the morning air.
>
> Yet were they not so shaken from the rest,
> But that the birds, perched on the utmost spray,
> Incessantly renewing their blithe quest,

With perfect joy received the early day,
Singing within the glancing leaves, whose sound
Kept a low burden to their roundelay,

Such as from bough to bough gathers around
The pine forest on bleak Chiassi's shore,
When Aeolus Sirocco has unbound.

My slow steps had already borne me o'er
Such space within the antique wood, that I
Perceived not where I entered any more,—

When, lo! A stream whose little waves went by,
Bending towards the left through grass that grew
Upon its bank, impeded suddenly

My going on. Water of purest hue
On earth, would appear turbid and impure
Compared with this, whose unconcealing dew,

Dark, dark, yet clear, moved under the obscure
Eternal shades, whose interwoven looms
The rays of moon or sunlight ne'er endure.

I moved not with my feet, but mid the glooms
Pierced with my charmed eye, contemplating
The mighty multitude of fresh May blooms

Which starred that night, when, even as a thing
That suddenly, for blank astonishment,
Charms every sense, and makes all thought take wing,—

A solitary woman! and she went
Singing and gathering flower after flower,
With which her way was painted and besprent.

"Bright lady, who, if looks had ever power
To bear true witness of the heart within,
Dost bask under the beams of love, come lower

"Towards this bank. I prithee let me win

This much of thee, to come, that I may hear
Thy song: like Proserpine, in Enna's glen,

"Thou seemest to my fancy, singing here
And gathering flowers, as that fair maiden when
She lost the Spring, and Ceres her, more dear."

Shelley keeps the *terza rima* (which Dante had invented) at some expense to the original's literal meaning, but he catches the surprises and splendor of the advent of Matilda, who has reversed the fall of Proserpine and of Eve, and who presages the imminent return of the vision of Beatrice to Dante. Shakespeare, in act 4, scene 4 of *The Winter's Tale*, may also hover in Shelley's memory, since Perdita is Shakespeare's equivalent of Matilda.

O Proserpina,
For the flowers now that frighted, thou let'st fall
From Dis's waggon! daffodils,
That come before the swallow dares, and take
The winds of March with beauty ...

Why Dante named this singing girl of a restored Eden Matilda (Matelda) is something of a puzzle, explained away differently by various scholars. Dante's Matilda makes only a brief appearance, but I perversely prefer her to Beatrice, who scolds and preaches, and is endlessly too good for Dante. Like Shakespeare's Perdita, Matilda charms us. Who but the ferocious Dante could fall in love again with the heavenly Beatrice? Who would not fall in love with Matilda, as translated here by William Merwin?

"and it tastes sweeter than any other,
and although your thirst might be completely
satisfied if I revealed no more.

"I will add a corollary, as a favor,
And I do not think my words will be less dear
To you because they go beyond my promise.

"Those who sang in ancient times of the age
Of gold and of its happy state saw this place,
Perhaps, in their dreams on Parnassus.

"Here the root of humankind was innocent.
Here Spring and every fruit lasted forever;
When they told of nectar this is what each meant."

Gracious and beautiful, the mysterious epitome of a young woman in love, Matilda walks with Dante through the meadows as though the Golden Age had returned. Matilda moves like a dancer, and we need not slow her pace by piling allegories upon her, or by relating her to historical noblewomen or blessed contemplatives. Dante, notoriously susceptible to the beauty of women, clearly would fall in love with Matilda, if the transmogrified Beatrice, as much chiding mother as image of desire, were not waiting for him in the next canto.

William Hazlitt, superb literary critic of British Romanticism, had a far more ambivalent reaction to Dante than Shelley and Byron did, yet Hazlitt caught at the truth of Dante's originality, the effect of Dante's genius:

> he interests only by his exciting our sympathy with the emotion by which he is himself possessed. He does not place before us the objects by which that emotion has been excited; but he seizes on the attention, by showing us the effect they produce on his feelings; and his poetry accordingly frequently gives us the thrilling and overwhelming sensation which is caught by gazing on the face of a person who has seen some object of horror.

Hazlitt was thinking of the *Inferno*, and not of Matilda in the *Purgatorio*, where the sensation is that of gazing upon a face who has seen an ultimate object of delight.

### The Divine Comedy

Dante, by common consent, stands with the supreme Western masters of literary representation: the Yahwist, Homer, Chaucer, Shakespeare, Cervantes, Milton, Tolstoy, Proust. Our ideas as to how reality can be represented by literary language depend, to a considerable extent, on this ninefold. Perhaps it can also be said that these writers have formed a large part of our experience of what is called reality. Certain aspects of reality might not be nearly so visible, had we not read these nine masters of mimesis. Setting the Yahwist and Homer aside as being both ancient and hypothetical, only Shakespeare, again by common consent, is judged to be

Dante's rival as a great Original in representation. But Shakespearean representation has naturalized us in its domain. Dante is now an immensely difficult poet partly because we are so much at home with Shakespeare.

Erich Auerbach, who with Charles S. Singleton and John Freccero makes up a celestial trinity of Dante interpreters, gave us the definitive opening description of Dante's ways of representing reality:

> Dante in the *Comedy* transcended tragic death by identifying man's ultimate fate with the earthly unity of his personality, and ... the very plan of the work made it possible, and indeed confronted him with the obligation, to represent earthly reality exactly as he saw it. Thus it became necessary that the characters in Dante's other world, in their situation and attitude, should represent the sum of themselves; that they should disclose, in a single act, the character and fate that had filled out their lives ...
>
> ... from classical theory Dante took over only one principle, the *sibi constare*, or consistency, of his persons; all other tenets had lost their literal meaning for him ... Dante's vision is a tragedy according to Aristotle's definition. In any event it is far more a tragedy than an epic, for the descriptive, epic elements in the poem are not autonomous, but serve other purposes, and the time, for Dante as well as his characters, is not the epic time in which destiny gradually unfolds, but the final time in which it is fulfilled.

If time is the final time, past all unfolding, then reality indeed can be represented in a single act that is at once character and fate. Dante's personages can reveal themselves totally in what they say and do, but they cannot change *because* of what Dante has them say and do. Chaucer, who owed Dante more than he would acknowledge, nevertheless departed from Dante in this, which is precisely where Chaucer most influenced Shakespeare. The Pardoner listens to himself speaking, listens to his own tale, and is darkly made doom-eager through just that listening. This mode of representation expands in Shakespeare to a point that no writer since has reached so consistently. Hamlet may be the most metamorphic of Shakespeare's people (or it may be Cleopatra, or Falstaff, or who you will), but as such he merely sets the mode. Nearly everyone of consequence in Shakespeare helps inaugurate a mimetic style we all now take too much for granted. They, like us, are strengthened or victimized, reach an apotheosis or are destroyed, by themselves reacting to what they say and do. It may be that we have learned to affect ourselves so strongly, in part because involuntarily we imitate Shakespeare's characters. We never imitate Dante's creatures because we do not live in finalities; we know that we are not fulfilled.

A literary text can represent a fulfilled reality only if it can persuade itself, and momentarily persuade us, that one text can fulfill another. Dante, as Auerbach demonstrated, relied upon the great Christian trope of *figura*, whose basis was the insistence that the Christian New Testament had fulfilled what it called "the Old Testament," itself a phrase deeply offensive to normative Jews who continue to trust in the Covenant as set forth in the Hebrew Bible. But the Hebrew Bible indeed must be the Old Testament, if Christianity is to retain its power. What must the New Testament be, if Dante's poem is to develop and maintain its force?

Auerbach, quoting the Church Father Tertullian's comments upon the renaming of Oshea, son of Nun, by Moses as Jehoshua (Joshua, Jesus), speaks of Joshua as "a figure of things to come." The definition of this figure of prophecy or *figura* by Auerbach is now classic: "*Figura* is something real and historical which announces something else that is real and historical." Equally classic is Auerbach's formulation of "figural interpretation":

> Figural interpretation establishes a connection between two events or persons, the first of which signifies not only itself but also the second, while the second encompasses or fulfills the first. The first two poles of the figure are separate in time, but both, being real events or figures, are within time, within the stream of historical life. Only the understanding of the two persons or events is a spiritual act, but this spiritual act deals with concrete events whether past, present, or future, and not with concepts or abstractions; these are quite secondary, since promise and fulfillment are real historical events, which have either happened in the incarnation of the word, or will happen in the second coming.

What happens when figural interpretation is transferred from sacred to secular literature? When Dante takes the historical Virgil and reads him as a *figura* of which Dante's character, Virgil, is the fulfillment, are we seeing the same pattern enacted as when Tertullian reads Joshua as the *figura* of which Jesus Christ was the fulfillment? Auerbach's answer is "yes," but this is a dialectical affirmative: "Thus Virgil in the *Divine Comedy* is the historical Virgil himself, but then again he is not; for the historical Virgil is only a *figura* of the fulfilled truth that the poem reveals, and this fulfillment is more real, more significant than the *figura*." Auerbach, writing on *figura* back in 1944, thought back to his book on Dante as poet of the secular world (1929), from which I quoted earlier, and insisted that he had acquired "a solid historical grounding" for his view of fifteen years before.

I am not certain that the earlier Auerbach is not to be preferred to the later. In secularizing *figura*, Auerbach dangerously idealized the relationship between literary texts. Appropriating the historical, Virgil is not an idealizing gesture, as John Freccero shows in his superb essay, "Manfred's Wounds and the Poetics of the *Purgatorio*." Poetic fathers die hard, and Dante understood that he had made the historical Virgil the *figura*, and his own Virgil the fulfillment, partly in order to suggest that he himself was the poet Virgil's true fulfillment. Great poets are pragmatists when they deal with precursors; witness Blake's caricature of Milton as the hero of his poem *Milton*, or James Merrill's loving and witty portrayal of Stevens and Auden in *The Changing Light at Sandover*. Dante's Virgil is no more the historical Virgil than Blake's Milton is the historical Milton. If texts fulfill one another, it is always through some self-serving caricature of the earlier text by the later.

## II

Charles S. Singleton, carefully reminding us that "Beatrice is not Christ," expounds Dante's use of the principle of analogy which likens the advent of Beatrice to the advent of Christ:

> Thus it is that the figure of a rising sun by which Beatrice comes at last to stand upon the triumphal chariot is the most revealing image which the poet might have found not only to affirm the analogy of her advent to Christ's in the present tense, but to stress, in so doing, the very basis upon which that analogy rests: the advent of light.

Whitman, certainly a poet antithetical to Dante, opposed himself to the rising sun as a greater rising sun:

> Dazzling and tremendous how quick the sun-rise would kill me,
> If I could not now and always send sun-rise out of me.

> We also ascend dazzling and tremendous as the sun,
> We found our own O my soul in the calm and cool of the daybreak.

This is not analogy but a subversive mode akin to Nietzsche's, and learned from Emerson. The figure of the Whitmanian sun here is not an advent of Christ ("a great defeat" Emerson called that advent) but is "now and always," a perpetual dawning ("we demand victory," as Emerson said for his Americans, prophesying Whitman). The figure of Beatrice, to Whitman, might as well have been the figure of Christ. Can we, with Singleton, accept her as an analogy, or is she now the principal embarrassment of Dante's poem? As a fiction she retains her force, but does not Dante present her as more than a fiction? If Dante wrote, as Singleton says, the allegory of the theologians rather than the allegory of the poets, how are we to recapture Dante's sense of Beatrice if we do not accept the analogy that likens her advent to Christ's?

Singleton's answer is that Beatrice is the representation of Wisdom in a Christian sense, or the light of Grace. This answer, though given in the allegorical language of the theologians rather than that of the poets, remains a poetic answer because its analogical matrix is light rather than Grace. Dante persuades us not by his theology but by his occult mastery of the trope of light, in which he surpasses even the blind Milton among the poets:

> There is a light up there which makes the Creator visible to the creature, who finds his peace only in seeing Him.
> (*Paradiso* XXX, 100–102)

This, as Singleton says, is the Light of Glory rather than the Light of Grace, which is Beatrice's, or the Natural Light, which is Virgil's. Dante's peculiar gift is to find perpetually valid analogies for all three lights. Since his poem's fiction of duration is not temporal, but final, all three modes of light must be portrayed by him as though they were beyond change. And yet an unchanging fiction cannot give pleasure, as Dante clearly knew. What does he give us that more than compensates for his poem's apparent refusal of temporal anguish?

Auerbach, in his essay on St. Francis of Assisi in the *Commedia*, turned to *figura* again as his answer. To the medieval reader, according to Auerbach, the representations of forerunning and after-following repetitions were as familiar as the trope of "historical development" is (or was, to those who believe that Foucault forever exposed the trope). To us, now, "forerunning and after-following repetitions" suggest, not *figura* and its fulfillment, but the Freudian death-drive as the "fulfillment" of the compulsion-to-repeat. The repetition-compulsion perhaps is the final Western *figura*, prophesying our urge to drive beyond the pleasure principle. That is to say, for us the only text that can fulfill earlier texts, rather than correct or negate them, is what might be called "the text of death," which is totally opposed to what Dante sought to write.

### III

What saves Dante from the idealizing lameness that necessarily haunts the allegorizing of the theologians? The earlier Auerbach was on the track of the answer when he meditated upon Dante's originality in the representation of persons. As seer, Dante identified character and fate, *ethos* and *daemon*, and what he saw in his contemporaries he transferred precisely to the three final worlds of *Inferno*, *Purgatorio*, and *Paradiso*. Dante's friends and enemies alike are presented, without ambiguity or ambivalence, as being consistent with themselves, beyond change, their eternal destinies over-determined by their fixed characters.

There are endless surprises in his poem for Dante himself, as for us, but there are no accidents. Farinata standing upright in his tomb, as if of Hell he had a great disdain, is heroic because he is massively consistent with himself, in his own tomb, can be nothing but what he is. His marvelous disdain of Hell represents a kind of necessity, what Wallace Stevens called the inescapable necessity of being that inescapable animal, oneself. Such a necessity is presented by Dante as being the judgment of Heaven upon us.

In Shakespeare, there are always accidents, and character can be as metamorphic as personality. Hamlet yields himself up to accident, at the last, perhaps because he has all but exhausted the possibilities for change that even his protean character possesses. This is our mode of representation, inherited by us from Shakespeare, and we no longer are able to see how original it originally was. Shakespeare therefore seems "natural" to us, even though we live in the age of Freud, who suspected darkly that there were no accidents, once we were past infancy. Dante no longer can be naturalized in our imaginations. His originality has not been lost for us, and yet his difficulty or strangeness for us is probably not caused by his authentic originality.

The allegory of the theologians simply is not an available mode for us, despite the labors of Auerbach and Singleton. Freccero has replaced them as the most relevant of Dante critics because he has returned Dante to what may be the truest, because least idealizing, allegory of the poets, which is the agon of poet against poet, the struggle for imaginative priority between forerunner and latecomer. Despite a marvelous parody by Borges, theologians are not primarily agonists. Dante understood that poets were. The light of glory, the light of grace, the light of nature are not competing lights, and yet all tropes for them necessarily compete, and always with other tropes.

Singleton, rejecting the allegory of the poets, said that it would reduce Dante's Virgil to a mere personification of Reason:

> For if this is the allegory of poets, then what Virgil does, like what Orpheus does, is a fiction devised to convey a hidden meaning which it ought to convey all the time, since only by conveying that other meaning is what he does justified at all. Instead, if this action is allegory as theologians take it, then this action must always have a literal sense which is historical and no fiction; and thus Virgil's deeds as part of the whole action may, in their turn, be as words signifying other things, but they do not have to do this all the time, because, being historical, those deeds exist simply in their own right.

But what if Virgil, as allegory of the poets, were to be read not as Reason, the light of nature, but as the trope of that light, reflecting among much else the lustres of the tears of universal nature? To say farewell to Virgil is to take leave not of Reason, but of the pathos of a certain natural light, perhaps of Wordsworth's "light of common day." Dante abandons Virgil not so as to substitute grace for reason, but so as to find his own image of voice, his own trope for all three lights. In the oldest and most authentic allegory of the poets, Virgil represents not reason but poetic fatherhood, the Scene of Instruction that Dante must transcend if he is to complete his journey to Beatrice.

IV

The figure of Beatrice, in my own experience as a reader, is now the most difficult of all Dante's tropes, because sublimation no longer seems to be a human possibility. What is lost, perhaps permanently, is the tradition that moves between Dante and Yeats, in which sublimated desire for a woman can be regarded as an enlargement of existence. One respected feminist critic has gone so far as to call Beatrice a "dumb broad," since she supposedly contemplates the One without understanding Him. What James Thurber grimly celebrated as the War between Men and Women has claimed many recent literary casualties, but none perhaps so unmerited as Dante's Beatrice. Dante, like tradition, thought that God's Wisdom, who daily played before His feet, was a woman, even as Nietzsche, with a gesture beyond irony, considered Truth to be a woman, presumably a deathly one. We possess art in order not to perish from the truth, Nietzsche insisted, which must mean that the aesthetic is a way of not being destroyed by a woman. Dante hardly would have agreed.

Beatrice is now so difficult to apprehend precisely because she participates both in the allegory of the poets and in the allegory of the philosophers. Her advent follows Dante's poetic maturation, or the vanishing of the precursor, Virgil. In the allegory of the poets, Beatrice is the Muse, whose function is to help the poet remember. Since remembering, in poetry, is the major mode of cognition, Beatrice is Dante's power of invention, the essence of his art. That means she is somehow the highest of the Muses, and yet far above them also, since in Dante's version of the allegory of the poets, Beatrice has "a place in the objective process of salvation," as Ernst Robert Curtius phrased it. Curtius rightly emphasized the extent of Dante's audacity:

> Guido Guinicelli (d. 1276) had made the exaltation of the beloved to an angel of paradise a topos of Italian lyric. To choose as guide in a poetic vision of the otherworld a loved woman who has been thus exalted is still within the bounds of Christian philosophy and faith. But Dante goes much further than this. He gives Beatrice a place in the objective process of salvation. Her function is thought of as not only for himself but also for all believers. Thus, on his own authority, he introduces into the Christian revelation an element which disrupts the doctrine of the church. This is either heresy—or myth.

It is now customary to speak of Dante as *the* Catholic poet, even as Milton is called *the* Protestant poet. Perhaps someday Kafka will be named as *the* Jewish writer, though his distance from normative Judaism was infinite. Dante and Milton were not less idiosyncratic, each in his own time, than Kafka was in ours, and the figure of Beatrice would be heresy and not myth if Dante had not been so strong a poet that the Church of later centuries has been happy to claim him. Curtius centered upon Dante's vision of himself as a prophet, even insisting that Dante expected the prophecy's fulfillment in the immediate future, during his own lifetime. Since Dante died at the age of fifty-six, a quarter-century away from the "perfect" age of eighty-one set forth in his *Convivio*, the literal force of the prophecy presumably was voided. But the prophecy, still hidden from us, matters nevertheless, as Curtius again maintains:

Even if we could interpret his prophecy, that would give it no meaning for us. What Dante hid, Dante scholarship need not now unriddle. But it must take seriously the fact that Dante believed that he had an apocalyptic mission. This must be taken into consideration in interpreting him. Hence the question of Beatrice is not mere idle curiosity. Dante's system is built up in the first two cantos of the *Inferno*, it supports the entire *Commedia*. Beatrice can be seen only within it. The Lady Nine has become a cosmic power which emanates from two superior powers. A hierarchy of celestial powers which intervene in the process of history—this concept is manifestly related to Gnosticism: as an intellectual construction, a schema of intellectual contemplation, if perhaps not in origin. Such constructions can and must be pointed out. We do not know what Dante meant by Lucia. The only proper procedure for the commentator, then, is to admit that we do not know and to say that neither the ophthalmological explanation nor the allegorical interpretations are satisfactory. Exegesis is also bound to give its full weight to all the passages at the end of the *Purgatorio* and in the *Paradiso* which are opposed to the identification of Beatrice with the daughter of the banker Portinari. Beatrice is a myth created by Dante.

Very little significant criticism of Dante has followed this suggestion of Curtius, and a distorted emphasis upon Dante's supposed orthodoxy has been the result. Curtius certainly does not mean that Dante was a Gnostic, but he does remind us that Dante's Beatrice is the central figure in a purely personal gnosis. Dante indeed was a ruthless visionary, passionate and willful, whose poem triumphantly expresses his own unique personality. The *Commedia*, though one would hardly know this from most of its critics (Freccero is the sublime exception), is an immense trope of pathos or power, the power of the individual who was Dante. The pathos of that personality is most felt, perhaps, in the great and final parting of Beatrice from her poet, in the middle of Canto XXXI of the *Paradiso*, at the moment when her place as guide is transferred to the aged St. Bernard:

Already my glance had taken in the whole general form of Paradise but had not yet dwelt on any part of it, and I turned with new-kindled eagerness to question my Lady of things on which my mind was in suspense. One thing I intended, and another encountered me: I thought to see Beatrice, and I saw an old man, clothed like that glorious company. His eyes and his cheeks were suffused with a gracious gladness, and his aspect was of such kindness as befits a tender father. And "Where is she?" I said in haste; and he replied: "To end thy longing Beatrice sent me from my place; and if thou took up into the third circle from the highest tier thou shalt see her again, in the throne her merits have assigned to her."

Without answering, I lifted up my eyes and saw her where she made for herself a crown, reflecting from her the eternal beams. From the highest region where it thunders no mortal eye is so far, were it lost in the depth of the sea, as was my sight there from Beatrice; but to me it made no difference, for her image came down to me undimmed by aught between.

"O Lady in whom my hope has its strength and who didst bear for my salvation to leave thy footprints in Hell, of all the things that I have seen I acknowledge the grace and the virtue to be from thy power and from thy goodness. It is thou who hast drawn me from bondage into liberty by all those ways, by every means for it that was in thy power. Preserve in me thy great bounty, so that my spirit, which thou hast made whole, may be loosed from the body well-pleasing to thee." I prayed thus; and she, so far off as she seemed, smiled and looked at me, then turned again to the eternal fount.

It is difficult to comment upon the remorseless strength of this, upon its apparent sublimation of a mythmaking drive that here accepts a restraint which is more than rhetorical. Freud in his own great *summa*, the essay of 1937, "Analysis Terminable and Interminable," lamented his inability to cure those who could not accept the cure:

A man will not be subject to a father-substitute or owe him anything and he therefore refuses to accept his cure from the physician.

Dante too would not owe any man anything, not even if the man were Virgil, his poetic father. The cure had been accepted by Dante from his physician, Beatrice. In smiling and looking at him, as they part, she confirms the cure.

# Geoffrey Chaucer

## (1343–1400)

CHAUCER—AS DONALD HOWARD ELOQUENTLY SHOWED US—LED ALMOST too interesting an outer life: fighting in two wars, endless travels in Europe, personal dealings with the kings and leading nobles of his time, and literary relations with most writers of note. Shakespeare, the only English writer who surpassed Chaucer, fought no wars, was never out of England, and for the most part confined his relations with people of power carefully to the theatrical sphere. It is not that Shakespeare's world was void of violence, but Shakespeare evaded angry events as best he could. We have comprehensive legal records concerning him, and they are virtually all commercial. There is nothing like the somewhat sensational document in which one Cecily Champain released Chaucer from legal actions concerning her rape: Chaucer doubtless had disbursed a large cash settlement.

In the 1380s, when Chaucer was in his prime, Richard II struggled desperately for power, and England was in turmoil. During the decade 1389-99, Richard gradually lost ascendancy, while Chaucer remained his faithful servant. Though the deposing of Richard by Henry IV possibly cost Chaucer nothing in patronage, it must have saddened him. In any case, a year later the great poet died.

There is a curious difference, almost a gap, between what we know of Chaucer's life and era, and his poetry. The age was violent, but Chaucer was an ironist of genius, and *The Canterbury Tales* and *Troilus and Criseyde* transcend their historical context. G.K. Chesterton remarked that Chaucer's irony was so large that sometimes we have trouble even seeing it. Chaucer is sublimely sly, whether in expressing his own pathos, or in acknowledging his authentic literary precursors, Dante and Boccaccio. Boccaccio particularly made Chaucer possible, in some of the same ways that Chaucer enabled Shakespeare to people a world. Chaucer's tales are *about* tale-telling, because Boccaccio had perfected the kind of fiction that is aware of itself as fiction. Stories rhetorically conscious that they *are* rhetoric behave very differently from stories that mask such consciousness. Clearly, Chaucer's heightened sense of story has some relation, however evasive, to the *Decameron.*

Chaucer likes to cite imaginary authorities, while avoiding any mention of Boccaccio, but that returns us to Chaucerian irony. Unlike Boccaccio, Chaucer will not admit to his own passional misadventures, except as jests, or as self-parodies. We are made confidants by Dante, Petrarch, and Boccaccio: Chaucer's anguish stays well within him. Part of Chaucer's genius emerges as self-distancing and comic perspectivism, anticipations of Shakespearean irony. What is extraordinary in Chaucer's own invention is his sense of personality, which allows the Wife of Bath, the Pardoner, even the Prioress (whom I just do not like!) each to speak in her or his own voice. The miracle of mature Shakespeare, which is the individualization of voice in Falstaff, Hamlet, Iago, Cleopatra and their peers, relies upon Chaucer's provocation to Shakespeare's developing genius. Sir John Falstaff is the Wife of Bath's son, as it were, and Iago's superb nihilism is anticipated by the Pardoner's joy in his own power of manipulation.

E. Talbot Donaldson, shrewdest of modern Chaucerians, illuminated Chaucer's two principal *personae*, Chaucer the Pilgrim in *The Canterbury Tales* and the narrator of *Troilus and Criseyde*. Chaucer the Pilgrim is everyone's favorite: friendly, more than tolerant, exuberantly receptive to every colorful scoundrel with whom he travels, but also always prepared to admire authentic goodness. The speaker of *Troilus and Criseyde*, presented as a would-be but unlucky lover, falls so intensely in love with Criseyde that most of us (men anyway) come to love her as Chaucer evidently does. Chaucer the Pilgrim is the greater ironist; the narrator of *Troilus and Criseyde* is finally so heartbroken that he transcends his own ironies.

## The Canterbury Tales

Chaucer is one of those great writers who defeat almost all criticism, an attribute he shares with Shakespeare, Cervantes, and Tolstoy. There are writers of similar magnitude—Dante, Milton, Wordsworth, Proust—who provoke inspired commentary (amidst much more that is humdrum) but Chaucer, like his few peers, has such mimetic force that the critic is disarmed, and so is left either with nothing or with everything still to do. Much criticism devoted to Chaucer is merely historical, or even theological, as though Chaucer ought to be read as a supreme version of medieval

Christianity. But I myself am not a Chaucer scholar, and so I write this only as a general critic of literature and as a common reader of Chaucer.

Together with Shakespeare and a handful of the greater novelists in English, Chaucer carries the language further into unthinkable triumphs of the representation of reality than ought to be possible. The Pardoner and the Wife of Bath, like Hamlet and Falstaff, call into question nearly every mode of criticism that is now fashionable. What sense does it make to speak of the Pardoner or the Wife of Bath as being only a structure of tropes, or to say that any tale they tell has suspended its referential aspect almost entirely? The most Chaucerian and best of all Chaucer critics, E. Talbot Donaldson, remarks of the General Prologue to the *Canterbury Tales* that:

> The extraordinary quality of the portraits is their vitality, the illusion that each gives the reader that the character being described is not a fiction but a person, so that it seems as if the poet has not created but merely recorded.

As a critical remark, this is the indispensable starting-point for reading Chaucer, but contemporary modes of interpretation deny that such an illusion of vitality has any value.

Last June, I walked through a park in Frankfurt, West Germany, with a good friend who is a leading French theorist of interpretation. I had been in Frankfurt to lecture on Freud; my friend had just arrived to give a talk on Joyce's *Ulysses*. As we walked, I remarked that Joyce's Leopold Bloom seemed to me the most sympathetic and affectionate person I had encountered in any fiction. My friend, annoyed and perplexed, replied that Poldy was *not* a person and that my statement therefore was devoid of sense. Though not agreeing, I reflected silently that the difference between my friend and myself could not be reconciled by anything I could say. To him, *Ulysses* was not even persuasive rhetoric, but was a system of tropes. To me, it was above all else the personality of Poldy. My friend's deconstructionism, I again realized, was only another formalism, a very tough-minded and skeptical formalism. But all critical formalism reaches its limits rather quickly when fictions are strong enough. L.C. Knights famously insisted that Lady Macbeth's children were as meaningless a critical issue as the girlhood of Shakespeare's heroines, a view in which Knights followed E.E. Stoll who, whether he knew it or not, followed E.A. Poe. To Knights, Falstaff "is not a man, but a choric commentary." The paradox, though, is that this "choric commentary" is more vital than we are, which teaches us that Falstaff is neither trope nor commentary, but a representation of what a human being *might* be, if that person were even wittier than Oscar Wilde, and even more turbulently high-spirited than Zero Mostel. Falstaff, Poldy, the Wife of Bath: these are what Shelley called "forms more real than living man."

Immensely original authors (and they are not many) seem to have no precursors, and so seem to be children without parents. Shakespeare is the overwhelming instance, since he swallowed up his immediate precursor Christopher Marlowe, whereas Chaucer charmingly claims fictive authorities while being immensely indebted to actual French and Italian writers and to Boccaccio in particular. Yet it may be that Chaucer is as much Shakespeare's great original as he was Spenser's. What is virtually without precedent in Shakespeare is that his characters *change themselves by pondering upon what they themselves say.* In Homer and the Bible and Dante, we do not find sea-changes in particular persons brought about by those persons' own language, that is, by the differences that individual diction and tone make as speech produces further speech. But the Pardoner and the Wife of Bath are well along the mimetic way that leads to Hamlet and Falstaff. What they say to others, and to themselves, partly reflects what they already are, but partly engenders also what they will be. And perhaps even more subtly and forcefully, Chaucer suggests ineluctable transformations going on in the Pardoner and the Wife of Bath through the effect of the language of the tales they choose to tell.

Something of this shared power in Chaucer and Shakespeare accounts for the failures of criticism to apprehend them, particularly when criticism is formalist, or too given over to the study of codes, conventions, and what is now called "language" but might more aptly be called applied linguistics, or even psycholinguistics. A critic addicted to what is now called the "priority of language over meaning" will not be much given to searching for meaning in persons, real or imagined. But persons, at once real *and* imagined, are the fundamental basis of the experiential art of Chaucer and Shakespeare. Chaucer and Shakespeare know, beyond knowing, the labyrinthine ways in which the individual self is always a picnic of selves. "The poets were there before me," Freud remarked, and perhaps Nietzsche ought to have remarked the same.

## II

Talbot Donaldson rightly insists, against the patristic exegetes, that Chaucer was primarily a comic writer. This need never be qualified, if we also judge the Shakespeare of the two parts of *Henry IV* to be an essentially comic writer, as well as Fielding, Dickens, and Joyce. "Comic writer" here means something very comprehensive, with the kind of "comedy" involved being more in the mode, say, of Balzac than that of Dante, deeply as Chaucer was indebted to Dante notwithstanding. If the Pardoner is fundamentally a comic figure, why, then, so is Vautrin? Balzac's hallucinatory "realism," a cosmos in which every janitor is a genius, as Baudelaire remarked, has its affinities with the charged vitalism of Chaucer's fictive world. The most illuminating exegete of the General Prologue to the *Canterbury Tales* remains William Blake, whose affinities with Chaucer were profound. This is the Blake classed by Yeats, in *A Vision*, with Rabelais and Aretino; Blake as an heroic vitalist whose motto was "Exuberance is Beauty," which is an apt Chaucerian slogan also. I will grant that the Pardoner's is a negative exuberance, and yet Blake's remarks show us that the Wife of Bath's exuberance has its negative aspects also.

Comic writing so large and so profound hardly seems to admit a rule for literary criticism. Confronted by the Wife of Bath or Falstaff or the suprahumane Poldy, how shall the critic conceive her or his enterprise? What is there left to be done? I grimace to think of the Wife of Bath and Falstaff deconstructed, or of having their life-augmenting contradictions subjected to a Marxist critique. The Wife of Bath and difference (or even "differance")? Falstaff and surplus value? Poldy and the dogma that there is nothing outside the text? Hamlet and Lacan's Mirror Phase? The heroic, the vitalizing pathos of a fully human vision, brought about through a supermimesis not of essential nature, but of human possibility, demands a criticism more commensurate with its scope and its color. It is a matter of aesthetic tact, certainly, but as Oscar Wilde taught us, that makes it truly a moral matter as well. What devitalizes the Wife of Bath, or Falstaff, or Poldy, tends at last to reduce us also.

## III

That a tradition of major poetry goes from Chaucer to Spenser and Milton and on through them to Blake and Wordsworth, Shelley and Keats, Browning and Tennyson and Whitman, Yeats and Stevens, D.H. Lawrence and Hart Crane, is now widely accepted as a critical truth. The myth of a Metaphysical counter-tradition, from Donne and Marvell through Dryden, Pope, and Byron on to Hopkins, Eliot, and Pound, has been dispelled and seen as the Eliotic invention it truly was. Shakespeare is too large for any tradition, and so is Chaucer. One can wonder if even the greatest novelists in the language—Richardson, Austen, George Eliot, Dickens, Henry James, and the Mark Twain of *Huckleberry Finn* (the one true rival of *Moby-Dick* and *Leaves of Grass* as *the* American book or Bible), or Conrad, Lawrence, and Faulkner in this century—can approach Shakespeare and Chaucer in the astonishing art of somehow creating fictions that are more human than we generally are. Criticism, perhaps permanently ruined by Aristotle's formalism, has had little hope of even accurately describing this art. Aristophanes, Plato, and Longinus are apter models for a criticism more adequate to Chaucer and to Shakespeare.

Attacking Euripides, Aristophanes, as it were, attacks Chaucer and Shakespeare in a true prolepsis, and Plato's war against Homer, his attack upon mimesis, prophesies an unwaged war upon Chaucer and Shakespeare. Homer and Euripides, after all, simply are not the mimetic scandal that is constituted by Chaucer and Shakespeare; the *inwardness* of the Pardoner and Hamlet is of a different order from that of Achilles and Medea. Freud himself does not catch up to Chaucer and Shakespeare; he gets as far as Montaigne and Rousseau, which indeed is a long journey into the interior. But the Pardoner is the interior and even Iago, even Goneril and Regan, Cornwall and Edmund, do not give us a fiercer sense of intolerable resonance on the way down and out. Donaldson subtly observes that "it is the Pardoner's particular tragedy that, except in church, every one can see through him at a glance." The profound phrase here is "except in church." What happens to, or better yet, *within* the Pardoner when he preaches in church? Is that not parallel to asking what happens within the dying Edmund when he murmurs, "Yet Edmund was beloved," and thus somehow is moved to make his belated, futile attempt to save Cordelia and Lear? Are there any critical codes or methods that could possibly help us to sort out the Pardoner's more-than-Dostoevskian intermixture of supernatural faith and preternatural chicanery? Will semiotics or even Lacanian psycholinguistics anatomize Edmund for us, let alone Regan?

Either we become experiential critics when we read Chaucer and Shakespeare, or in too clear a sense we never read them at all. "Experiential" here necessarily means humane observation both of others and of ourselves, which leads to testing such observations in every context that indisputably is relevant. Longinus is the ancestor of such experiential criticism, but its masters are Samuel Johnson, Hazlitt and Emerson, Ruskin, Pater, and Wilde. A century gone mad on method has given us no critics to match these, nor are they likely to come again soon, though we still have Northrop Frye and Kenneth Burke, their last legitimate descendants.

IV

Mad on method, we have turned to rhetoric, and so much so that the best of us, the late Paul de Man, all but urged us to identify literature with rhetoric, so that criticism perhaps would become again the rhetoric of rhetoric, rather than a Burkean rhetoric of motives or a Fryean rhetoric of desires. Expounding the Nun's Priest's Tale, Talbot Donaldson points to "the enormous rhetorical elaboration of the telling" and is moved to a powerful insight into experiential criticism:

> Rhetoric here is regarded as the inadequate defense that mankind erects against an inscrutable reality; rhetoric enables man at best to regard himself as a being of heroic proportions—like Achilles, or like Chauntecleer—and at worst to maintain the last sad vestiges of his dignity (as a rooster Chauntecleer is carried in the fox's mouth, but as a hero he rides on his back), rhetoric enables man to find significance both in his desires and in his fate, and to pretend to himself that the universe takes him seriously. And rhetoric has a habit, too, of collapsing in the presence of simple common sense.

Yet rhetoric, as Donaldson implies, if it is Chaucer's rhetoric in particular, can be a life-enhancing as well as a life-protecting defense. Here is the heroic pathos of the Wife of Bath, enlarging existence even as she sums up its costs in one of those famous Chaucerian passages that herald Shakespearean exuberances to come:

> But Lord Crist, whan that it remembreth me
> Upon my youthe and on my jolitee,
> It tikleth me aboute myn herte roote—
> Unto this day it dooth myn herte boote
> That I have had my world as in my time.
> But age, allas, that al wol envenime,
> Hath me biraft my beautee and my pith—
> Lat go, farewel, the devel go therwith!
> The flour is goon, ther is namore to telle:
> The bren as I best can now moste I selle;
> But yit to be right merye wol I fonde.
>     (*WBP*, 1.475; E.T. Donaldson, 2d ed.)

The defense against time, so celebrated as a defiance of time's revenges, is the Wife's fierce assertion also of the will to live at whatever expense. Rhetorically, the center of the passage is in the famously immense reverberation of her great cry of exultation and loss, "That I have had my world as in my time," where the double "my" is decisive, yet the "have had" falls away in a further intimation of mortality. Like Falstaff, the Wife is a grand trope of pathos, of life defending itself against every convention that would throw us into death-in-life. Donaldson wisely warns us that "pathos, however, must not be allowed to carry the day," and points to the coarse vigor of the Wife's final benediction to the tale she has told:

> And Jesu Crist us sende
> Housbondes meeke, yonge, and fresshe abedde—
> And grace t'overbide hem that we wedde.
> And eek I praye Jesu shorte hir lives
> That nought wol be governed by hir wives,
> And olde and angry nigardes of dispence—
> God sende hem soone a verray pestilence!
> (*WBT*, 1. 402)

Blake feared the Wife of Bath because he saw in her what he called the Female Will incarnate. By the Female Will, Blake meant the will of the natural woman or the natural man, a prolepsis perhaps of Schopenhauer's rapacious Will to Live or Freud's "frontier concept" of the drive. Chaucer, I think, would not have quarreled with such an interpretation, but he would have scorned Blake's dread of the natural will or Schopenhauer's horror of its rapacity. Despite every attempt to assimilate him to a poetry of belief, Chaucer actually surpasses even Shakespeare as a celebrant of the natural heart, while like Shakespeare being beyond illusions concerning the merely natural. No great poet was less of a dualist than Chaucer was, and nothing makes poetry more difficult for critics, because all criticism is necessarily dualistic.

The consolation for critics and readers is that Chaucer and Shakespeare, Cervantes and Tolstoy, persuade us finally that everything remains to be done in the development of a criticism dynamic and comprehensive enough to represent such absolute writers without reduction or distortion. No codes or methods will advance the reading of Chaucer. The critic is thrown back upon herself or himself, and upon the necessity to become a vitalizing interpreter in the service of an art whose burden is only to carry more life forward into a time without boundaries.

## V

The Knight's Tale is a chivalric romance, or purports to be; it is as much genial satire as romance, a triumph of Chaucer's comic rhetoric, monistic and life-enhancing. Talbot Donaldson charmingly sums up the poem's ethos as being rather more Stoic than Christian: "No matter how hard we look, we cannot hope to see why Providence behaves as it does; all we can do is our best, making a virtue of necessity, enjoying what is good, and remaining cheerful." Applied to most other authors, Donaldson's comments might seem banal. Chaucer's overwhelming representation of an immediate reality, in which we ride with the protagonists, enjoy what is good, and certainly become more cheerful, gives Donaldson's amiable observations their edge of precision. Since Chaucer the Pilgrim rides along with us, allowing his own narrative voice full scope, despite the authority of his storytellers, we hear more than the Knight's tonalities in the telling of his tale.

Donald R. Howard, admirably setting forth "the idea" of the *Canterbury Tales*, the totality of its vision, reminds us that Chaucer himself may be in a skeptical stance towards the Knight's Tale, if only because the voice of the Knight, as narrator, is so much at variance with Chaucer's larger idea or vision:

> And the work, because of this idea, discourages us from assenting to the tales, from giving them credence. Almost very tale is presented in circumstances which discredit it. Even the Knight's Tale, a high-minded story told by an ideal figure, gives us reason to approach it skeptically. In it ... Chaucer permits his own voice to intrude upon the Knight's. These ironic intrusions may discredit the tale itself, or the Knight, or the style and manner of its telling, or the cultural and literary tradition it represents. However explained, this ironic element raises questions in the reader's mind which the tale never settles. In other instances what we know about the pilgrim raises such questions. The Miller's Tale parodies the Knight's and holds some of its values up to ridicule; but the Miller does not get the last word and there is no reason to think Chaucer sided with him more than another—he is, we are told, a drunk and a churl. Besides, the Reeve's tale "quits" the Miller and his tale, discrediting both with another churlish viewpoint. Tales discredit each other, as with the Friar and Summoner. The Nun's Priest subtly discredits the Monk's tale and other tales which have preceded it. Whole groups of tales discredit one another by presenting various viewpoints in conflict—the sequence Knight-Miller-Reeve is an example, as is the "marriage group."

Talbot Donaldson places a particular emphasis upon one crucial couplet of the Knight's:

It is ful fair a man to bare him evene,
For alday meeteth men at unset stevene.

I remember walking once with the late and much mourned Donaldson, on an ordinary evening in New Haven, and hearing him quote that couplet, and then repeat his own superb paraphrase of it: "It is a good thing for a man to bear himself with equanimity, for one is constantly keeping appointments one never made." That certainly seems the Knight's ethos, and may have been Chaucer's, and doubtless does reflect *The Consolation of Philosophy* of Boethius. Yet Chaucer, as Donaldson helped teach us, is a very great comic writer—like Rabelais, Cervantes, Shakespeare. As a poet, Chaucer is larger than any formulation we can bring to bear upon him, and, again like Shakespeare, he tends to transcend genres also.

F. Anne Payne argues cogently that "the Knight's Tale, a philosophical parody with the *Consolation* and the romance as its models, belongs to the seriocomic tradition of Menippean satire." Less a genre than a grab bag, Menippean satire is essentially typified by Lucian, whose dialogues turn their mockery in several directions at once. Lucian is less a satirist than an extreme ironist, who exploits precisely that aspect of irony that the late Paul de Man termed "a permanent parabasis of meaning." The irony of irony, with its destruction of any fixed meaning, is the irony of the Knight's Tale, where nothing can be settled and much must be accepted. Donaldson. In his splendid final book, *The Swan at the Well: Shakespeare Reading Chaucer*, relates the irony of romantic love in *A Midsummer Night's Dream* to the irony of the Knight's Tale. Puck's "Lord, what fools these mortals be" falls short of the irony of Chaucer's Theseus: "who maie be a foole, but if he love?" The destruction of friendship by love, Chaucer's overt story, is itself Chaucer's metaphor for the dispersion of meaning by a love of philosophical disputation, which the Knight's Tale converts into a mockery. That must be why Shakespeare based his own Theseus more on Chaucer's Knight than on Chaucer's Theseus. The Knight is no philosopher but rather a chivalric skeptic, and so is Shakespeare's Theseus, who like the Knight will not go beyond his own experience.

Though the Knight's skepticism does not extend to his own tale-telling, there is always a remarkable gap between the complexity of his narrative and his own insistence that it is all a quite simple if rather sad matter. Donaldson compares this stance to that of the Nun's Priest, who blandly

urges us to take the pith of his tale while ignoring its rhetorical reverbera-
tions, that alone give it power and universality. The Knight has tied up generations of Chaucerians with his famous red herring of a moral question:

> You lovers axe I now this questioun:
> Who hath the worse, Arcite or Palamoun?

As Donaldson remarks, the question is wrong because there is no
authentic difference between the two love-crazed worthies. The Knight
may be no Chaucerian ironist, but the gap between the Knight's experience
of life and that of most among us necessarily and ironically defeats every
attempt we could make to answer the question, unless indeed we qualify as
experiential critics. No Formalist or method-based reading will be able to
turn the Knight's question into its implied realization, which is that all of
us must confront and absorb the possible worst, however unlooked-for and
undeserved.

### VI

Chaucer, writing at our American moment, would have written "The
TV Evangelist's Tale, " rather than "The Pardoner's Tale." Alas, we have
no contemporary Chaucer to give us "The TV Evangelist's Prologue" and
"The TV Evangelist's Epilogue," for which so much superb material has
been provided in recent revelations. That is the context, aside from all his-
toricisms, old and new, in which Chaucer's Pardoner should be seen. He is
at once obscenely formidable and a laughable charlatan, thus arousing in
us ambivalences akin to those provoked by certain eminent preachers on
our home screens.

In the General Prologue to the *Canterbury Tales* we first encounter the
Pardoner as the Summoner's lustful companion, boisterously singing the
tavern air, "Come hither. Love, to me," and producing, with his Summoner
friend, a sound surpassing the trumpet's cry. With his wax-like yellow hair,
hanging like a lank of flax, thin and fine, and his piercing high voice, and his
lack of beard, the Pardoner is the very type of the eunuch. We understand
then why he hangs close to the authentically obscene Summoner, so as to
pick up some sexual coloring, as it were. Beneath the overcompensation of
lustful behavior, which fools nobody, the Pardoner is dangerously close to
being an emblem of death, like the uncanny old man of his tale. The association of castration, blindness, and death, so crucial in Freud, is already a
given in Chaucer, just as the strangely authentic power of the Pardoner's
sermon, which transcends his overt tricksterism, testifies to the weird

prolepsis of Dostoevsky in the *Canterbury Tales*. A professional hypocrite who yet can invoke the terror of eternity, truly despite himself, the Pardoner is the most powerful representation of depravity we can find in English before the creation of Shakespeare's Iago and Edmund. Even Talbot Donaldson underestimates, I think, the Pardoner's depth of self-destructiveness:

> But the Pardoner's secret is, of course, a secret only to himself: at any rate Chaucer the pilgrim guessed it at once. But as long as the secret remains unspoken the Pardoner dwells securely in his own delusion, so that the secret remains valid for him. Yet at the end of his frightening story he wantonly imperils—and destroys—the fragile structure on which his self-confidence depends. Whatever his reasons—avarice, good-fellowship, humor—he concludes his sermon with an offer to sell his pardon to the pilgrims even after all he has told about his own fraudulence. Ironically he picks the worst possible victim, that rough, manly man who might be supposed to have a natural antipathy for the unmasculine Pardoner. The insult to the Host's intelligence is the first and last failure of the Pardoner's intelligence, for the Host's violently obscene reaction reveals the Pardoner's secret. Thereupon the man whose clever tongue has seemed to give him control of every situation is reduced to furious silence.

I do not think that "avarice, good-fellowship, humor" are the only reasons why the Pardoner so brazenly insults Harry Bailly, the most likely of all his listeners to give the brutal and inevitable riposte. Moved by the extraordinary intensity of his own tale-telling. The Pardoner achieves a kind of vertigo that mixes pride in his own swindling with something dangerously authentic out of the supernatural order of grace:

> O cursed sinne of alle cursednesse!  
> O traitours homicide, a wikkednesse!  
> O glotonye, luxure, and hasardrye!  
> Thou blasphemour of Crist with vilainye  
> And othes grete of usage and of pride!  
> Allas, mankinde, how may it bitide  
> That to thy Creatour which that thee wroughte,  
> And with his precious herte blood thee boughte,  
> Thou art so fals and so unkinde, allas?

Now goode men, God foryive you youre trespas,
And ware you fro the sinne of avarice:
Myn holy pardon may you alle warice—
So that ye offre nobles or sterlinges,
Or elles silver brooches, spoones, ringes.
Boweth your heed under this holy bulle!
Cometh up, ye wives, offreth of youre wolle!
Youre name I entre here in my rolle: anoon
Into the blisse of hevene shul ye goon.
I you assoile by myn heigh power—
Ye that wol offer—as clene and eek as cleer
As ye were born.—And lo, sires, thus I preche.
And Jesu Crist that is oure soules leeche
So graunte you his pardon to receive,
For that is best—I wol you nat deceive.
                                    (*PT*, II. 567–90)

A desperate good-fellowship and a kind of gallows humor certainly
are present in those closing lines. What is also present is a sense that the
Pardoner has been carried away, and by more than his tale's strength or his
own rough eloquence as a preacher. A kind of madness or enthusiasm takes
possession of him and drives him to the social suicide that Freud would
have regarded as "moral masochism," the need for punishment due to an
unconscious sense of guilt, perhaps even a retroactive self-recognition that
might account for his emasculate condition. The drive for destruction
again turns inward and rages against the self, so that in courting a kind of
social death the Pardoner receives premonitions of the spiritual death he
has earned. That perhaps explains the outrageousness of the Pardoner's
address to his fellow-pilgrims:

It is an honour to everich that is heer
That ye mowe have a suffisant pardoner
T'assoile you in contrees as ye ride,
For aventures whiche that may bitide:
Paraventure ther may falle oon or two
Down of his hors and breke his nekke atwo;
Looke which a suretee is it to you alle
That I am in youre felaweshipe yfalle
That may assoile you, bothe more and lasse,
Whan that the soule shal fro the body passe.
                                    (*PT*, II. 603–12)

What can the Pardoner have expected as response to this outburst? The need for rebuke surely dominates the Pardoner's address to the Host, which asks for more than trouble:

> I rede that oure Hoste shal biginne,
> For he is most envoluped in sinne.
> Com forth, sire Host, and offer first anoon,
> And thou shalt kisse the relikes everichoon,
> Ye, for a grote: unbokele anoon thy purs.
> (II. 613–17)

The Host's splendidly violent response, with its images of kissing the Pardoner's stained fundament and slicing off and carrying away his testicles, is precisely what the Pardoner was too shrewd not to expect. But the shrewdness here belongs to the Pardoner's unconscious death drive; the merely conscious ego of the wretch is stricken as silent as Iago was to be. Iago ends by saying that from this time forth he never will speak a word. His true precursor, the sublimely damned yet still comic Pardoner, also answered not a word: "So wroth he was no word ne wolde he saye."

# Edmund Spenser

## (c. 1552–1599)

... if the whole man be trained perfectly, and his mind calm, consistent, and powerful, the vision which corner to him is seen as in a perfect mirror, serenely, and in consistence with the rational power; but if the mind be imperfect and ill trained, the vision is seen as in a broken mirror, with strange distortions and discrepancies, all the passions of the heart breathing upon it in cross ripples, till hardly a trace of it remains unbroken. So that, strictly speaking, the imagination is never governed; it is always the ruling and Divine power.... And thus *Iliad*, *the Inferno*, the *Pilgrim's Progress*, the *Faerie Queene*, are all of them true dreams; only the sleep of the men to whom they came was the deep, living sleep which God sends, with a sacredness in it, as of death, the revealer of secrets.

—RUSKIN

OF ALL THE MAJOR POETS IN ENGLISH, EDMUND SPENSER IS, AT THIS TIME, the last read and, in proportion to his merits, the least valued. As a living presence in the poetry of the last twenty years he is scarcely to be felt, for since the death of Yeats the English-speaking world has had no poet even in part educated by Spenser, no poetry directly affected by *The Faerie Queene*. Spenser has been abandoned to the academies, and within them he has become increasingly peripheral. When the critical sensibility that prevailed in Britain and America during these last decades turned to Spenser, it found little in him to justify the eminence he had held for three hundred years. His long poem was dismissed as the product of the will usurping the work of the imagination. The Shakespearean critic, Derek Traversi, may be taken as representative of still prevalent (though waning) taste when he judged Spenser to have made "splendid pieces of rhetorical decoration" devoid of deep personal content, and to have mastered a style which "tends irresistibly to become an instrument of disintegration, furthering the dissolution of the declared moral intention into mere rhythmical flow." The distance between such a verdict and an accurate judgment of Spenser's achievement is so great that a lover of Spenser's poetry is compelled to resist a reaction into overpraise of "the Prince of Poets in his time." One is tempted to maintain that a reader who cannot apprehend Spenser's voice as being at its best the voice of poetry itself is not capable of reading adequately any poetry whatsoever. But too much rhetoric of that dismissing kind has been used by critics over the past decades; admirers of Spenser, of Milton, of Blake and Wordsworth and Shelley, have been assured, all too frequently, that the life of English poetry was elsewhere, and that the Romantic and mythopoeic tradition was an aberration. It was curiously necessary for the admirers of metaphysical verse to deprecate everything in English poetry that was most unlike Donne, but the poetry of Spenser and the tradition he inaugurated are too firmly central to require any polemic against a rival tradition.

John Hughes, who edited the works of Spenser in 1715, remarked of *The Faerie Queene* that "the chief merit of this Poem consists in that surprizing Vein of fabulous Invention, which runs thro it." We no longer commend poets specifically for their invention, but that seemed the essence of poetry from the Renaissance critics through Dr. Johnson and on into the Romantic period. The manner in which the invention was handled received only equal weight with the rarity of the fictive matter itself in Renaissance criticism, but gradually has come (in modern criticism) to crowd out the proper valuing of invention. In a period of revived mythopoeic poetry, the age of Yeats and Rilke, the poets are attended as exegetes by rhetorical critics, many of them hostile to the autonomy demanded by the inventive faculty, the mythopoeic power that Spenser possessed in greater measure than any poet in English except for Blake.

Hughes observed that "Spenser's Fable, tho often wild, is ... always emblematical," and commended his poet for thus turning romance to the uses of allegory. The conventions of romance and the problematical nature of allegory have alike provided barriers between Spenser and many modern readers, but the poet's artistry as a romantic allegorist is informed by the exuberance of his invention. To consider Spenser under the arbitrary divisions of romance, allegory and myth-making, as I shall now proceed to do, is to endanger the integrity of his sustained vision, but one of the virtues of reading and discussing Spenser is to be taught a healthy fear of discursive reduction, of the organized translation of poetry into prose that criticism can so easily become. Yet one learns also, more from Spenser than from any poet, that all criticism of poetry tends towards allegorizing, and that the consciously allegorical poet is not content to leave the reader and critic without a guide in his interpretation.

W.L. Renwick has said of Spenser that "we must regard his work as part of a cultural movement of European extent, as fruit of general and not merely personal experience." Certainly any attempt to understand the genesis of Spenser's poetry and that poetry's intentions must look on it as Renwick suggests, yet Spenser in his best poetry stands very much apart from his fellow-poets of Renaissance Europe. There are very crucial elements in his poetry that make it more akin in certain ways to Blake and Shelley and Keats, writing two hundred years later, than to Ariosto and Du Bellay and Sidney, all of whom influenced him. To account for the emergence of those elements is perhaps not possible, since an imagination as full and powerful as Spenser's is strictly not accountable; we can see what it was and where it went but may never surmise its origins. Scholars of the history of ideas and historical critics of poetry think otherwise, but they tend to read all poetry by allegorizing it into concepts, on the implied assumption that the minds of great poets work as theirs do. It must be granted that Spenser thought of himself as being, among other things, a philosophical poet. Philosophically he was eclectic and richly confused, in the fortunate manner of his time, which could still believe in the ultimate unity of all knowledge, pagan and Christian, natural and revealed. The intricate tangle of his conceptual borrowings is a delight to the source-hunter but irrelevant to a reader who seeks what a poet alone can give him. Again, Spenser conceived of his poetic function as being a uniquely national one; he wished to write an English poem that would match if not surpass the classical epic of Homer and Virgil and the contemporary romance of Ariosto and Tasso. The thrust towards national identity and international greatness that typified Elizabethan aspiration at its most intense is a vital component in Spenser's conscious poetic purpose. But where his poem is most national, most the work of the courtier, it is least interesting as a poem, and hopelessly mired in a now disheartening historical allegory, which Dr. Johnson's "common reader" can safely ignore.

Yeats, who knew better, but was moved by an understandable Irish grudge against Spenser, spoke of him as "the first poet struck with remorse, the first poet who gave his heart to the State." Insofar as *The Faerie Queene* so gives its heart, it ceases to be a poem, and does fasten its knights and ladies "with allegorical nails to a big barn door of common sense, of merely practical virtue," as Yeats maintained. But Spenser never gave all his heart to anything less than that imaginative vision in which the unattainable ideals of Protestant humanism were displaced into a poetic world where all good things and their dialectical counterparts were made simultaneously possible. Yeats was more accurate about Spenser and the value of his poetry when he realized how Spenser's visions, supposedly forgotten, "would rise up before me coming from I knew not where." Yeats's best criticism of Spenser is in his own poetry where he makes use of him, as when *The Ruins of Time* and the *Prothalamion* together with certain stanzas in *The Faerie Queene*, help form *Leda and the Swan* and *The Wild Swans at Coole*. More is to be teamed about what is most relevant to us in Spenser's poetry by seeing how it was used by Drayton, Milton, Blake, Shelley, Keats, Tennyson and Yeats than by reading the bulk of past and present Spenserian criticism. There have been excellent Spenser critics, from Hughes and Thomas Warton to C.S. Lewis and Northrop Frye, but the extraordinary sense in which Spenser is truly the poet's poet is best brought out in a great poem like Shelley's *The Witch of Atlas*, where the world of *The Faerie Queene* is relied upon as being the universe of poetry itself.

To understand the unique nature of Spenser's poetry is to understand also something vital about how poets influence one another; indeed the study of Spenser's poetry is the best introduction available to the fascinating problem of what there is about poetry that can bring more poetry into being, for no poet has made so many other men into poets as Spenser has. What so many poets have learned from Spenser is not a style of writing but a mode of poetry, and a sense of the poet's self-recognition in regard to his own poem. The mode is that of the poem as heterocosm, the other or possible world of the poem as it exists in relation to the too-probable world of the reader. Coleridge acutely noted "the marvellous independence and true imaginative absence of all particular space or time in *The Faerie Queene*. It is in the domains neither of history or geography; it is ignorant of all artificial boundary, all material obstacles; it is truly in land of Faery, that is, of mental space." Dante comes closest to Spenser in creating such a world, but Dante's three worlds are categorical and sharply distinguished from one another. The persuasiveness of Spenser's imagined world is in the treachery of its boundaries; its heavens and hells, purgatories and earthly paradises, undergo a continual transmemberment, yet its appearances are either supremely delusive or absolutely truthful and no honest reader could tell the difference between one and the other on the basis of imagistic vividness. What Spenser had, better I think than any poet before or since, was the power to project both the object of desire and the shape of nightmare with equal imaginative freedom. That power gives its possessor the control of the literary realm of romance or idealized narrative, a domain with a potential ranging from the most primordial and almost childlike to the most sophisticated of perspectives. Romance, Northrop Frye suggestively states, is the Mythos of Summer, the narrative of quest for a lost paradise, the proper story for the man of whom Wallace Stevens could say: "He had studied the nostalgias." So have we all, and when we find ourselves most impatient of romance we are most susceptible to it, rejecting the wish but falling somehow into its fulfilling dream. Between the invaluable chaos of nostalgia and the achieved form of romance only the capable imagination can mediate, and the fully capable imagination must be uninhibited. Why Spenser's liberty to imagine existed at all we cannot know, but we can see how the circumstances of his life and time conspired to make him more free than his greater disciple, Milton, ever came to be.

Spenser, like Milton after him, is a Protestant poet, and the Spenserian tradition in English poetry has been a Protestant one, with a progressive movement to what could be called the visionary left wing; radical in politics, individualist in religion and insisting upon the unsupported imagination as its own warrant. The movement in religion is from the moderate Puritanism of Spenser, with its prophetic strain conflicting with a residue of medieval sacramentalism, to the militant Puritanism and prophetic self-identification of Milton on to the displaced Protestantism of Romantic myth-making: the naturalistic humanism of Keats, the natural supernaturalism (as M.H. Abrams terms it) of Wordsworth, the apocalyptic vitalism of Blake, and the despairing yet heroic agnosticism of the prophetic Shelley, most Spenserian of them all in the effect of his major poems. In our own time the Spenserian and Romantic tradition is directly manifested in Yeats's eclectic "system" of belief, and indirectly in the American late Romanticism of Wallace Stevens (who returns to Wordsworth and Keats) and of Hart Crane, very much the Shelley of our age and the legitimate claimant to the sad dignity of being the Last Romantic. Extreme as this statement is, *Notes Towards A Supreme Fiction* and *The Bridge* are Spenserian poems, for the conception of the poem pointing to itself as poem in *Notes* and the terrified quest of the poet in *The Bridge* are both in lineal descent from *The Faerie Queene*. Crane trapped in the purgatorial maze of *The Tunnel* seems a symbolic figure far removed from Spenser's knight lost in the labyrinth of Error's wood, but the kinship is clear enough when we consider the binding figures in the middle of the tradition, the young poets of Shelley's *Alastor* and Keats's *Endymion* questing through the baffling mazes of the natural world. Stevens, meditating in his subtle variations on the theme of "the origin of the major man," and uncovering at last "how simply the fictive hero becomes the real," seems far indeed from Spenser laboring "to fashion a gentleman or noble person in vertuous and gentle discipline," but again the connecting link is in the Romantic tradition, in Blake's fictive hero, Los, the refiner in imaginative fire who labors to humanize man, or in Wordsworth's attempt through poetry to fashion a man in the nobility of a reciprocal generosity with nature.

Spenser and Milton were Christian humanists and, except for Wordsworth in his poetic decline, this can scarcely be said of any of their poetic descendants, but the lineage remains not only clear but illuminatingly inevitable in its progression. The Protestant aesthetic, as Malcolm M. Ross has shown, shifts from tradition to innovation in Milton's poetry, but the process can be traced earlier in *The Faerie Queene*, although certainly more ambiguously. Spenser did not allow himself to be inhibited either by the fear that a universal symbolism founded on sacramentalism might betray him into Catholic poetry, or that his own fictive covering might obscure the truths of Scriptural revelation. No one else has so cheerfully and astonishingly compounded pagan mythology, Christian symbolism and personal myth-making while remaining centrally in a main doctrinal tradition of Christianity.

Spenser had the humanist belief that classical thought and poetic form did not conflict with Christian truth; for him all myths merged, as all mirrored a unity of truth. Yet his personal attitude towards mythology is confusing because his sense of history is poetically pragmatic; he seems to seek the relevant, the story he can use, whether it arouses his unrivalled powers for sensuous description or because it might illuminate his allegory of sanctification, and usually because it can do both. The golden world seemed past to him, and although he heralded the greatest single period of English poetry he evidently had as dark a view of his country's immediate literary prospects as any unimaginative moralist might have assumed. Like Sidney, Spenser believed that a poet shared in the creativity of God, and therefore believed also in the poet's responsibility to bring his creation into a meaningful relationship with the moral order of God's creation. Such a belief led Spenser into the writing of allegory, and finally into the ambitious enterprise of his allegorical epic-romance.

Much recent prejudice against *The Faerie Queene* is simply a prejudice against all allegory whatsoever. Works that declare themselves overtly as simple allegories, like *The Pilgrim's Progress*, now tend to go unread, while complex allegorists like Dante, Blake and Melville are studied frequently as if they had not consciously modulated the contexts in which their meanings were to be interpreted. Allegory is now associated for many with mere moralizing, while symbolism has the prestige of the legitimate about it. The Romantic descendants of Spenser, from Blake to Yeats, are partially responsible for this curious confusion. Blake was a great critic, but his distinction between "Allegory & Vision" was not a very happy one: "Fable or

Allegory are a totally distinct & inferior kind of Poetry. Vision or Imagination is a Representation of what Eternally Exists, Really & Unchangeably." Indeed, he could not rest in his own distinction, for his own poetry fits his earlier and positive use of the word: "Allegory address'd to the Intellectual powers, while it is altogether hidden from the Corporeal Understanding, is My Definition of the Most Sublime Poetry." On this definition a proper defence of Spenser's poetry, as well as Blake's can and should be made. The "Corporeal Understanding" is Blake's phrase for any empirical approach that is not open to vision or imaginative apprehension. The unity and, to a good extent, the value of Spenser's masterpiece are certainly hidden from the investigation of much Spenserian scholarship, with its empiricist presuppositions. What Blake means by "the Intellectual powers" is everything the reader's mind is capable of bringing to self-integration as the reader experiences the poem. If the poem falls short of the reader's potential for wholeness the reader will learn it in time, but patience and good will are necessities if the effort is to be made.

Edwin Honig usefully finds "the allegorical quality in a twice-told tale written in rhetorical, or figurative, language and expressing a vital belief." So broad a way of approaching allegory seems the best antidote to the modern suspicion of allegory, a distrust reducing a complex relation between image and idea to the simple deception of an image masking an idea. For allegory in Spenser is neither a discourse in disguised ideas nor a pattern of familiar events deliberately (and momentarily) distorted. Spenser's allegory, in its totality and frequently in its details, reverberates into further meanings by its capability and adequacy as a poem, its strength in self-containment and completeness. *The Faerie Queene* is a more diffuse work than *Paradise Lost* or Blake's *Jerusalem*, more diffuse even than *Finnegans Wake* (with which it curiously has much in common) but the manner of its metamorphic extension justifies the seeming lack of cohesiveness. For Spenser begins with sustained allegory and ends (he died before conclusion) with an imagined world, a world containing as many of the total possibilities of literature within it as any other professed allegory up to his own time. His apocalyptic Book I may be his masterpiece, but I pass over it here so as to consider the centers of vision elsewhere in his great romance, and in the best of his minor poems.

II

The artistic completeness of Book I compels Spenser to an altogether fresh start in Book II, in which the literary context shifts from the Bible to the classical epic and the theme from experience in the order of grace to experience in the order of nature, a change best analyzed by A.S.P. Woodhouse. Sir Guyon, the quester in Book II, exemplifies heroic virtue more directly and fully than St. George could ever represent sanctification, since the classical virtues are wholly within the natural realm. Though Guyon is spared the fearful purgations of Spenser's first hero, his triumph is necessarily a less definitive one, and the disinterested reader of poetry is rather less likely to be unequivocal in appreciating that triumph, the overthrow of the sensual delights of Acrasia and her Bower of Bliss.

Frequently noted is the clear parallel in narrative structure between the first two books, usefully explained by Woodhouse's frame of reference, the contrast between the two orders, nature and grace. The knight of faith, guided by a veiled but still effectual truth, overcomes his earlier opponents, but falls victim (through his own credulity) to deception and is tempted by an irrevocable despair. The knight of temperance, guided by an invulnerable and moderate wisdom, undergoes temptation but resists it, and falls only through natural exhaustion. Roused again, his awakened nature accomplishes an ethical triumph without direct heavenly aid, unlike the knight of faith who must be rescued by grace, and then refreshed by it in the climactic battle.

Where Book I is dominated by scenes of struggle climaxing in the strife between death and resurrection, the actual battles in Book II are of only secondary importance. The first event in Book I is the Red Cross Knight's victory over Error; the parallel event in Book II is a fight that does not take place, as Guyon recognizes the error of his wrath before fully attacking the Red Cross Knight. Guyon already has the temperate virtues, and needs only to realize them by bringing them into activity in response to a wide range of temptations. By doing so, he becomes the prototype of Milton's Christ in *Paradise Regained*, for his is the task of a Hercules greater than the Herculean heroes of classical epic. Guyon and Milton's Christ must transform a passive consciousness of heroic virtue into an active awareness that knows itself fully because it becomes more itself in the act of confronting temptation. Guyon is of course only a man, and fortunately for the poem he can be tempted, although one sometimes wishes he could be tempted to a greater degree of dramatic indecisiveness as he quests remorselessly on.

The quest of Book II begins with the powerful episode of Amavia and Mortdant, both slain indirectly by the sexual witchery of Acrasia, a Circe-like enchantress. Guyon vows to avenge their death, and begins this process by attempting to care for Ruddymane, the infant abandoned by their self-destructiveness. The ineffectuality of merely natural means to accomplish fully any moral quest is shown immediately by Guyon's inability to wash the babe's hands free of guilty human blood, a frightening symbolic parody of the sacrament of baptism.

The image of the babe's bloody hands haunts the rest of Book II, for the babe's equivocal innocence is an epitome of how closely original sin and the possibility of natural virtue dwell together in the experiential world. The adventures of Guyon are a series of encounters between his temperate affections and the excessive humors leading to "outrageous anger" or lust, or excessive desire of any kind. In these encounters Guyon goes on foot, and his victories are indecisive, for he is more skilled at resisting evils than at abolishing them. Temperance, as Northrop Frye observes, is deliberately displayed as a pedestrian virtue, and Guyon is memorable for what he rightfully declines to do, until the very close of his book when he acts to destroy the Bower of Acrasia.

III

The most remarkable instance of Guyon's passive heroism is Canto VII, the descent into the Cave of Mammon, an episode that renews the archetype of the classical hero's descent to Avernus, as in *Aeneid*, VI. Parted from his moral guide, the prudent Palmer, Guyon undergoes a three day trial in the underworld that seems essentially to be an initiation, a parallel experience to the Red Cross Knight's three day fight with the dragon. This extraordinary myth-making of the Cave of Mammon is partly to be read as the supreme instance in Book II of the negative virtue of temperate endurance, but the invention of Spenser is too absolute to be interpreted only in terms of moral intention.

Charles Lamb noted the dream-atmosphere of the Mammon episode, and praised Spenser for a creation replete with violent transitions and incongruities "and yet the waking judgment ratifies them." The Mammon episode is vision and not dream, for the poetic content is manifest in the images, and not latent in a depth-pattern hidden from the imagination. Milton is the best guide to the Cave of Mammon and Bower of Bliss alike when he writes in *Areopagitica* that Guyon is brought through these places "that he might see and know, and yet abstain." Even Guyon must be purified by trial "and trial is by what is contrary." Guyon must "scout into the regions of sin and falsity," and so it is just and necessary that he accompany Mammon into the depths, even as Christ must undergo the temptations of Satan in *Paradise Regained*.

Mammon offers Guyon the wealth of this world, as well as his daughter Philotime, who is the equivalent of Lucifera in Book I, as Frank Kermode notes. In courteously declining Philotime, Guyon puts from himself all aspiration towards merely worldly honor, as earlier he rejects worldly goods. By passing through the Garden of Proserpina without eating of its fruit, Guyon avoids the fate of Tantalus, who suffers in hell for impiously seeking divinely concealed secrets. The punishment of Tantalus is a demonic parody of the refreshment of St. George by the Tree of Life, just as the punishment of his companion Pilate parodies St. George's being revived by immersion in the Water of Life. (The image of Pilate reminds us also of the Ruddymane episode.) Like Tantalus, the bloody-handed Pilate sinned against the truth, and Guyon, in refusing the fruit of unlawful knowledge, has separated himself from this fundamental consequence of natural depravity.

All through his ordeal Guyon is shadowed by a fiend who would rend him apart at the least yielding to temptation, a persuasive symbol of the spectral self, the dark aspect of nature that must be purged from every man. The silver stool which is Guyon's last temptation, "to rest thy weary person in the shadow coole," was suggestively related by the eighteenth century editor Upten to the forbidden seat in the Eleusinian mysteries, a suggestion elaborated by Kermode as "a punitive chair of oblivion" for those who pervert divine knowledge.

Like Christ in the temptations by Satan, Guyon voluntarily submits to the blandishments of Mammon, and shows his heroism negatively, by a firm resistance. Guyon's is the Miltonic fortitude of patience, the virtue Adam must learn if he is to be saved. As a Christian knight, Guyon does not achieve the revelation granted to St. George, but he does overtake the Homeric and Virgilian heroes by attaining to a perfect control over his own nature through a descent into the underworld. His achieved virtue is heroic but not supernatural; it hesitates on the edge of the world of grace, but does not cross over into the revealed order. At the triumphant end of his ordeal Guyon faints, not because he has been in any way intemperate, but because he has carried his heroism to a verge of the natural condition, and has exhausted nature in doing so. He has not harrowed hell, but he has seen and known the mysteries of hell, and been saved from them by his abstinence. He falls out of his vision back into nature, and as with Keats's Endymion, the first touch of earth again comes nigh to killing him. We are left with the dark splendor of his ordeal, a pattern directly relevant to our society as it was to Spenser's. What Guyon has rejected is what Spenser sought and most men compulsively seek, a glory that shines beautifully because it is surrounded by darkness, a kingdom where the only wealth is death. The moral is an aesthetically powerful dimension of the myth not only because it is universal but because it is observation rather than admonition. Spenser knew himself to be no Hercules, and Guyon's escape is not the victory of an Everyman. The strength of Spenser's fiction is in its deathly attraction; the reader is not Guyon. A knight of Temperance humanistically fulfills his nature, and faints into the light of every day. The necessarily intemperate reader yields to the imagination, which desires to be indulged. We remain to some extent in the Cave, not because it is the best of places, or even because we are overwhelmingly tempted, but because we are poor; we lack the only wealth which is life.

IV

Probably no section of *The Faerie Queene* so directly identifies its poets as Canto XII of Book II, the account of the voyage towards and the overthrow of Acrasia's Bower of Bliss. Hazlitt praised the "voluptuous pathos" of the Bower, and implied that what was most poetic in Spenser was most at home in the Bower. This is a partial truth and certainly more valuable than the moralistic insistence of many commentators that the Bower is altogether a degraded as well as a degrading place. The Bower is a "horrible enchantment," but an enchantment nevertheless.

The most persuasive modern enemy of the Bower is C.S. Lewis, who has severely insisted that Acrasia's garden is artificial rather than natural, as contrasted to the natural and spontaneous profusion of the Gardens of Adonis. The Bower, again according to Lewis, shows the whole sexual nature in sterile suspension: "There is not a kiss or an embrace in the island: only male prurience and female provocation." To this Lewis again contrasts the Gardens of Adonis, with its teeming sexual life. On this reading, one has got to be something of a *voyeur* to be attracted by the Bower, to be delighted as our "wanton eies do peepe" at Acrasia and her naked damsels.

Lewis is reacting against those critics who have charged Spenser with "actual sensuality and theoretical austerity." Spenser is subtler and more varied in his art than either his moralistic attackers or defenders have been willing to notice. Part of the contrast between the Gardens of Adonis and the Bower of Bliss is certainly due to the element of artifice in the Bower, yet the Bower remains very much within the natural world. Indeed its natural beauty is what we as readers are first asked to notice, and precisely what Guyon must first resist. He wonders much "at the fayre aspect of that sweet place," but does not suffer any delight "to sincke into his sence, nor mind affect." The Bower is nature *mixed* with art, as one might expect of any sophisticated sensuality. Some of its fruits are of burnished gold, yet its boughs hang always heavy with the ripeness of nature. Acrasia and her victim-lover are not caught by Guyon and the Palmer in the act of love, but it will not do to maintain that there are no embraces in the Bower. Acrasia is seen in the "langour of her late sweet toyle," and her spent lover sleeps in her arms in what is intended as a demonic parody of the sleep of Adonis, a vision that would be pointless if it testified only to "male prurience and female provocation." No; whatever the Bower is, it is scarcely a picture of the whole sexual nature in disease. Moral criticism of poetry is self-defeating if it denies Satan his heroic courage, Iago his serpentine insight, or Acrasia her genuine attractiveness, the fierce vigor of her unsanctified sexual nature, presented as its own self-justifying goal. Even the peeping-Tom element in the Bower, which is undeniable, is an equivocal element throughout the poem. Spenser's vision always points us in towards a center in any scene, sexual or otherwise; his is the art of the cynosure, and no poet has yielded so fully to the tyranny of the bodily eye. His heroes long to gaze upon a variety of glories, and to fulfill themselves in that vision. Acrasia's wanton damsels, inviting the gaze of Guyon, are a parody of the Faerie Queene's granting-of-herself in vision to Arthur, and more directly of all Spenser's exposed heroines upon whom we so delightedly spy.

Guyon is not more or less natural than the Bower he overthrows, any more than his resistance to the temptations of Mammon is more or less natural than a surrender to the Cave's wealth would have been. It is because both Guyon and Acrasia are natural possibilities that Spenser is capable of bringing them into an imaginatively meaningful juxtaposition. What Guyon destroys is not evil in itself, but is rather a good that has luxuriated into dangerous excess because it has denied all context. Guyon is faithful to a context in which sexual love can humanize and not merely naturalize, but Acrasia's love robs men of their human nature. If the reader is more inclined towards naturalism than Spenser was, he still need not suspend his disbelief in Guyon's context, for Spenser's poem stands in its own right as a making, rather than as an adornment to a moral order complete without the imaginings of the poet. Acrasia is like Keats's Belle Dame or Blake's maidens of the Crystal Cabinet or the Golden Net, weaving an enchantment horrible only because it pretends to offer a final reality or inmost form within sexual experience alone. The ruined quester becomes a beast of the field, or starves, or enters into a baffled state unable to comprehend his loss. Keats and Blake are more humanistic in their implications as to what a saving context might be, but the mythic pattern they give us is Spenserian.

There is a curious bitterness in the final stanzas of Book II, as Spenser confronts Guyon and the Palmer with the stubborn Gryll, who had been happy as a hog. It was for this Gryll's sake, as for his fellows, that Guyon and the Palmer had surpassed the voyages of Odysseus, had risked the terrors of the sea so magnificently set forth in the earlier stanzas of Canto XII. The temperate voyager has shown the power of a Hercules and the endurance of an Odysseus; with "rigor pittilesse" he has broken down a great work of mixed art and nature, sparing no part of "their goodly workmanship." Part of his immediate reward is the hoggish lament of a Gryll, and the incongruity of this response provokes the abruptness of the canto's end. If there is bitterness here, there is a sour humor as well. Spenser usually spares himself (and us) the Miltonic contempt for "the donghill kinde" of all-too-natural men, but he has something of the Miltonic horror at any forgetfulness of the excellence of man's creation. The Bower is finally seen as a complement to Mammon's cave, as yet another instrumentality for the dehumanization of man. We are asked to believe that the fruit of Acrasia, eaten for its own sake, destroys as surely as the fruit of Proserpina's garden. There is a natural resistance to so harsh a judgment, within Spenser as within ourselves. Gryll is the warning made not to overcome that resistance but to offer a speaking picture that may trouble even the self-indulging imagination.

V

It is in the *Two Cantos of Mutabilitie* that Spenser troubles his own imagination most, by the strongest of his pictures. *The Mutabilitie Cantos* were not published until 1609, a decade after Spenser's death. Though this greatest of poetic fragments was printed as Cantos VI and VII (and two stanzas of Canto VIII) of Book VII of *The Faerie Queene*, one is tempted to read it as a complete unit in itself, a finishing coda to the otherwise unfinished poem. Certainly the fragment's last two stanzas could not have begun anything; what they yearn for is finality, and they proclaim a poet's farewell to his art and his life.

Various commentators have traced (or thought they traced) the effect of Empedocles, of Lucretius and of Bruno on the *Mutabilitie Cantos*, but Spenser is here more than ever inventive, dealing imaginatively with his own obsessional theme of change and decay in the phenomenal world. Probably he owes the debate form of the fragment to Chaucer's *Parlement of Foules*, but *Mutabilitie* is a very un-Chaucerian comedy, with a profound anguish underlying the ebullient surface.

C.S. Lewis has maintained that Spenser's Titaness Mutabilitie "despite her beauty, is an evil force," an enemy of Spenserian health and concord, and indeed an incarnation of corruption and sin, but this is an over-reading through excessive simplification. Part of the immense power of Spenser's fragment is lost if the Titaness is denied all justice, however much of a shudder must accompany the dramatic sympathy. What is poetically most important about Mutabilitie is what we find most surprising—that Spenser had made her beautiful. This is part of our involuntary sympathy with her, and wins even Jove's momentary (and mistaken) indulgence. Another part is in the genesis of the Titanic myth itself; her claim through lineage is better than Jove's. But most crucial is that Mutabilitie is more human than the gods she challenges; if she is tainted by earthly sin, we of course are too, and her mounting up into the sphere of the moon has its Promethean element.

The corruption of Mutabilitie is primarily decay rather than sin, for morality is not very relevant to this fragment. If it were, then Jove might be given power over Mutabilitie, or his ultimate rule over her realm be implied. But Spenser, for once in *The Faerie Queene*, is not giving us a vision of possibility, but a lament of experience, and the phenomenal sway of Mutabilitie is an experiential truth. The beauty of Mutabilitie is part of that truth, as is the virtual identity of Mutabilitie and human existence itself. The charming episode of Faunus and Molanna is an effective digression because the mischief of its natural spirits towards Diana shows a gentler aspect of the revolt against heavenly rule by Mutabilitie. We suffer with poor Faunus, are pleased by Molanna's river-marriage, and are not very edified by Diana's curse on the region around Arlo-hill. On a larger scale, we have some degree of involvement in Mutabilitie's quest against Cynthia, much as we desire the verdict to go against the rebel.

Yet even the verdict is ambiguous, with something of the mythopoeic complexity we have encountered earlier in the Gardens of Adonis. The poetic synthesis of Spenser is indeed conceptually simpler, more sensuous and more passionate than any philosophical resolution of the problem of change and decay could have been. One element in that synthesis is almost a palinode, which emerges most clearly in the two final stanzas, perhaps the most moving Spenser wrote. The close of Chaucer's *Troilus and Criseyde* provides a rough but useful parallel to Spenser's last stanzas, but the heavenly laughter of Troilus is what Spenser seeks, not what he has already found.

The metamorphic land of Faerie is by turns a humanized nature and a demonic labyrinth, but the land of the *Mutabilitie Cantos* is our generative world, neither redeemed nor doomed, but perpetually subject to alteration, some of it cyclic and expected, like that portrayed in the pageant of the months, but some portion totally unexpected, and running generally to the worse. On the simplest and most human level of his subject Spenser is complaining for all men, and the dignity of the universal is deeply invested in his tone. Proud Mutabilitie is unquestioned mistress of all moral things; from her "all living wights have learned to die." When she turns her ambitions to the heavens she projects our deathly desires towards the eternal world, and menaces an orderly alteration with our disorderly and corrupt beauty. Spenser's uniqueness as a poet, which he bequeaths to Keats especially among his descendants, is in the sensuous immediacy of all his imagined worlds. Mutabilitie is descended from chaos and from earth, and so are we. She carries up with her to the moon's sphere the menace of chaos and the beauty of earth, and the supposed right of capability. The relation of poetry to morality has always been a troubled one, but it seems clear that energy and resolution are always poetic virtues, however unlawful or evil their ends may be in actual existence. Spenser's aspiring Titaness has something of the vigor of Milton's greatest creation, the Satan of *Paradise Lost*, and something in consequence, of Satan's aesthetic hold upon us.

Her appeal is made past Jove to "the god of Nature," who appears only through the veiled presence of his surrogate, Nature herself, perhaps suggested to Spenser by the Wisdom of Proverbs 8:22–31, brought forth by God "before his works of old." The judging voice of Spenser's Nature is his version of the voice of the Hebrew God, for Spenser was poetically subtler than Milton, and too involved in the glory of invention to risk a portrayal of God in His proper person. So Spenser's Nature, though a "great goddess" is not to be seen by us as being either man or women, terror or beauty. Yet her shrouding garment burns with the light of the Transfiguration, and her words are to be respected as definitive by Mutabilitie herself.

The Titaness, by her direct appeal to Nature, affords Spenser the opportunity for one of his most brilliant set-pieces, the Cycle of the Seasons and Months. The tone of Spenser in this chant is complex, for much of the alteration he evidences is benevolent towards men. Even Mutabilitie's account of Earth's function is close to that given in the Gardens of Adonis, and her vision of the other elements suggests the lament of Ecclesiastes. When Spenser comes to the seasons, his voice suggests the tragic naturalism of Keats, who must have learned from these stanzas. In the pageant of the months Spenser fuses joyful images of human labor with the dignified and mixed sadness of classical mythology, as he follows out the course of the vegetative (and Christian) year, till he comes to December, with its Christian paradox of a divine birth in the dead of winter. From this point his stately chant is dominated by dialectical images, with Day and Night, Life and Death, in a creative opposition, preparing the way for the apocalyptic longings of the final stanzas.

The judgment of Nature turns the evidence of Mutabilitie against itself, and makes of phenomenal change and decay an emblem of faith, in reply to the skepticism of the insurgent Titaness: "But what we see not, who shall us perswade?" Everything changes, and yet but dilates being, for natural existence constantly though gradually works towards the revelation of a more human nature. Mutabilitie seeks more palpable sway, yet her desire is self-destructive, for time in Spenser as in Blake or Shelley is the mercy of eternity, and the agent of prophetic redemption. Spenser's humanism is liberated into an imaginative vitalism through Nature's assurances that states of being survive though all things must endure change. The time that shall come, in bringing about the uncovering of all things, will bring also the perfection that reigns over change. Until that time comes, Nature vanishes, leaving Mutabilitie dominant in the lower world beneath the moon, and Jove as ordered change still reigning in the heavens above.

Had Spenser ended there, his fragment would have a curiously cold climax for so turbulent and piercing a work. The poet's voice at its most personal breaks into his poem, weighing the speech of Mutabilitie and desperately granting the pragmatic strength of her claim to all the human world. Renouncing the beauty and pride of the only life we can lead, he turns to the speech of Nature for some comfort, and the urgency of his prayer reverberates strangely against the humanism and love celebrated throughout his poem. Yet even here, as he prays for a sight of the eternal sabbath, he does not allow himself to denigrate the experience of living. All shall rest with God, but meanwhile "all that moveth doth in change *delight.*" The pride of life is "so fading and so fickle" and must yield to "short time," but while it lasts it remains a "*flowring* pride."

# John Milton

## (1608–1674)

AFTER SHAKESPEARE AND CHAUCER, JOHN MILTON IS THE MOST EMINENT poet in the English language. Since he is an immensely learned poet, Milton becomes increasingly difficult for most readers at a time when we are less deeply educated than many of us were in the past. After a half-century at Yale University, I am aware that no one remarks to me of a colleague that she or he is remarkably "learned." Erudition is hardly in fashion.

John Milton may be the most radical instance I know of the work in a writer, or the influence of an exemplary mind upon itself. No other great poet, even Dante, began with so clear and systematic an intention to devote himself entirely to poetry, with the ambition of surpassing all forerunners. And no other major poet ever has read so deeply and extensively as Milton did. He desired a life cloistered but secular, in which poetry and learning, fused together, were to be his central preoccupations. Until he was thirty-three, he lived his dream, at Cambridge University, and at Horton, his father's country estate near Windsor, and then in a long Italian tour in 1638–1639. From 1640 on, he lived in London, teaching at his own school, and continuing his preparation for epic accomplishment.

The struggle against the monarchy and its bishops began, for Milton, in 1841, when he took the side of Protestantism and Parliament in the gathering conflict that led to the English Civil War. For twenty years—before, during, and after his service to Cromwell and the Commonwealth as Secretary for Foreign Tongues to the Council of State—Milton devoted his creative energies to polemical prose tracts.

Let us begin by looking at Milton's poetry up through 1637, when it culminated in *Lycidas*, a year before his Italian tour. His greatness is first manifested in *L'Allegro* and *Il Penseroso*, matched extended lyrics in tetrameter couplets that still retain their extraordinary freshness and originality. Immensely playful, they resonate with intimations of a giant art to come:

> Lap me in soft Lydian airs,
> Married to immortal verse,
> Such as the meeting soul may pierce
> In notes with many a winding bout
> Of linked sweetness long drawn out,
> With wanton heed and giddy cunning,
> The melting voice through mazes running,
> Untwisting all the chains that tie
> The hidden soul of harmony;
> That Orpheus' self may heave his head
> From golden slumber on a bed
> Of heaped Elysian flowers, and hear
> Such strains as would have won the ear
> Of Pluto, to have quite set free
> His half-regained Eurydice.
> These delights if thou canst give,
> Mirth, with thee I mean to live.

This conclusion might be called Milton's Song of Innocence, to be contrasted with the close of *Il Penseroso* as a Song of Experience:

> There let the pealing organ blow
> To the full-voiced quire below,
> In service high and anthems clear,
> As may with sweetness, through mine ear,
> Dissolve me into ecstasies,
> And bring all heaven before mine eyes.
> And may at last my weary age
> Find out the peaceful hermitage,
> The hairy gown and mossy cell,
> Where I may sit and rightly spell
> Of every star that heaven doth shew,
> And every herb that sips the dew,
> Till old experience do attain
> To something like prophetic strain.
> These pleasures, Melancholy, give,
> And I with thee will choose to live.

This is Milton at twenty-three or twenty-four, sublimely picturing himself as a new Orpheus, with all the imaginative world still before him. In 1634, Milton's pastoral masque, *Comus*, with music by his friend Henry Lawes, was performed. It remains a work of enduring beauty, strongly influenced by Shakespeare's *A Midsummer Night's Dream*, *The Winter's Tale* and *The Tempest*. So astonishing was the young Milton's artistry that *Comus* is able to absorb Shakespeare at his pastoral perfection without being destroyed by this strongest of precursors.

The culmination of Milton's early poetry is *Lycidas*, the superb pastoral elegy written when the poet was twenty-nine, soon after the death of his mother. *Lycidas*, an extended canzone of one hundred and ninety-three lines, is quite possibly the best shorter poem in the language, and is properly one of the most demanding. The true subject of *Lycidas* is neither Edward King, a young poet drowned in the Irish Sea, and a classmate of Milton at Cambridge, nor the evaded death of the mother. Rather, the poem contemplates Milton's dread of being cut off before he had time to compose the major poems he lived to write:

> Alas! What boots it with uncessant care
> To tend the homely slighted shepherd's trade,
> And strictly meditate the thankless Muse?
> Were it not better done as others use,
> To sport with Amaryllis in the shade,
> Or with the tangles of Neaera's hair?
> Fame is the spur that the clear spirit doth raise
> (That last infirmity of noble mind)
> To scorn delights, and love laborious days;
> But the fair guerdon when we hope to find,
> And think to burst out into sudden blaze,
> Comes the blind Fury with the abhorred shears,
> And slits the thin-spun life.

This did not happen, and Milton survived to write *Paradise Lost* (1658–1665), *Paradise Regained* (1667–1670), and *Samson Agonistes* (possibly 1670–1671). By 1652, in his mid-forties, Milton was completely blind. In 1660, the monarchy was restored: Milton's books were burned by the hangman in London, and the defiant poet was arrested and locked up from October to December. Fortunately, the government of Charles II released him, though he could have been hanged as a defender of regicide. When Milton died, in early November, 1674, he was just short of sixty-six. His personal life (three marriages, and three resentful daughters) had not been particularly happy, and his religious and political hopes for his nation had been destroyed, but *Paradise Lost* and *Samson Agonistes* were triumphant accomplishments, absolute fulfillments of his lifelong ambitions.

The influence of Milton's mind upon itself best can be conveyed, in my judgment, by bringing together portions of the four invocations to *Paradise Lost*, that commence Books I, III, VII, and IX of the only epic that can rival the *Iliad* and the *Odyssey*. I give a cento drawn from the invocations:

> And chiefly thou, O Spirit, that dost prefer
> Before all temples the upright heart and pure,
> Instruct me, for thou knowest; thou from the first
> Wast present, and with mighty wings outspread
> Dove-like sat'st brooding on the vast abyss
> And mad'st it pregnant: what in me is dark
> Illumine, what is low raise and support ...
> (I.17–23)

> Then feed on thoughts that voluntary move
> Harmonious numbers, as the wakeful bird
> Sings darkling, and in shadiest covert hid
> Tunes her nocturnal note. Thus with the year
> Seasons return; but not to me returns
> Day, or the sweet approach of even or morn,
> Or sight of vernal bloom, or summer's rose,
> Or flocks, or herds, or human face divine;
> But cloud instead, and ever-during dark
> Surrounds me, from the cheerful ways of men
> Cut off, and for the book of knowledge fair
> Presented with a universal blank
> Of Nature's works to me expunged and razed,
> And wisdom at one entrance quite shut out.
> So much the rather thou, celestial Light,
> Shine inward, and the mind through all her powers
> Irradiate, there plant eyes, all mist from thence
> Purge and disperse, that I may see and tell
> Of things invisible to mortal sight ...
> (III.37–55)

> Up led by thee
> Into the heaven of heavens I have presumed,
> An earthly guest, and drawn empyreal air,

Thy tempering; with like safety guided down,
Return me to my native element ...
(VII.12–16)

If answerable style I can obtain
Of my celestial patroness, who deigns
Her nightly visitation unimplored,
And dictates to me slumbering, or inspires
Easy my unpremeditated verse,
Since first this subject for heroic song
Pleased me long choosing, and beginning late ...
(IX.20–26)

What Milton has taught Milton is the fruit of thirty years and more of profound meditation upon extraordinary learning and native genius. Not blindness, disgrace, imprisonment, or danger, or a life filled with marital and familial discord, has prevented a great consciousness from expanding to its limits. Milton more than earned the magnificent final line of *Samson Agonistes*:

And calm of mind, all passion spent.

### Paradise Lost

By 1652, before his forty-fourth birthday and with his long-projected major poem unwritten, Milton was completely blind. In 1660, with arrangements for the Stuart Restoration well under way, the blind poet identified himself with the prophet Jeremiah, as if he would "tell the very soil itself what her perverse inhabitants are deaf to," vainly warning a divinely chosen people "now choosing them a captain back for Egypt, to bethink themselves a little, and consider whither they are rushing." These words are quoted from the second edition of *The Ready and Easy Way*, a work which marks the end of Milton's temporal prophecy and the beginning of his greater work, the impassioned meditations upon divine providence and human nature. In these [meditations] Milton abandons the field of his defeat, and leaves behind him also the songs of triumph he might have sung in praise of a reformed society and its imaginatively integrated citizens. He changes those notes to tragic, and praises, when he praises at all, what he calls the better fortitude of patience, the hitherto unsung theme of Heroic Martyrdom. Adam, Christ and Samson manifest an internal mode of heroism that Satan can neither understand nor overcome, a heroism that the blind Puritan prophet himself is called upon to exemplify in the England of the Restoration.

Milton had planned a major poem since he was a young man, and he had associated his composition of the poem with the hope that it would be a celebration of a Puritan reformation of all England. He had prophesied of the coming time that "amidst the hymns and hallelujahs of the saints some one may perhaps be heard offering at high strains in new and lofty measures to sing and celebrate thy divine mercies and marvellous judgements in the land throughout all ages." This vision clearly concerns a national epic, very probably on a British rather than a Biblical theme. That poem, had it been written, would have rivaled the great poem of Milton's master, Spenser, who in a profound sense was Milton's "Original," to cite Dryden's testimony. *Paradise Lost* is not the poem that Milton had prophesied in the exuberance of his youth, but we may guess it to be a greater work than the one we lost, for the unwritten poem would not have had the Satan who is at once the aesthetic glory and the moral puzzle of Milton's epic of loss and disillusion.

The form of *Paradise Lost* is based on Milton's modification of Vergil's attempt to rival Homer's *Iliad*, but the content of Milton's epic has a largely negative relation to the content of the *Iliad* or the *Aeneid*. Milton's "one greater Man," Christ, is a hero who necessarily surpasses all the sons of Adam, including Achilles and Aeneas, just as he surpasses Adam or archetypal Man himself. Milton delights to speak of himself as soaring above the sacred places of the classical muses and as seeking instead "thee *Sion* and the flow'ry brooks beneath," Siloam, by whose side the Hebrew prophets walked. For *Paradise Lost*, despite C.S. Lewis's persuasive assertions to the contrary, is specifically a Protestant and Puritan poem, created by a man who finally became a Protestant church of one, a sect unto himself. The poem's true muse is "that eternal Spirit who can enrich with all utterance and knowledge, and sends out his seraphim, with the hallowed fire of his altar, to touch and purify the lips of whom he pleases." This Spirit is one that prefers for its shrine, in preference to all Temples of organized faith, the upright and pure heart of the isolated Protestant poet, who carries within himself the extreme Christian individualism of the Puritan Left Wing. Consequently, the poem's doctrine is not "the great central tradition" that Lewis finds it to be, but an imaginative variation on that tradition. Milton believed in the doctrines of the Fall, natural corruption, regeneration through grace, an aristocracy of the elect, and Christian Liberty, all of them fundamental to Calvinist belief, and yet Milton was no orthodox Calvinist, as Arthur Barker has demonstrated. The poet refused to make a sharp distinction between the natural and the spiritual in man, and broke from Calvin in his theory of regeneration. Milton's doctrine of predestination, as seen in *Paradise Lost*, is both general and conditional; the Spirit does not make particular and absolute choices. When regeneration comes, it heals not only man's spirit but his nature as well, for Milton could not abide in dualism. Barker makes the fine contrast between Milton and Calvin that in Calvin even good men are altogether dependent upon God's will, and not on their own restored faculties, but in Milton the will is made free again, and man is restored to his former liberty. The hope for man in *Paradise Lost* is that Adam's descendants will find their salvation in the fallen world, once they have accepted Christ's sacrifice and its human consequences, by taking a middle way between those who would deny the existence of sin altogether, in a wild freedom founded upon a misunderstanding of election, and those who would repress man's nature that spirit might be more free. The regenerated descendants of Adam are to evidence that God's grace need not provide for the abolition of the natural man.

To know and remember this as Milton's ideal is to be properly prepared to encounter the dangerous greatness of Satan in the early books of *Paradise Lost*. The poem is a theodicy, and like *Job* seeks to justify the ways of Jehovah to man, but unlike the poet of *Job* Milton insisted that reason could comprehend God's justice, for Milton's God is perfectly reasonable and the perfection of man in Christ would raise human reason to a power different only in degree from its fallen status. The poet of *Job* has an aesthetic advantage over Milton, for most readers rightly prefer a Voice out of a Whirlwind, fiercely asking rhetorical questions, to Milton's sophistical Schoolmaster of Souls in Book III of *Paradise Lost*. But Milton's God is out of balance because Satan is so magnificently flawed in presentation, and to account for the failure of God as a dramatic character the reader is compelled to enter upon the most famous and vexing of critical problems concerning *Paradise Lost*, the Satanic controversy itself. Is Satan in some sense heroic, or is he merely a fool?

The anti-Satanist school of critics has its great ancestor in Addison, who found Satan's sentiments to be "suitable to a created being of the most exalted and most depraved nature.... Amid those impieties which this enraged spirit utters ... the author has taken care to introduce none that is not big with absurdity, and incapable of shocking a religious reader." Dr. Johnson followed Addison with more eloquence: "The malignity of Satan foams in haughtiness and obstinacy; but his expressions are commonly general, and no otherwise offensive than as they are wicked." The leading modern anti-Satanists are the late Charles Williams, and C.S. Lewis, for whom Milton's Satan is to some extent an absurd egoist, not altogether unlike Meredith's Sir Willoughby Patterne. So Lewis states "it is a mistake to demand that Satan, any more than Sir Willoughby, should be able to rant and posture through the whole universe without, sooner or later, awaking the comic spirit." Satan is thus an apostle of Nonsense, and his progressive degeneration in the poem is only the inevitable working-out of his truly absurd choice when he first denied his status as another of God's creatures.

> The Satanist school of critics finds its romantic origins in two very great poets profoundly and complexly affected by Milton, Blake and Shelley. This tradition of romantic Satanism needs to be distinguished from the posturings of its Byronic-Napoleonic cousin, with which anti-Satanists have loved to confound it. The greatest of anti-Satanists (because the most attracted to Satan), Coleridge, was himself guilty of this confusion. But though he insisted upon reading into Milton's Satan the lineaments of Bonaparte, Coleridge's reading of the Satanic character has never been equaled by any modern anti-Satanist: But in its utmost abstraction and consequent state of reprobation, the will becomes Satanic pride and rebellious self-idolatry in the relations of the spirit to itself, and remorseless despotism relatively to others; the more hopeless as the more obdurate by its subjugation of sensual impulses, by its superiority to toil and pain and pleasure; in short, by the fearful resolve to find in itself alone the one absolute motive of action, under which all other motives from within and from without must be either subordinated or crushed.

Against this reading of the Satanic predicament we can set the dialectical ironies of Blake in *The Marriage of Heaven and Hell* and the imaginative passion of Shelley in his Preface to *Prometheus Unbound* and *A Defence of Poetry*. For Blake the Satan of Books I and II supremely embodies human desire, the energy that alone can create. But desire restrained becomes passive, until it is only a shadow of desire. God and Christ in *Paradise Lost* embody reason and restraint, and their restriction of Satan causes him to forget his own passionate desires, and to accept a categorical morality that he can only seek to invert. But a poet is by necessity of the party of energy and desire; reason and restraint cannot furnish the stuff of creativity. So Milton, as a true poet, wrote at liberty when he portrayed Devils and Hell, and in fetters when he described Angels and God. For Hell is the active life springing from energy, and Heaven only the passive existence that obeys reason.

Blake was too subtle to portray Satan as being even the unconscious hero of the poem. Rather, he implied that the poem can have no hero because it too strongly features Milton's self-abnegation in assigning human creative power to its diabolical side. Shelley went further, and claimed Satan as a semi-Promethean or flawed hero, whose character engenders in the reader's mind a pernicious casuistry of humanist argument against theological injustice. Shelley more directly fathered the Satanist school by his forceful statement of its aesthetic case: "Nothing can exceed the energy and magnificence of Satan as expressed in *Paradise Lost*." Whatever else, Shelley concluded, might be said for the Christian basis of the poem, it was clear that Milton's Satan as a moral being was far superior to Milton's God.

Each reader of *Paradise Lost* must find for himself the proper reading of Satan, whose appeal is clearly all but universal. Amid so much magnificence it is difficult to choose a single passage from *Paradise Lost* as surpassing all others, but I incline to the superlative speech of Satan on top of Mount Niphates (Book IV, ll.32–113), which is the text upon which the anti-Satanist, Satanist or some compromise attitude must finally rest. Here Satan makes his last choice, and ceases to be what he was in the early books of the poem. All that the anti-Satanists say about him is true *after* this point; all or almost all claimed for him by the Satanists is true *before* it. When this speech is concluded, Satan has become Blake's "shadow of desire," and he is on the downward path that will make him "as big with absurdity" as ever Addison and Lewis claimed him to be. Nothing that can be regenerated remains in Satan, and the rift between his self-ruined spirit and his radically corrupted nature widens until he is the hissing serpent of popular tradition, plucking greedily at the Dead Sea fruit of Hell in a fearful parody of Eve's Fall.

It is on Mount Niphates again that Satan, now a mere (but very subtle) tempter, stands when he shows Christ the kingdoms of this world in the brief epic, *Paradise Regained*. "Brief epic" is the traditional description of this poem (published in 1671, four years after *Paradise Lost*), but the description has been usefully challenged by several modern critics. E.M.W. Tillyard has warned against judging the poem by any kind of epic standard and has suggested instead that it ought to be read as a kind of Morality play, while Arnold Stein has termed it an internal drama, set in the Son of God's mind. Louis L. Martz has argued, following Tillyard, that the poem is an attempt to convert Vergil's *Georgics* into a mode for religious poetry, and ought therefore to be read as both a didactic work and a formal meditation on the Gospel. *Paradise Regained* is so subdued a poem when compared to *Paradise Lost* that we find real difficulty in reading it as epic. Yet it does resemble *Job*, which Milton gave as the possible model for a brief epic, for like *Job* it is essentially a structure of gathering self-awareness, of the protagonist and hero recognizing himself in his relation to God. Milton's Son of Man is obedient where Milton's Adam was disobedient; Job was not quite either until God spoke to him and demonstrated the radical incompatibility involved in any mortal's questionings of divine purpose. Job, until his poem's climax, is an epic hero because he has an unresolved conflict within himself, between his own conviction of righteousness and his moral outrage at the calamities that have come upon him despite his righteousness. Job needs to overcome the temptations afforded him by this conflict, including those offered by his comforters (to deny his own righteousness) and by his finely laconic wife (to curse God and die). The temptations of Milton's Son of God (the poet's fondness for this name of Christ is another testimony to his Hebraic preference for the Father over the Son) are not easy for us to sympathize with in any very dramatic way, unlike the temptations of Job, who is a man like ourselves. But again Milton is repeating the life-long quest of his poetry; to see man as an integrated unity of distinct natures, body and soul harmonized. In Christ these natures are perfectly unified, and so the self-realization of Christ is an image of the possibility of human integration. Job learns not to tempt God's patience too far; Christ learns who he is, and in that moment of self-revelation Satan is smitten with amazement and falls as by the blow of a Hercules. Milton had seen himself in *Paradise Lost* as Abdiel, the faithful Angel who will not follow Satan in rebellion against God, defying thus the scorn of his fellows. Less consciously, something crucial in Milton had found its way into the Satan of the opening books, sounding a stoic defiance of adversity. In *Paradise Regained* Milton, with genuine humility, is exploring the Jobean problem within himself. Has he, as a Son of God also, tried God's patience too far, and can he at length overcome the internal temptations that beset a proud spirit reduced to being a voice in the wilderness? The poet's conquest over himself is figured in the greater Son of God's triumphant endurance, and in the quiet close of *Paradise Regained*, where the Savior returns to his mother's house to lead again, for a while, the private life of contemplation and patience while waiting upon God's will, not the public life forever closed to Milton.

Published with *Paradise Regained* in 1671, the dramatic poem *Samson Agonistes* is more admired today than the brief epic it accompanied. The poem's title, like the *Prometheus Bound* of Aeschylus, refers to the episode in the hero's life upon which the work is centered. The reference (from the Greek for athletic contestants in public games) is to Samson's ordeal before the Philistines at their Feast of Dagon, where he is summoned for their sport to demonstrate his blind strength, and where his faith gives him light enough to destroy them. Samson is Milton's Christian modification of Athenian drama, as *Paradise Lost* had been of classical epic. Yet Milton's drama is his most personal poem, in its experimental metric and in its self-reference alike. Modern editors cautiously warn against overstressing the extent to which Samson represents Milton, yet the representation seems undeniable, and justly so, to the common reader. Milton's hatred of his enemies does not seem particularly Christian to many of his modern critics, but its ferocious zeal fits both the Biblical story of Samson and the very bitter situation that the blind Puritan champion had to face in the first decade of the Restoration. The crucial text here is the great Chorus, ll.652–709, in which Milton confronts everything in the world of public events that had hurt him most. The theodicy of *Paradise Lost* seems abstract compared to the terrible emotion conveyed in this majestic hymn. The men solemnly elected by God for the great work of renovation that is at once God's glory and the people's safety are then evidently abandoned by God, and indeed thrown by Him lower than He previously exalted them on high. Milton had lived to see the bodies of his great leaders and associates, including Cromwell, dug up and hanged on the gallows to commemorate the twelfth anniversary of the execution of Charles I. Sir Henry Vane, for whom Milton had a warm and especial admiration, had been executed by order of "the unjust tribunals, under change of times, / And condemnation of the ingrateful multitude." *Samson Agonistes* give us not only the sense of having experienced a perfectly proportioned work of art, but also the memory of Milton's most moving prayer to God, which follows his account of the tribulations of his fellow Puritans:

> So deal not with this once thy glorious Champion,
> The Image of thy strength, and mighty minister.
> What do I beg? how hast thou dealt already?
> Behold him in this state calamitous, and turn
> His labours, for thou canst, to peaceful end.

# William Wordsworth

## (1770–1850)

There is a human loneliness,
A part of space and solitude,
In which knowledge cannot be denied.
In which nothing of knowledge fails,
The luminous companion, the hand,
The fortifying arm, the profound
Response, the completely answering voice....
—WALLACE STEVENS

THE PRELUDE WAS TO BE ONLY THE ANTECHAPEL TO THE GOTHIC CHURCH of *The Recluse*, but the poet Wordsworth knew better than the man, and *The Prelude* is a complete and climactic work. The key to *The Prelude* as an internalized epic written in creative competition to Milton is to be found in those lines (754–860) of the *Recluse* fragment that Wordsworth prefaced to *The Excursion* (1814). Wordsworth's invocation, like Blake's to the Daughters of Beulah in his epic *Milton*, is a deliberate address to powers higher than those that inspired *Paradise Lost*:

Urania, I shall need
Thy guidance, or a greater Muse, if such
Descend to earth or dwell in highest heaven!
For I must tread on shadowy ground, must sink
Deep—and, aloft ascending, breathe in worlds
To which the heaven of heavens is but a veil.

The shadowy ground, the depths beneath, and the heights aloft are all in the mind of man, and Milton's heaven is only a veil, separating an allegorical unreality from the human paradise of the happiest and best regions of a poet's mind. Awe of the personal Godhead fades before the poet's reverence for his own imaginative powers:

> All strength—all terror, single or in bands,
> That ever was put forth in personal form—
> Jehovah—with his thunder, and the choir
> Of shouting Angels, and the empyreal thrones—
> I pass them unalarmed.

Blake, more ultimately unorthodox than Wordsworth as he was, had yet too strong a sense of the Bible's power to accept this dismissal of Jehovah. After reading this passage, he remarked sardonically:

> Solomon, when he Married Pharaoh's daughter & became a Convert to the Heathen Mythology, talked exactly in this way of Jehovah as a Very inferior object of Man's Contemplations; he also passed him by unalarm'd & was permitted. Jehovah dropped a tear & follow'd him by his Spirit into the Abstract Void; it is called the Divine Mercy.

To marry Pharaoh's daughter is to marry Nature, the Goddess of the Heathen Mythology, and indeed Wordsworth will go on to speak of a marriage between the Mind of Man and the goodly universe of Nature. Wordsworth is permitted his effrontery, as Solomon the Wise was before him, and, like Solomon, Wordsworth wanders into the Ulro or Abstract Void of general reasoning from Nature, pursued by the ambiguous pity of the Divine Mercy. But this (though powerful) is a dark view to take of Wordsworth's reciprocal dealings with Nature. Courageously but calmly Wordsworth puts himself forward as a renovated spirit, a new Adam upon whom fear and awe fall as he looks into his own Mind, the Mind of Man. As befits a new Adam, a new world with a greater beauty waits upon his steps. The most defiant humanism in Wordsworth salutes the immediate possibility of this earthly paradise naturalizing itself in the here and now:

> Paradise, and groves
> Elysian, Fortunate Fields—like those of old
> Sought in the Atlantic Main—why should they be
> A history only of departed things,
> Or a mere fiction of what never was?
> For the discerning intellect of Man,

When wedded to this goodly universe
In love and holy passion, shall find these
A simple produce of the common day.

No words are more honorific for Wordsworth than "simple" and "common." The marriage metaphor here has the same Hebraic sources as Blake had for his Beulah, or "married land." The true Eden is the child of the common day, when that day dawns upon the great consummation of the reciprocal passion of Man and Nature. What Wordsworth desires to write is "the spousal verse" in celebration of this fulfillment:

                                        and, by words
Which speak of nothing more than what we are,
Would I arouse the sensual from their sleep
Of Death, and win the vacant and the vain
To noble raptures.

This parallels Blake's singing in *Jerusalem*:

Of the sleep of Ulro! and of the passage through
Eternal Death! and of the awaking to Eternal Life.

But Wordsworth would arouse us by speaking of nothing more than what we already are; a more naturalistic humanism than Blake could endure. Wordsworth celebrates the *given*—what we already possess, and for him it is as for Wallace Stevens

As if the air, the mid-day air, was swarming
With the metaphysical changes that occur,
Merely in living as and where we live.

For Wordsworth, as for Stevens, the earth is enough; for Blake it was less than that all without which man cannot be satisfied. We need to distinguish this argument between the two greatest of the Romantics from the simplistic dissension with which too many readers have confounded it, that between the doctrines of innate goodness and original sin. Wordsworth is not Rousseau, and Blake is not St. Paul; they have more in common with one another than they have with either the natural religionist or the orthodox Christian.

Wordsworth's Imagination is like Wallace Stevens's *Angel Surrounded by Paysans*: not an angel of heaven, but the necessary angel of earth, as, in its sight, we see the earth again, but cleared; and in its hearing we hear the still sad music of humanity, its tragic drone, rise liquidly, not harsh or grating, but like watery words awash, to chasten and subdue us. But the Imagination of Wordsworth and of Stevens is "a figure half seen, or seen for a moment." It rises with the sudden mountain mists, and as suddenly departs. Blake, a literalist of the Imagination, wished for its more habitual sway. To marry Mind and Nature is to enter Beulah; there Wordsworth and Blake are at one. Blake insisted that a man more fully redeemed by Imagination would not need Nature, would regard the external world as hindrance. The split between Wordsworth and Blake is not theological at all, though Blake expresses it in his deliberately displaced Protestant vocabulary by using the metaphor of the Fall where Wordsworth rejects it. For Wordsworth the individual Mind and the external World are exquisitely fitted, each to the other, even as man and wife, and with blended might they accomplish a creation the meaning of which is fully dependent upon the sexual analogy; they give to us a new heaven and a new earth blended into an apocalyptic unity that is simply the matter of common perception and common sexuality raised to the freedom of its natural power. Wordsworthian Man is Freudian Man, but Blake's Human Form Divine is not. "You shall not bring me down to believe such a fitting & fitted" is his reaction to Wordsworth's exquisite adjustings of the Universe and Mind. To accept Nature as man's equal is for Blake the ineradicable error. Blake's doctrine is that either the Imagination totally destroys Nature and puts a thoroughly Human form in its place, or else Nature destroys the Imagination. Wordsworth says of his task that he is forced to hear "Humanity in fields and groves / Pipe solitary anguish" and Blake reacts with ferocity:

> Does not this Fit, & is not Fitting most Exquisitely too, but to
> what?—not to Mind, but to the Vile Body only & to its Laws
> of Good & Evil & its Enmities against Mind.

This is not the comment of an embittered Gnostic. Blake constructs his poetry as a commentary upon Scripture; Wordsworth writes his poetry as a commentary upon Nature. Wordsworth, while not so Bible-haunted as Blake, is himself a poet in the Hebraic prophetic line. The visible body of Nature is more than an outer testimony of the Spirit of God to him; it is our only way to God. For Blake it is the barrier between us and the God within ourselves. Ordinary perception is then a mode of salvation for Wordsworth, provided that we are awake fully to what we see. The common earth is to be hallowed by the human heart's and mind's holy union with it, and by that union the heart and mind in concert are to receive their bride's gift of phenomenal beauty, a glory in the grass, a splendor in the flower. Until at last the Great Consummation will be achieved, and renovated Man will stand in Eden once again. The human glory of Wordsworth, which he bequeathed to Keats, is in this naturalistic celebration of the possibilities inherent in our condition, here and now. That Wordsworth himself, in the second half of his long life, could not sustain this vision is a criticism of neither the vision nor the man, but merely his loss—and ours.

*The Old Cumberland Beggar* (1797) is Wordsworth's finest vision of the irreducible natural man, the human stripped to the nakedness of primordial condition and exposed as still powerful in dignity, still infinite in value. The Beggar reminds us of the beggars, solitaries, wanderers throughout Wordsworth's poetry, particularly in *The Prelude* and *Resolution and Independence*. He differs from them in that he is not the agency of a revelation; he is not responsible for a sudden release of Wordsworth's imagination. He is not even of visionary utility; he is something finer, beyond use, a vision of reality in himself. I am not suggesting that *The Old Cumberland Beggar* is the best of Wordsworth's poems outside *The Prelude*; it is not in the sublime mode, as are *Tintern Abbey*, the Great Ode, *Resolution and Independence*. But it is the most Wordsworthian of poems, and profoundly moving.

Nothing could be simpler than the poem's opening: "I saw an aged Beggar in my walk." The Old Man (the capitalization is the poet's) has put down his staff, and takes his scraps and fragments out of a flour bag, one by one. He scans them, fixedly and seriously. The plain beginning yields to a music of love, the beauty of the real:

> In the sun,
> Upon the second step of that small pile,
> Surrounded by those wild unpeopled hills,
> He sat, and ate his food in solitude:
> And ever, scattered from his palsied hand,
> That, still attempting to prevent the waste,
> Was baffled still, the crumbs in little showers
> Fell on the ground; and the small mountain birds,
> Not venturing yet to peck their destined meal,
> Approached within the length of half his staff.

It is difficult to describe *how* this is beautiful, but we can make a start by observing that it is beautiful both because it is so matter of fact, and because the fact is itself a transfiguration. The Old Man is in his own state, and he is radically innocent. The "wild unpeopled hills" complement his own solitude; he is a phenomenon of their kind. And he is no more sentimentalized than they are. His lot is not even miserable; he is too absorbed into Nature for that, as absorbed as he can be and still retain human identity.

He is even past further aging. The poet has known him since his childhood, and even then "he was so old, he seems not older now." The Old Man is so helpless in appearance that everyone—sauntering horseman or toll-gate keeper or post boy—makes way for him, taking special care to keep him from harm. For he cannot be diverted, but moves on like a natural process. "He travels on, a solitary Man," Wordsworth says, and then repeats it, making a refrain for that incessant movement whose only meaning is that it remains human though at the edge of our condition:

> He travels on, a solitary Man;
> His age has no companion. On the ground
> His eyes are turned, and, as he moves along,
> *They* move along the ground; and, evermore,
> Instead of common and habitual sight
> Of fields with rural works, of hill and dale,
> And the blue sky, one little span of earth
> Is all his prospect.

He is bent double, like the Leech Gatherer, and his vision of one little span of earth recalls the wandering old man of Chaucer's *Pardoner's Tale*. But Chaucer's solitary longed for death, and on the ground he called his mother's gate he knocked often with his staff, crying, "Dear mother, let me in." Wordsworth's Old Man sees only the ground, but he is tenaciously alive, and is beyond desire, even that of death. He sees, and yet hardly sees. He moves constantly, but is so still in look and motion that he can hardly be seen to move. He is all process, hardly character, and yet almost stasis.

It is so extreme a picture that we can be tempted to ask, "Is this life? Where is its use?" The temptation dehumanizes us, Wordsworth would have it, and the two questions are radically dissimilar, but his answer to the first is vehemently affirmative and to the second an absolute moral passion. There is

> a spirit and pulse of good,
> A life and soul, to every mode of being
> Inseparably linked.

The Old Man performs many functions. The most important is that of a binding agent for the memories of good impulses in all around him. Wherever he goes,

> The mild necessity of use compels
> To acts of love.

These acts of love, added one to another, at last insensibly dispose their performers to virtue and true goodness. We need to be careful in our reaction to this. Wordsworth is not preaching the vicious and mad doctrine that beggary is good because it makes charity possible. That would properly invoke Blake's blistering reply in *The Human Abstract*:

> Pity would be no more
> If we did not make somebody Poor;
> And Mercy no more could be
> If all were as happy as we.

Wordsworth has no reaction to the Old Man which we can categorize. He does not think of him in social or economic terms, but only as a human life, which necessarily has affected other lives, and always for the better. In particular, the Old Man has given occasions for kindness to the very poorest, who give to him from their scant store, and are the kinder for it. Again, you must read this in its own context. Wordsworth's best poetry has nothing directly to do with social justice, as Blake's or Shelley's frequently does. The old beggar is a free man, at home in the heart of the solitudes he wanders, and he does not intend the humanizing good he passively causes. Nor is his social aspect at the poem's vital center; only his freedom is:

> —Then let him pass, a blessing on his head!
> And, long as he can wander, let him breathe
> The freshness of the valleys; let his blood
> Struggle with frosty air and winter snows;
> And let the chartered wind that sweeps the heath
> Beat his grey locks against his withered face.

Pity for him is inappropriate; he is pathetic only if shut up. He is a "figure of capable imagination," in Stevens's phrase, a Man perfectly complete in Nature, reciprocating its gifts by being himself, a being at one with it:

Let him be free of mountain solitudes;
And have around him, whether heard or not,
The pleasant melody of woodland birds.

Mountain solitudes and sudden winds are what suit him, whether he
reacts to them or not. The failure of his senses does not cut him off from
Nature; it does not matter whether he can hear the birds, but it is fitting
that he have them around him. He has become utterly passive toward
Nature. Let it be free, then, to come in upon him:

                          if his eyes have now
Been doomed so long to settle upon earth
That not without some effort they behold
The countenance of the horizontal sun,
Rising or setting, let the light at least
Find a free entrance to their languid orbs.

The Old Man is approaching that identity with Nature that the
infant at first knows, when an organic continuity seems to exist between
Nature and consciousness. Being so naturalized, he must die in the eye of
Nature, that he may be absorbed again:

And let him, *where* and *when* he will, sit down
Beneath the trees, or on a grassy bank
Of highway side, and with the little birds
Share his chance-gathered meal; and, finally,
As in the eye of Nature he has lived,
So in the eye of Nature let him die!

The poem abounds in a temper of spirit that Wordsworth shares
with Tolstoy, a reverence for the simplicities of *caritas*, the Christian
love that is so allied to and yet is not pity. But Tolstoy might have
shown the Old Cumberland Beggar as a sufferer; in Wordsworth he
bears the mark of "animal tranquillity and decay," the title given by
Wordsworth to a fragment closely connected to the longer poem. In
the fragment the Old Man travels on and moves not with pain, but with
thought:

              He is insensibly subdued
    To settled quiet ...
              He is by nature led

To peace so perfect that the young behold
With envy, what the Old Man hardly feels.

We know today, better than his contemporaries could, what led
Wordsworth to the subject of human decay, to depictions of idiocy,
desertion, beggars, homeless wanderers. He sought images of alienated
life, as we might judge them, which he could see and present as images
of natural communion. The natural man, free of consciousness in any of
our senses, yet demonstrates a mode of consciousness which both intends
Nature for its object and at length blends into that object. The hiding
places of man's power are in his past, in childhood. Only memory can
take him there, but even memory fades, and at length fades away. The
poet of naturalism, separated by organic growth from his own past, looks
around him and sees the moving emblems of a childlike consciousness in
the mad, the outcast, and the dreadfully old. From them he takes his
most desperate consolation, intimations of a mortality that almost ceases
to afflict.

### The Prelude

*The Prelude*, completed in 1805, was published after Wordsworth's death in
1850. The title was chosen by the poet's widow; for Wordsworth it was
simply "the poem to Coleridge." The 1850 text both suffers and gains by
nearly half a century of Wordsworth's revisions, for the poet of the decade
1798–1807 was not the Urizenic bard of the *Ecclesiastical Sonnets*, and the
attempts of the older Wordsworth to correct the younger are not always
fortunate. The 1850 text shows better craftsmanship, but it also sometimes
manifests an orthodox censor at work, straining to correct a private myth
into an approach at Anglican dogma. As Wordsworth's modern editor,
Ernest de Selincourt, has observed, nothing could be more significant than
the change of

I worshipped then among the depths of things
As my soul bade me ...
I felt and nothing else
(XI, 234–8, 1805)

to

Worshipping then among the depths of things
As piety ordained ...

I felt, observed, and pondered
(XII, 184–8, 1850)

In the transition between these two passages, Wordsworth loses his Miltonic heritage, an insistence upon the creative autonomy of the individual soul. With it he loses also an emphasis peculiar to himself, a reliance upon the *felt* experience, as distinguished from received piety or the abstraction that follows experience. In what follows I shall cite the 1850 text, but with reference, where it seems desirable, to the 1805 version.

The poem approximates epic structure, in that its fourteen books gather to a climax after a historical series of progressively more vital crises and renovations. The first eight books form a single movement, summed up in the title of Book Eight, "Retrospect—Love of Nature Leading to Love of Mankind." Books Nine, Ten, and Eleven carry this Love of Mankind into its natural consequence, Wordsworth's "Residence in France," and his involvement with the Revolution. Books Twelve and Thirteen deal with the subsequent crisis of Wordsworth's "Imagination, How Impaired and Restored." The "Conclusion," Book Fourteen, is the climax of Wordsworth's imaginative life and takes the reader back, in a full cycle, to the very opening of the poem. The "Conclusion" presents Wordsworth and Coleridge as "Prophets of Nature," joint laborers in the work of man's redemption:

> what we have loved,
> Others will love, and we will teach them how;
> Instruct them how the mind of man becomes
> A thousand times more beautiful than the earth
> On which he dwells.

Blake, had he read this, would have approved, though he might have wondered where Wordsworth had accounted for that "thousand times more beautiful." Blake's distrust of Wordsworth's dialectics of Nature is to some extent confirmed by Wordsworth himself. "Natural objects always did and now do weaken, deaden, and obliterate imagination in me," was Blake's comment on Wordsworth's fragment "Influence of Natural Objects" ... and Wordsworth does fall mute when the external stimulus is too clearly present. Geoffrey Hartman remarks that even in Wordsworth "poetry is not an act of consecration and Nature not an immediate external object to be consecrated." A natural object liberates Wordsworth's imagination only when it both ceases to be purely external and fades out of its object status.

The romantic metaphor of the correspondent breeze has [previously] been discussed. The wind of Beulah, creative and destructive, rises in the opening lines of *The Prelude*. Wordsworth need not call upon this spirit, for it precedes his invocation. It begins as a gentle breeze, and a blessing, half-conscious of the joy it gives to the new Moses who has escaped the Egypt that is London, and new Adam who can say:

> The earth is all before me. With a heart
> Joyous, nor scared at its own liberty,
> I look about; and should the chosen guide
> Be nothing better than a wandering cloud,
> I cannot miss my way.

Adam and Eve, scarcely joyous, go out hand in hand as loving children into all that is before them to choose a place of rest, with the Divine Providence as their guide. Wordsworth seeks a place where he will be lulled into the creative repose of epic composition, and he picks his own guide; nor need it be a Mosaic pillar, for he cannot miss his way. Nature, all before him, is generous, and his choice can only be between varying modes of good. *The Prelude* therefore opens without present anxiety: its crises are in the past. Unlike *Paradise Lost* and Blake's *Jerusalem*, *The Prelude* is a song of triumph rather than a song of experience. Wordsworth sings of what Blake called "organized innocence."

When the wind blows upon Wordsworth, he feels within a corresponding breeze, which rapidly becomes:

> A tempest, a redundant energy,
> Vexing its own creation.

Wordsworth's account of this vexing redundancy is that he is:

> not used to make
> A present joy the matter of a song

Although he tries again, aided by Eolian visitations, his harmony disperses in straggling sounds and, lastly, utter silence. What matters is his reaction. There is no despair, no sense of loss, only a quiet confidence based upon the belief that his inspiration is henceforward to be perpetual:

> "Be it so;
> Why think of anything but present good?"

We mistake *The Prelude*, then, if we seek to find a crisis, rather than the history of a crisis, within it. *The Prelude* is not a tragic poem but an autobiographical myth-making. Dominating *The Prelude* is the natural miracle of memory as an instrumentality by which the self is saved. Supreme among Wordsworth's inventions is the myth of renovating "spots of time," crucial in the "Intimations" ode and "Tintern Abbey," and the entire basis for the imaginative energy of *The Prelude*.

The story of *The Prelude* is mysterious only in that Wordsworthian Nature is now a mystery to most of us. For Wordsworth, Nature is first of all the sensuous *given*—what is freely offered for our discernment at all times. Like Blake, Wordsworth is preeminently a master of phenomenology, in the sense that he is able to read reality in appearances. Like Abraham, Wordsworth is the patriarch of a Covenant, made in the latter case between phenomenal appearance and the human heart. If the human heart, in its common, everyday condition, will love and trust the phenomenal world, then that world will never betray it. Betrayal here takes some of the force of its meaning from the context of sexuality and marriage. For man to betray Nature is to embrace one of the several modes in which the primacy of Imagination is denied. For Nature to betray man is to cease as a renovating virtue for man when he returns to it. Man turns from that loving embrace of nature which *is* in fact the supreme act of the Imagination, and takes the cruel mistress of discursiveness in her place. Nature turns from man by ceasing to be a Beulah state, and becoming instead a hostile and external object. What Wordsworth never considers is the more sinister manifestation of Nature-as-temptress, Blake's Vala or Keats's Belle Dame. Shelley climaxes his heritage from the Wordsworth tradition in "The Triumph of Life" by introducing Wordsworthian Nature as the deceptive "Shape all light," who tramples the divine sparks of Rousseau's imagination into the dust of death. Wordsworth's symbol of the covenant between man and nature, the rainbow, is employed by Shelley as the emblem that precedes the appearance of the beautiful but destructive Nature figure of "The Triumph of Life."

The inner problem of *The Prelude*, and of all the poetry of Wordsworth's great decade, is that of the autonomy of the poet's creative imagination. Indeed, as we have seen, it is the single most crucial problem of all that is most vital in English Romantic poetry. Even Wordsworth, the prophet of Nature, is uneasy at the prospect of his spirit's continual dependence upon it. He insists, like all prophets in the Hebraic tradition, upon the mutual dependence of the spiritual world and its human champion. The correspondent breeze is necessary because of natural decay; our mortality insists upon being redeemed by our poetry. To serve Nature in his early years, Wordsworth needed only to be wisely passive. But to sustain himself (and Nature?) in his maturity, an initiative from within is required. And yet if the initiative is too overt, as here at the opening of *The Prelude*, then Nature refuses to be so served, and the mutual creation that is the poem cannot go forward.

Hartman, analyzing this problem, says that "Nature keeps the initiative. The mind at its most free is still part of a deep mood of weathers." Wordsworth's problem is thus a dialectical one, for what he seeks is the proper first term that will yield itself readily to be transcended. The first term is not Poetry, for Nature at *The Prelude*'s onset will not have it so. Nor can the first term be Nature, for it will not allow itself to be subsumed even by the naturalizing imagination, at least *not immediately*. Blake has no patience for the Primary Imagination, but the whole of the secret discipline of Wordsworth's art is to wait upon it, confident that it will at last consent to dissolve into a higher mode.

Hartman speaks of the difficult first term of Wordsworth's dialectic as being "neither Nature nor Poetry. It is, rather, Imagination in embryo—muted yet strengthened by Nature's inadequacies." This is certainly the best balance to keep, unless we consent to a more radical review of Wordsworth's doctrine of Nature. Gorky said of Tolstoy's dealings with God that they reminded him of the old proverb "two bears in one den," and one can say the same of Wordsworth's relations with Nature. After a time, there is not quite room for both of them in Wordsworth's poetry if either is to survive full-size, and clearly it is Nature that makes room for Wordsworth. Yet the struggle, while concealed, inhibits Wordsworth and limits his achievement. There are unresolved antagonisms between Poetry and Divinity in Milton, but nothing so prolonged as the hidden conflict between Poetry and Nature in Wordsworth. But for this conflict, Wordsworth might have attempted national epic. Because of it, he was compelled to work in the mode of Rousseau, the long confessional work that might clarify his relation both to Nature and his own poetic calling.

The Nature of *The Prelude* is what Wordsworth was to become, a great teacher. Nature is so strong a teacher that it first must teach itself the lesson of restraint, to convert its immediacy into a presence only lest it overpower its human receiver. Wordsworth desires it as a mediating presence, a motion and a spirit. When it is too powerful, it threatens to become first, an object of worship, and second, like all such objects, an exhaustible agent of reality, a life that can be drained. Wordsworth knows well the dangers of idolatry, the sinister dialectic of mutual use. He desires only a relationship, a moment-to-moment confrontation of life by life, a dialogue. In this respect he is the direct ancestor of Shelley's vision of Nature.

*The Prelude* tries to distinguish between the *immediate* and the *remembered* external worlds. It is the paradoxical freedom of the Wordsworthian Imagination that it must avoid bondage to the immediate but seek the reign of the remembered world. In Blake the Imagination strives to be totally free of both, externals and memory, and delights only in the final excellence, the imagined land. Blake has no quest; only a struggle against everything within and without himself that is not pure Imagination. But Wordsworth has the quest that Blake's marginalia upon him gave clear warning of, the search for the autonomy of his own imagination. Hartman suggests that Nature's particular grace toward Wordsworth is to unfold *gradually* his own freedom to him, as his quest is largely an unwilling one; he does not want to be free of Nature. This suggestion is a displaced form of the Christian reading of history; for Wordsworth's "Nature" read St. Augustine's "History," as both are varieties of mercy presented as gradualism.

The hidden tragedy running through *The Prelude* is Wordsworth's resistance to his own imaginative emancipation. Wordsworth has clues enough, but usually declines to read them. In the presence of too eloquent a natural image, he is speechless. Nor does he attempt, after "Tintern Abbey," to particularize any local habitations for vision. He diffuses the secret strength of things over the widest possible landscape, in contrast to his disciple Shelley, who stands before Mont Blanc and cries "The power is there." Again, unlike their operations in Shelley and in Blake, the epiphanies in Wordsworth are not really sudden; there are no raptures of prophecy, but rather a slowly mounting intensity of baffled vision until at last the illumination greatly comes.

For Blake, and finally for Shelley, the Imagination's freedom from Nature is a triumph. It makes Wordsworth profoundly uneasy; he does not believe that time and space ought to be abandoned quite so prematurely. For Blake, the matter of common perception, the world of Primary Imagination, is hindrance, not action, but for Wordsworth it is something better than action; it is contemplation, and to see something clearly is already to have made some sense out of the diffuse and chaotic world of sensation. To mold a few of these clear things into a simpler and still clearer unity is to have made imaginative sense out of sensation. Blake's protest is absolute. He saw both these operations as passive, as a surrender to the living death of a world too small to contain the expansive vision of a more human Man.

The world of *The Prelude* is exquisitely fitted to the individual mind of the young Wordsworth. Even when it works upon him by frustration or fear, it continues to teach the young poet. The passages at the opening of the poem concerning the frustrating of composition have been examined above. Though he puts aside these failures, which are due to the immediacy of his inspiration, he is more troubled by the greater frustration of seemingly finding no subject for sustained epic. Even this vacant musing is redeemed by Nature, for in reproving himself he is carried back into remembrances, and these not only give him his only proper subject but begin the genuine forward movement of his poem. The growth of a poet's mind, as fostered by the goodly universe around him, becomes the inevitable subject as he sustains a gentle self-chastisement:

> Was it for this
> That one, the fairest of all rivers, loved
> To blend his murmurs with my nurse's song.

As the Derwent river once flowed along his dreams, now it stirs a flow of memory, carrying the mature poet back into the salvation of things past. The image of the coursing river runs through the entire poem, and provides the analogue for the flowing progress of the long work. Wordsworth speaks of "the river of my mind," and warns that its portions cannot be traced to individual fountains, but rather to the whole flow of the sensuous generosity of external phenomena.

The first two books of the poem show the child as encountering unknown modes of being, the life of Nature which is both one with us and yet dwells apart in its tranquillity. The primordial strength of Wordsworth's mind, its closeness to the myth-makings of early cultures and of children, is revealed in the incident in which an early wrong-doing is followed by hints of natural nemesis:

> and when the deed was done
> I heard among the solitary hills
> Low breathings coming after me, and sounds
> Of undistinguishable motion, steps
> Almost as silent as the turf they trod.

We make a mistake if we read this as a projection of the child's conscience upon the external world. That he heard it is warrant enough for its reality. Similarly, when he hangs above the raven's nest, sustained by the grip of finger tips, he hears a strange utterance in the wind, and perceives a motion unlike any ordinary one, in a sky that does not seem a sky of earth. At such a moment he belongs more to the universe of elemental forces, of motions and spirits, than he does to ours.

These early incidents of participation in other modes of being climax in the famous episode of the stolen boat, "an act of stealth and troubled pleasure." There is a muffled sexual element in this boyish escapade. The moon shines on the child as he lustily dips his oars into the silent lake. Suddenly, from behind a craggy steep that had been till then the horizon's bound:

> a huge peak, black and huge,
> As if with voluntary power instinct,
> Upreared its head.

The grim shape, with its own purpose and the measured motion of a living thing, comes striding after him. He flees, returns the boat, and for many days is haunted by a sense of "unknown modes of being":

> No familiar shapes
> Remained, no pleasant images of trees,
> Of sea or sky, no colours of green fields;
> But huge and mighty forms, that do not live
> Like living men, moved slowly through the mind
> By day, and were a trouble to my dreams.

This is a fundamental paganism, so primitive that it cannot yield to any more sophisticated description without distortion. It is like the Titanism of Blake, with its Giant Forms like the Zoas wandering a world substantially our own. Worth particular attention is the momentary withdrawal of the given world of Nature from the boy, for it hints that familiar natural beauty is a gift, not to be retained by the unnatural.

The theme of reciprocity is introduced in this passage and strengthened by the skating incident, where the giving of one's body to the wind is repaid by being allowed to see, in a sense, the motion of earth in her diurnal round.

Summing up the first book, Wordsworth sees his mind as revived, now that he has found "a theme / Single and of determined bounds." Yet the most vital passage of the second book breaks beyond bounds, and makes clear how ultimately ambitious the theme is:

> and I would stand,
> If the night blackened with a coming storm,
> Beneath some rock, listening to notes that are
> The ghostly language of the ancient earth,

Or make their dim abode in distant winds.
Thence did I drink the visionary power

Listening to the wind is a mode of primitive augury, but it is not gross prophecy of the future that the boy aspires toward as he hears the primordial language of earth. The exultation involved, Wordsworth goes on to say, is profitable, not because of its content:

> but that the soul,
> Remembering how she felt, but what she felt
> Remembering not, retains an obscure sense
> Of possible sublimity, whereto
> With growing faculties she doth aspire,
> With faculties still growing, feeling still
> That whatsoever point they gain, they yet
> Have something to pursue.

No passage in *The Prelude* is more central, and nothing is a better description of Wordsworth's poetry. *What* his soul felt in different encounters with Nature, he will not always remember. *How* it felt is recalled, and this retains that obscure sense of possible sublimity that colors all of the poetry of the Great Decade. As the soul's faculties grow, the soul is in danger of becoming content, of ceasing to aspire, but is saved from such sleep by the sense of possible sublimity. This sublimity, in its origins, has little to do with love or sympathy for others, and has small relation to human suffering. It is a sense of individual greatness, of a joy and a light yet unknown even in the child's life. *The Prelude*, until the eighth book, devotes itself largely to an inward world deeply affected only by external nature, but with a gradually intensifying sense of others held just in abeyance.

The soul in solitude moves outward by encountering other solitaries. Solitude, Wordsworth writes in Book Four, is most potent when impressed upon the mind with an appropriate human center. Having escorted a wandering old soldier to shelter, Wordsworth entreats him to linger no more on the roads, but instead to ask for the help that his state requires. With a "ghastly mildness" on his face the vagrant turns back the reproof:

> "My trust is in the god of Heaven,
> And in the eye of him who passes me!"

From this first lesson in human reciprocity, Wordsworth's narrative flows inward again, but this time to make clear the imaginative relation between Nature and literature (Book Five), which centers on a dream of apocalypse and survival. Sitting by the seaside, reading *Don Quixote*, he begins to muse on poetry and mathematics as being the ultimate apprehenders of reality, and having the "high privilege of lasting life." He falls asleep, and dreams. Around him is a boundless, sandy, wild plain, and distress and fear afflict him, till a Bedouin appears upon a dromedary. He bears a lance, and carries a stone beneath one arm, and holds a shell of surpassing brightness in the opposite hand. The Arab tells him that the stone is "Euclid's Elements" and the shell "is something of more worth," poetry. When Wordsworth puts the shell to his ear, as commanded, he hears:

> A loud prophetic blast of harmony;
> An Ode, in passion uttered, which foretold
> Destruction to the children of the earth
> By deluge, now at hand.

The Arab's mission is to bury "these two books," stone and shell, against the day when the flood shall recede. The poet attempts to join him in this enterprise, but he hurries off. Wordsworth follows, baffled because the Arab now looks like Don Quixote, then an Arab again, and then "of these was neither, and was both at once." The waters of the deep gather upon them, but in the aspect of "a bed of glittering light." Wordsworth wakes in terror, to view the sea before him and the book at his side.

The dream is beautifully suggestive, and invites the kind of symbol-building that W.H. Auden performs with it in his lively exercise in Romantic iconography, *The Enchafed Flood*. Unlike the use of water symbolism in most of Wordsworth, the deluge here threatens both Imagination and abstract reason, and the semi-Quixote flees the waters of judgment that Wordsworth, like the prophet Amos, elsewhere welcomes. Wordsworth puts Imagination at the water line in the marvelous passage about the children sporting on the shore which provides the "Intimations" ode with its liberating epiphany. The seashell participates in both the land of reasoning and the sea of apocalypse, of primal unity, which makes it an ideal type of the poetic Imagination. Though the Arab says that the shell is of more worth than the stone, the passage clearly sets high value on geometric as well as instinctual truth. Yet the stone as a symbol for mathematical reason is very close to Blake's Urizenic symbolism; the Ulro is associated with slabs of stone. Wallace Stevens's use of "the Rock" as symbol is closer to Wordsworth in spirit. The Rock, like the stone, is the gray particular of man's life, which poetry must cause to flower.

One can either pursue an investigation of the dream properties in this incident, which is endless, or else turn to Wordsworth's own reading of it, which takes us closer again to the design of *The Prelude*. The most important point is how close Wordsworth comes to identifying himself with the Arab Quixote. He fancies him a living man, "crazed by love and feeling, and internal thought protracted among endless solitudes." This is a fate that Wordsworth feared for himself, had his sensibility taken too strong control of his reason. For the Arab's mission, though the poet calls it mad, "that maniac's fond anxiety," is very like Wordsworth's own in *The Prelude*. Both desire to save Imagination from the abyss of desert and ocean, man's solitary isolation from and utter absorption into Nature. But the Arab is quixotic; he pursues a quest that is hopeless, for the deluge will cover all. Wordsworth hopes that his own quest will bring the healing waters down, as he pursues his slow, flowing course toward his present freedom.

The first of the major breakthroughs of the Imagination in *The Prelude* comes soon after this dream. The poet, in Book Six, describes a summer expedition to the Alps. He desires to cross the Alps for reasons obscure even to himself. It may be a desire to emancipate his maturing Imagination from Nature by overcoming the greatest natural barrier he can encounter. He draws an explicit parallel between his Alpine expedition and the onset of the French Revolution:

> But Nature then was sovereign in my mind,
> And mighty forms, seizing a youthful fancy,
> Had given a charter to irregular hopes.
> In any age of uneventful calm
> Among the nations, surely would my heart
> Have been possessed by similar desire;
> But Europe at that time was thrilled with joy,
> France standing on the top of golden hours,
> And human nature seeming born again.

The rebirth of human nature heralds Wordsworth's own "irregular hope." He does not seem conscious altogether of the personal revolution he seeks to effect for his own imagination. He speaks of it as "an underthirst," which is "seldom utterly allayed," and causes a sadness different in kind from any other. To illustrate it, he cites the incident of his actual crossing of the Alps. He misses his path, and frustrates his "hopes that pointed to the clouds," for a peasant informs him that he has crossed the Alps without even being aware of the supposed achievement. This moment of baffled aspiration is suddenly seen as the agent of a transfiguration:

> Imagination—here the Power so called
> Through sad incompetence of human speech,
> That awful Power rose from the mind's abyss
> Like an unfathered vapour that enwraps,
> At once, some lonely traveller.

The mind's thwarted expectation makes it a shapeless abyss; the Imagination *rises from it*, and is self-begotten, like the sudden vapor, "unfathered," that enwraps the lonely traveler. Yet the Imagination remains ours, even if at the time of crisis it seems alien to us:

> I was lost;
> Halted without an effort to break through;
> But to my conscious soul I now can say—
> "I recognise thy glory"

The vertigo resulting from the gap between expectation and fulfillment halts Wordsworth at the moment of his disappointment, and leaves him without the will to transcend his frustration. But *now*, in recollection, he recognizes the glory of the soul's triumphant faculty of expectation:

> in such strength
> Of usurpation, when the light of sense
> Goes out, but with a flash that has revealed
> The invisible world, doth greatness make abode,
> There harbours; whether we be young or old,
> Our destiny, our being's heart and home,
> Is with infinitude, and only there;
> With hope it is, hope that can never die,
> Effort, and expectation, and desire,
> And something evermore about to be.

Even here, in a passage bordering the realm of the mystical, the poet's emphasis is naturalistic. Imagination usurps the place of the baffled mind, and the light of sense momentarily goes out: that is, the object world is not perceived. *But*, and this proviso is the poet's, the flash of greater illumination that suddenly reveals the invisible world is itself due to the flickering light of sense. Nature is overcome by Nature, and the senses are transcended by a natural teaching. The transcendence is the vital element in this passage, for in the Imagination's strength to achieve transcendence is the abode and harbor of human greatness. "More! More! is the cry of a

mistaken Soul. Less than All cannot satisfy Man," is Blake's parallel statement. Wordsworth stresses infinitude because he defines the imaginative
as that which is conversant with or turns upon infinity. In a letter to the
poet Landor (January 21, 1824) he defines an imaginative passage as one
in which "things are lost in each other, and limits vanish, and aspirations
are raised." To the earlier statement in *The Prelude* celebrating "an obscure
sense of possible sublimity" (II, 317–8), we can add this passage's sense of
"something evermore about to be." Such a sense constitutes for the soul its
"banners militant," under which it seeks no trophies or spoils, no self-grat-
ification, for it is

> blest in thoughts
> That are their own perfection and reward,
> Strong in herself and in beatitude
> That hides her, like the mighty flood of Nile
> Poured from his fount of Abyssinian clouds
> To fertilise the whole Egyptian plain.

This is a tribute to the autonomy of the creative soul, and to its ultimate value as well. The soul in creation rises out of the unfathered vapor
just as the flood of the Nile rises from its cloud-shrouded heights. The
waters of creation pour down and fertilize the mind's abyss, giving to it
something of the soul's strength of effort, expectation, and desire.

Directly after this revelation, Wordsworth is free to trace the "characters of the great Apocalypse." As he travels through a narrow chasm in
the mountains, Nature reveals to him the unity between its constant outer
appearances and the ultimate forms of eternity:

> The immeasurable height
> Of woods decaying, never to be decayed,
> The stationary blasts of waterfalls,
> And in the narrow rent at every turn
> Winds thwarting winds, bewildered and forlorn,
> The torrents shooting from the clear blue sky,
> The rocks that muttered close upon our ears,
> Black drizzling crags that spake by the way-side
> As if a voice were in them, the sick sight
> And giddy prospect of the raving stream,
> The unfettered clouds and region of the Heavens,
> Tumult and peace, the darkness and the light—
> Were all like workings of one mind, the features

Of the same face, blossoms upon one tree;
Characters of the great Apocalypse,
The types and symbols of Eternity,
Of first, and last, and midst, and without end.

So much is brought together so magnificently in this that we can read it as a summary of what the poet has to say about the final relation between phenomena and the invisible world. The woods are constantly in process of decay, but the process will never cease; it will continue into Apocalypse. The waterfalls descend, and yet give the appearance of being stationed where they are, not to be moved. The winds are antithetical, balancing one another in the narrow chasm. Thwarted, bewildered, forlorn; they are humanized by this description. Torrents, rocks, crags participate in this speaking with tongues, and the raving stream takes on attributes of human disorder. Above, the unbound Heavens contrast their peace to this torment, their light to this darkness. The above and the below are like the workings of one unified mind, and are seen as features of the same face, blossoms upon one tree, either and both together. For the human and the natural are alike characters of the great unveiling of reality, equal types and symbols of the everlasting. The power that moves Man is the power that impels Nature, and Man and Nature, taken together, are the true form, not to be transcended even by a last judgment. This intimation of survival is given to Wordsworth under Nature's guidance, but the point of revelation is more human than natural. What the poet describes here is not Nature but the force for which he lacks a name, and which is at one with that "something far more deeply interfused" celebrated in "Tintern Abbey."

After this height in Book Six, the poem descends into the abyss of residence in London in Book Seven.

Imagination rises for Wordsworth in solitude, and yet "Tintern Abbey" puts a very high value upon "the still, sad music of humanity," a love of men that depends upon societies. F.A. Pottle remarks of Wordsworth in this context that though the poet "had the best of intentions, he could never handle close-packed, present, human crowds in the mode of imagination. If he were to grasp the life of a great city imaginatively, it had to be at night or early in the morning, while the streets were deserted; or at least in bad weather, when few people were abroad." As Wordsworth goes along the overflowing street, he is oppressed by a sense that the face of everyone he passes is a mystery to him. Suddenly he is smitten with the view:

Of a blind Beggar, who, with upright face,
Stood, propped against a wall, upon his chest

Wearing a written paper, to explain
His story, whence he came, and who he was.
Caught by the spectacle my mind turned round
As with the might of waters

The huge fermenting mass of humankind does not set the poet's imagination in motion, but the sight of one solitary man among them does. Wordsworth says that the pathetic label the beggar wears is an apt type of the utmost we can know, either of the universe or of ourselves, but this is not the imaginative meaning of the Beggar's sudden manifestation. Like the old Leech Gatherer of "Resolution and Independence," he causes the mind to assume the condition of the moving waters of Apocalypse, to receive a hint of the final communion between Man and Nature. The Leech Gatherer does this merely by being what he is, a reduced but still human form thoroughly at peace in a landscape reduced to naked desolation, but still natural. The blind Beggar's landscape is the noise of the crowd around him. He sits "with upright face"; the detail suggests the inner uprightness, the endurance of the outwardly bent Leech Gatherer. Amid the shock for eyes and ears of what surrounds him, his label affords a silent vision of human separateness, of the mystery of individual being.

From this bleak image, the poet retires with joy in Book Eight, which both heralds his return to Nature and chronicles the course of the first half of the poem, the stages by which love of Nature has led to love for Man. The figure linking the first love to the second is the shepherd, endowed by the boy Wordsworth with mythical powers and incarnating the virtues of Natural Man, an Adam who needs no dying into life, no second birth. The shepherd affects his own domain by intensifying its own characteristics:

I felt his presence in his own domain,
As of a lord and master, or a power,
Or genius, under Nature, under God,
Presiding; and severest solitude
Had more commanding looks when he was there.

This figure gives Wordsworth the support he needs for his "trust in what we may become." The shepherd, like Michael, like even the Old Cumberland Beggar, is a figure of capable imagination, strong in the tie that binds him to the earth.

Natural love for Man leads Wordsworth where it led the French followers of the prophet Rousseau, to Revolution in the name of the Natural Man. His particular friend in that cause, Michel Beaupuy (or Beaupuis, as

Wordsworth spells it, Book Nine, line 419), fighting for the Revolution as a high officer, says to him on encountering a hunger-bitten girl, "'Tis against *that* that we are fighting." As simply; Wordsworth says of him: "Man he loved as man."

The 1850 *Prelude* omits the tragic story of Wordsworth's love affair with Annette Vallon, told under the disguise of the names Vaudracour and Julia in the 1805 *Prelude*. It is not likely that Words worth excluded the affair for aesthetic reasons, though much of it makes rather painful reading. Yet parts of it have a rich, almost passionate tone of excited recollection, and all of it, even as disguised, is crucial for the growth of this poet's soul, little as he seems to have thought so. Nowhere else in his poetry does Wordsworth say of himself, viewing a woman and not Nature, that:

> his present mind
> Was under fascination; he beheld
> A vision, and he lov'd the thing he saw.

Nor does one want to surrender the charm of the prophet of Nature accomplishing a stolen interview at night "with a ladder's help."

Wordsworth was separated from Annette by the war between England and France. In the poem, Vaudracour and Julia are parted by parental opposition. The effects of the parting in life were largely hidden. Wordsworth the man made a happy marriage; Wordsworth the poet did not do as well. Julia goes off to a convent, and Vaudracour goes mad. Either in *The Prelude* or out of it, by presence or by absence, the story is a gap in the poem. Memory curbed was dangerous for Wordsworth; memory falsified was an imaginative fatality.

From the veiled account of his crisis in passion Wordsworth passes, in Books Ten and Eleven, to the crisis in his ideological life, the supreme test of his moral nature. When England went to war against the France of the Revolution, Wordsworth experienced the profound shock of having to exult "when Englishmen by thousands were o'erthrown," and the dark sense:

> Death-like, of treacherous desertion, felt
> In the last place of refuge—my own soul.

The profounder shock of the Terror and of France's career as an external aggressor followed. Wordsworth was adrift, his faith in the Revolution betrayed, and he sought to replace that faith by abstract speculation, and a blind trust in the supreme efficacy of the analytical faculty. He fell, by his own account, into the Ulro of the mechanists and materialists, a rationalism utterly alien to his characteristic modes of thinking and feeling:

> now believing,
> Now disbelieving; endlessly perplexed
> With impulse, motive, right and wrong, the ground
> Of obligation, what the rule and whence
> The sanction; till, demanding formal *proof*,
> And seeking it in every thing, I lost
> All feeling of conviction, and, in fine,
> Sick, wearied out with contrarieties,
> Yielded up moral questions in despair.

Love of Nature had led to love of Man, love of Man to revolutionary hope for Man, and the thwarting of that hope to this unnatural abyss. From these depths the poet's sister was to rescue him, maintaining "a saving intercourse with my true self," as he prays her to do in "Tintern Abbey." In an extraordinary outburst of love for Coleridge, to whom the poem is addressed, the poet invokes a parallel salvation for his friend, to restore him "to health and joy and pure contentedness." He then proceeds, in Books Twelve and Thirteen, to tell of the final stages of his crisis of dejection, the impairment of his Imagination and Taste, and their eventual restoration.

"A bigot to the new idolatry," he:

> Zealously laboured to cut off my heart
> From all the sources of her former strength

The final mark of his fall is to begin to scan the visible universe with the same analytical view he has applied to the moral world. In the aesthetic contemplation pictured in "Tintern Abbey," we see into the life of things because the eye has learned a wise passivity. It has been made quiet by the power of harmony, and the deep power of joy. Bereft of these powers, the poet in his crisis yields to the tyranny of the eye:

> I speak in recollection of a time
> When the bodily eye, in every stage of life
> The most despotic of our senses, gained
> Such strength in me as often held my mind
> In absolute dominion.

This fear of visual appearance is at one with Wordsworth's worship of the outward world, though it presents itself as paradox. For the visual surfaces of natural reality are mutable, and Wordsworth desperately quests for a natural reality that can never pass away. That reality, for him, lies just within natural appearance, and the eye made generously passive by nature's generosity is able to trace the lineaments of that final reality, and indeed "half create" it, as "Tintern Abbey" says. The eye must share, and not seek to appropriate for its own use, for where there is self-appropriation there can be no reality, no covenant of mutual giving. The apocalyptic sense therefore tends to be hearing, as it is in the "Intimations" ode, or that sense of organic fusion, seeing-hearing, which Wordsworth attributes to the infant in that poem. Hartman usefully sums this up as "a vision in which the mind knows itself almost without exterior cause or else as no less real, here, no less indestructible than the object of its perception."

Two agents rescue Wordsworth from the tyranny of the bodily eye, and the consequent impairment of his imagination. One, already spoken of, is Dorothy. The other is the creative doctrine or myth that the poet calls "spots of time":

> There are in our existence spots of time,
> That with distinct pre-eminence retain
> A renovating virtue, whence ...
>                                          ... our minds
> Are nourished and invisibly repaired

This virtue lurks in those episodes of life which tell us precisely how and to what point the individual mind is master of reality, with outward sense merely the mind's servant. Wordsworth gives two incidents as examples, both from his own childhood, as we would expect. In the first he is learning to ride, in the hills, encouraged and guided by his father's servant. Separated by mischance, he dismounts in fear, and leads his horse down the rough and stony moor. He stumbles on a bottom, where once a murderer had hung on a gibbet. Most evidences of an execution place are gone, but local superstition continually clears away the grass, and marks the murderer's name in monumental characters upon the turf. The boy sees them and flees, faltering and faint, losing the road:

> Then, reascending the bare common, saw
> A naked pool that lay beneath the hills,
> The beacon on the summit, and, more near,
> A girl, who bore a pitcher on her head,

And seemed with difficult steps to force her way
Against the blowing wind. It was, in truth,
An ordinary sight; but I should need
Colours and words that are unknown to man,
To paint the visionary dreariness
Which, while I looked all round for my lost guide,
Invested moorland waste and naked pool,
The beacon crowning the lone eminence,
The female and her garments vexed and tossed
By the strong wind.

The boy's fear of the fresh characters in the turf, and of the moldered gibbet mast, is "natural," as we would say, in these circumstances. But the "visionary dreariness" is a more complex sensation. The common is bare, the pool naked beneath the hills, as open to the eye of heaven as is the pool by which Wordsworth will encounter the Leech Gatherer in "Resolution and Independence," a poem built around a "spot of time." The girl bearing the pitcher struggles against the wind, as winds thwarted winds in the apocalyptic passage in Book Six. Everything that the boy beholds, waste moorland and naked pool, the solitary beacon on the lone eminence, the girl and her garments buffeted by the wind, is similarly dreary, but the nudity and vulnerability of these phenomena, their receptivity to the unchecked power of Nature, unite them in a unified imaginative vision. They blend into one another and into the power to which they offer themselves.

The boy finds no consolation in the scene of visionary dreariness at the time he views it, but he retains it in his memory. Later he returns to the same scene, in the happy hours of early love, his beloved at his side. Upon the scene there falls the gleam of Imagination, with radiance more sublime for the power these remembrances had left behind:

So feeling comes in aid
Of feeling, and diversity of strength
Attends us, if but once we have been strong.

The soul, remembering how it felt, but what it felt remembering not, has retained the power of a sense of possible sublimity. Imagination, working through memory, appropriates the visionary power and purges the dreariness originally attached to it in this instance. The power is therefore an intimation of the indestructible, for it has survived both initial natural dreariness and the passage of time.

The power is indestructible, but can the poet retain it? We hear again the desperate forebodings of loss:

> The days gone by
> Return upon me almost from the dawn
> Of life: the hiding-places of man's power
> Open; I would approach them, but they close.
> I see by glimpses now; when age comes on,
> May scarcely see at all

The function of the spots of time is to enshrine the spirit of the Past for future restoration. They are meant to be memorials in a lively sense, giving substance and life to what the poet can still feel. That they become memorials in the sepulchral sense also is a sadly unintentional irony.

The poet gives a second example of a spot of time, more complex than the first. Away from home with his brothers, he goes forth into the fields, impatient to see the led palfreys that will bear him back to his father's house. He goes to the summit of a crag overlooking both roads on which the palfreys can come:

> 'twas a day
> Tempestuous, dark, and wild, and on the grass
> I sate half-sheltered by a naked wall;
> Upon my right hand couched a single sheep,
> Upon my left a blasted hawthorn stood

With these companions he watches, as the mist gives intermitting prospect of the plain beneath. Just after this episode, his father dies, and he thinks back to his vigil, with its anxiety of hope:

> And afterwards, the wind and sleety rain,
> And all the business of the elements,
> The single sheep, and the one blasted tree,
> And the bleak music from that old stone wall,
> The noise of wood and water, and the mist
> That on the line of each of those two roads
> Advanced in such indisputable shapes;
> All these were kindred spectacles and sounds
> To which I oft repaired, and thence would drink,
> As at a fountain

What does he drink there? We recognize first in this episode the characteristic quality of the nakedness of the natural scene. The boy is only half sheltered by the naked wall. Beside him, seeking this exposed shelter from the wind, is a single sheep, and on the other side a hawthorn, blasted by the elements. The mist rises all about, blending the landscape into a unity. What can be drunk from this fountain of vulnerable natural identity is, as before, the consciousness of immutable existence, of a life in Nature and in Man which cannot die. This one life within us and abroad must bear the weather, however tempestuous, dark, and wild, but it will not be destroyed if it holds itself open to the elements in loving trust.

Thus "moderated" and "composed" by the spots of time, his faith in Nature restored, the poet is able to say in triumph:

> I found
> Once more in Man an object of delight,
> Of pure imagination, and of love

He is prepared now for his poem's apocalyptic conclusion, the ascent of Mount Snowdon and the vision vouchsafed him there, in Book Fourteen. The poem's structure comes to rest on a point of epiphany, located on a mountain top and associated with the moon and all the mutable world below it, but also with the immutable world above. Girt round by the mist of rising Imagination, the poet looks up to see the Moon hung naked in the azure firmament. The mist stretches in solid vapors, a still ocean as far as the eye can see. In the midst of this ocean, a rift appears, and through the gap:

> Mounted the roar of waters, torrents, streams
> Innumerable, roaring with one voice?
> Heard over earth and sea, and, in that hour,
> For so it seemed, felt by the starry heavens.

The mist, which has for so long figured as an emblem of Imagination in Wordsworth's poetry, now moves to an identity with the emblem of apocalypse, the gathering waters of judgment. The voice of mighty waters makes its strength felt past the point of epiphany, and momentarily influences even the starry heavens. Of this vision the poet says:

> it appeared to me the type
> Of a majestic intellect, its acts
> And its possessions, what it has and craves,

What in itself it is, and would become.
There I beheld the emblem of a mind
That feeds upon infinity, that broods
Over the dark abyss, intent to hear
Its voices issuing forth to silent light
In one continuous stream; a mind sustained
By recognitions of transcendent power

The whole scene before him is the "type of a majestic intellect," while the moon is the emblem of a mind brooding over the dark abyss. The moon, governing all that is mutable beneath it, feeds upon the infinity of the larger vision to gain an intimation of what is beyond mutability. The moon is like the poet's aroused consciousness, looking up to the indestructible heavens and down at the sea of mist which intimates both the impermanence of the world as we know it (the hint is that it will be flooded again) and its final endurance, after the judgment of the waters. Caught at what Eliot calls "the still point of the turning world," Wordsworth attains to an apprehension of the relation between his moonlike consciousness and the majestic intellect, which now feels the human mind's reciprocal force but which transcends both the human and the natural. What Wordsworth is giving us here is his vision of God, akin to Dante's tremendous vision at the close of the *Paradiso*, except that the mode of this manifestation is still extraordinarily naturalistic. Though not Nature but the power that moves her is revealed, the power's showing forth is not miracle but rather intensification of natural process and visual appearance. Later, in *The Excursion*, Wordsworth will not trust the powers of poetry enough to make so autonomous a statement, to see so human a vision. Here, as he gathers *The Prelude*'s many currents together, he shows a confidence both in his art and in his personal myth of natural salvation. In this confidence he has created a major poem that refreshes life, that is, as Wallace Stevens wrote:

An elixir, an excitation, a pure power.
The poem, through candor, brings back a power again
That gives a candid kind to everything.

# Samuel Taylor Coleridge

## (1772-1834)

COLERIDGE, THE YOUNGEST OF FOURTEEN CHILDREN OF A COUNTRY clergyman, was a precocious and lonely child, a kind of changeling in his own family. Early a dreamer and (as he said) a "character," he suffered the loss of his father (who had loved him best of all the children) when he was only nine. At Christ's Hospital in London, soon after his father's death, he found an excellent school that gave him the intellectual nurture he needed, as well as a lifelong friend in the future essayist Charles Lamb. Early a poet, he fell deeply in love with Mary Evans, a schoolfellow's sister, but sorrowfully nothing came of it.

At Jesus College, Cambridge, Coleridge started well, but temperamentally he was not suited to academic discipline and failed of distinction. Fleeing Cambridge, and much in debt, he enlisted in the cavalry under the immortal name of Silas Tomkyn Comberback but kept falling off his horse. Though he proved useful to his fellow dragoons at writing love letters, he was good for little else but stable-cleaning, and the cavalry allowed his brothers to buy him out. He returned to Cambridge, but his characteristic guilt impeded academic labor and when he abandoned Cambridge in 1794 he had no degree.

A penniless young poet, radical in politics, original in religion, he fell in with the then equally radical bard Robert Southey, remembered today as the Conservative Laureate constantly savaged in Byron's satirical verse. Like our contemporary communards, the two poetical youths projected what they named a "pantisocracy." With the right young ladies and, hopefully, other choice spirits, they would found a communistic agrarian-literary settlement on the banks of the Susquehanna in exotic Pennsylvania. At Southey's urging, Coleridge made a pantisocratic engagement to the not very brilliant Miss Sara Fricker, whose sister Southey was to marry.

Pantisocracy died aborning, and Coleridge in time woke up miserably to find himself unsuitably married, the greatest misfortune of his life.

He turned to Wordsworth, whom he had met early in 1795. His poetry influenced Wordsworth's and helped the latter attain his characteristic mode. It is not too much to say that Coleridge's poetry disappeared into Wordsworth's. We remember *Lyrical Ballads* (1798) as Wordsworth's book, yet about a third of it (in length) was Coleridge's, and "Tintern Abbey," the crown of the volume except for "The Rime of the Ancient Mariner," is immensely indebted to Coleridge's "Frost at Midnight." Nor is there much evidence of Wordsworth admiring or encouraging his friend's poetry; toward "The Ancient Mariner" he was always very grudging, and he was discomfited (but inevitably so) by both "Dejection: An Ode" and "To William Wordsworth." Selfless where Wordsworth's poetry was concerned, Coleridge had to suffer his closest friend's neglect of his own poetic ambitions.

This is not an easy matter to be fair about, since literature necessarily is as much a matter of personality as it is of character. Coleridge, like Keats (and to certain readers, Shelley), is lovable. Byron is at least always fascinating, and Blake in his lonely magnificence is a hero of the imagination. But Wordsworth's personality, like Milton's or Dante's, does not stimulate affection for the poet in the common reader. Coleridge has, as Walter Pater observed, a "peculiar charm"; he seems to lend himself to myths of failure, which is astonishing when the totality of his work is contemplated.

Yet it is his life, and his self-abandonment of his poetic ambitions, that continue to convince us that we ought to find in him parables of the failure of genius. His best poetry was all written in the year and half in which he saw Wordsworth daily (1797–8), yet even his best poetry, with the single exception of "The Ancient Mariner," is fragmentary. The pattern of his life is fragmentary also. When he received an annuity from the Wedgwoods, he left Wordsworth and Dorothy to study language and philosophy in Germany (1798–9). Soon after returning, his miserable middle years began, though he was only twenty-seven. He moved near the Wordsworths again and fell in love, permanently and unhappily, with Sara Hutchinson, whose sister Mary was to become Wordsworth's wife in 1802. His own marriage was hopeless, and his health rapidly deteriorated, perhaps for psychological reasons. To help endure the pain he began to drink laudanum, liquid opium, and thus contracted an addiction he never entirely cast off. In 1804, seeking better health, he went to Malta but returned two years later in the worst condition of his life. Separating from Mrs. Coleridge, he moved to London and began another career as lecturer, general man-of-letters, and periodical editor, while his miseries augmented.

The inevitable quarrel with Wordsworth in 1810 was ostensibly reconciled in 1812, but real friendship was not reestablished until 1828.

From 1816 on, Coleridge lived in the household of a physician, James Gillman, so as to be able to keep working and thus avoid total breakdown. Prematurely aged, his poetry period over, Coleridge entered into a major last phase as critic and philosopher, upon which his historical importance depends; but this, like his earlier prose achievements, is beyond the scope of an introduction to his poetry. It remains to ask, What was his achievement as a poet, and extraordinary as that was, why did his poetry effectively cease after about 1807? Wordsworth went on with poetry after 1807 but mostly very badly. The few poems Coleridge wrote, from the age of thirty-five on, are powerful but occasional. Did the poetic will not fail in him, since his imaginative powers did not?

Coleridge's large poetic ambitions included the writing of a philosophic epic on the origin of evil and a sequence of hymns to the sun, moon, and elements. These high plans died, slowly but definitively, and were replaced by the dream of a philosophic *Opus Maximum*, a huge work of synthesis that would reconcile German idealist philosophy with the orthodox truths of Christianity. Though only fragments of this work were ever written, much was done in its place—speculations on theology, political theory, and criticism that were to influence profoundly conservative British thought in the Victorian period and, in quite another way, the American transcendentalism led by Emerson and Theodore Parker.

Coleridge's actual achievement as poet divides into two remarkably diverse groupings—remarkable because they are almost simultaneous. The daemonic group, necessarily more famous, is the triad of "The Ancient Mariner," "Christabel," and "Kubla Khan." The "conversational" group includes the conversation poem proper, of which "The Eolian Harp" and "Frost at Midnight" are the most important, as well as the irregular ode, such as "Dejection" and "To William Wordsworth." The late fragments, "Limbo" and "Ne Plus Ultra," are a kind of return to the daemonic mode. For a poet of Coleridge's gifts to have written only nine poems that really matter is a sorrow, but the uniqueness of the two groups partly compensates for the slenderness of the canon.

The daemonic poems break through the orthodox censor set up by Coleridge's moral fears of his own imaginative impulses. Unifying the group is a magical quest-pattern which intends as its goal a reconciliation between the poet's self-consciousness and a higher order of being, associated with Divine forgiveness; but this reconciliation fortunately lies beyond the border of all these poems. The Mariner attains a state of purgation but cannot get beyond that process. Christabel is violated by Geraldine, but this too is a purgation rather than a damnation, as her utter innocence is her only flaw. Coleridge himself, in the most piercing moment in his poetry, is tempted to assume the state of an Apollo-rebirth—the youth with flashing eyes and floating hair—but he withdraws from his vision of a poet's paradise, judging it to be only another purgatory.

The conversational group, though so immensely different in mode, speaks more directly of an allied theme: the desire to go home, not to the past but to what Hart Crane beautifully called "an improved infancy." Each of these poems, like the daemonic group, verges upon a kind of vicarious and purgatorial atonement in which Coleridge must fail or suffer so that someone he loves may succeed or experience joy. There is a subdued implication that somehow the poet will yet be accepted into a true home this side of the grave if he can achieve an atonement.

Where Wordsworth, in his primordial power, masters the subjective world and aids his readers in the difficult art of feeling, Coleridge deliberately courts defeat by subjectivity and is content to be confessional. But though he cannot help us to feel, as Wordsworth does, he gives us to understand how deeply felt his own sense of reality is. Though in a way his poetry is a testament of defeat, a yielding to the anxiety of influence and to the fear of self-glorification, it is one of the most enduringly poignant of such testaments that literature affords us.

## II

"Psychologically," Coleridge observed, "consciousness is the problem"; and he added somberly: "Almost all is yet to be achieved." How much he achieved Kathleen Coburn and others are showing us. My concern here is the sadder one of speculating yet again about why he did not achieve more as a poet. Walter Jackson Bate has meditated, persuasively and recently, upon Coleridge's human and literary anxieties, particularly in regard to the burden of the past and its inhibiting poetic splendors. I swerve away from Bate to center the critical meditation upon what might be called the poetics of anxiety, the process of misprision by which any latecomer strong poet attempts to clear an imaginative space for himself.

Coleridge could have been a strong poet, as strong as Blake or Wordsworth. He could have been another mighty antagonist for the Great Spectre Milton to engage and, yes, to overcome, but not without contests as titanic as those provided by Blake's *The Four Zoas* and Wordsworth's *The Excursion*, and parental victories as equivocal as those achieved with Blake's *Jerusalem* and Wordsworth's *The Prelude*. But we have no such poems by Coleridge. When my path winds home at the end of this Introduction, I will speculate as to what these poems should have been. As critical fathers for my quest I invoke first Oscar Wilde, with his glorious principle that the highest criticism sees the object as in itself it really is not, and second, Wilde's critical father, Walter Pater, whose essay of 1866 on "Coleridge's Writings" seems to me still the best short treatment of Coleridge, and this after a century of commentary. Pater, who knew his debt to Coleridge, knew also the anxiety Coleridge caused him, and Pater therefore came to a further and subtler knowing. In the Organic analogue, against which the entire soul of the great Epicurean critic rebelled, Pater recognized the product of Coleridge's profound anxieties as a creator. I begin therefore with Pater on Coleridge, and then will move immediately deep into the Coleridgean interior, to look upon Coleridge's fierce refusal to take on the ferocity of the strong poet.

This ferocity, as both Coleridge and Pater well knew, expresses itself as a near-solipsism, and Egotistical Sublime, or Miltonic godlike stance. From 1795 on, Coleridge knew, loved, envied, was both cheered and darkened by the largest instance of that Sublime since Milton himself. He studied constantly, almost involuntarily, the glories of the truly modern strong poet, Wordsworth. Whether he gave Wordsworth rather more than he received, we cannot be certain; we know only that he wanted more from Wordsworth than he received, but then it was his endearing though exasperating weakness that he always needed more love than he could get, no matter how much he got: "To be beloved is all I need, / And whom I love, I love indeed."

Pater understood what he called Coleridge's "peculiar charm," but he resisted it in the "sacred name of what he called the "relative" spirit against Coleridge's archaizing "absolute" spirit. In gracious but equivocal tribute to Coleridge he observed:

> The literary life of Coleridge was a disinterested struggle against the application of the relative spirit to moral and religious questions. Everywhere he is restlessly scheming to apprehend the absolute; to affirm it effectively; to get it acknowledged. Coleridge failed in that attempt, happily even for him, for it was a struggle against the increasing life of the mind itself.... How did his choice of a controversial interest, his determination to affirm the absolute, weaken or modify his poetic gift.

To affirm the absolute, Pater says—or, as we might say, to reject all dualisms except those sanctioned by orthodox Christian thought—is not *materia poetica* for the start of the nineteenth century, and if we think of a poem like the "Hymn before Sun-Rise, in the Vale of Chamouni," we are likely to agree with Pater. We will agree also when he contrasts Wordsworth favorably with Coleridge, and even with Goethe, commending Wordsworth for "that flawless temperament ... which keeps his conviction of a latent intelligence in nature within the limits of sentiment or instinct, and confines it to those delicate and subdued shades of expression which perfect art allows." Pater goes on to say that Coleridge's version of Wordsworth's instinct is a philosophical idea, which means that Coleridge's poetry had to be "more dramatic, more self-conscious" than Wordsworth's. But this in turn, Pater insists, means that for aesthetic success ideas must be held loosely, in the relative spirit. One idea that Coleridge did not hold loosely was the Organic analogue, and it becomes clearer as we proceed in Pater's essay that the aesthetic critic is building toward a passionate assault upon the Organic principle. He quotes Coleridge's description of Shakespeare as "a nature humanized, a genial understanding, directing self-consciously a power and an implicit wisdom deeper even than our consciousness." "There," Pater comments, with bitter eloquence, "'the absolute' has been affirmed in the sphere of art; and thought begins to congeal." With great dignity Pater adds that Coleridge has "obscured the true interest of art." By likening the work of art to a living organism, Coleridge does justice to the impression the work may give us, but he "does not express the process by which that work was produced."

M.H. Abrams, in his *The Mirror and the Lamp*, defends Coleridge against Pater by insisting that Coleridge knew his central problem "was to use analogy with organic growth to account for the spontaneous, the inspired, and the self-evolving in the psychology of invention, yet not to commit himself as far to the elected figure as to minimize the supervention of the antithetic qualities of foresight and choice." Though Abrams calls Pater "short-sighted," I am afraid the critical palms remain with the relative spirit, for Pater's point was not that Coleridge had no awareness of the dangers of using the Organic analogue but rather that awareness, here as elsewhere, was no salvation for Coleridge. The issue is whether Coleridge, not Shakespeare, was able to direct "self-consciously a power and an implicit wisdom deeper than consciousness." Pater's complaint is valid because Coleridge, in describing Shakespeare, Dante, Milton, keeps repeating his absolute formula that poems grow from within themselves, that their "wholeness is not in vision or conception, but in an inner feeling of totality and absolute being." As Pater says, "that exaggerated inwardness is barren" because it "withdraws us too far from what we can see, hear, and feel," because it cheats the senses and emotions of their triumph. I urge

Pater's wisdom here not only against Coleridge, though I share Pacer's love for Coleridge, but against the formalist criticism that continued in Coleridge's absolute spirit.

What is the imaginative source of Coleridge's disabling hunger for the Absolute? On August 9, 1831, about three years before he died, he wrote in his Notebook: "From my earliest recollection I have had a consciousness of Power without Strength—a perception, an experience, of more than ordinary power with an inward sense of Weakness.... More than ever do I feel this now, when all my fancies still in their integrity are, as it were, drawn *inward* and by their suppression and compression rendered a mock substitute for Strength—" Here again is Pater's barren and exaggerated inwardness, but in a darker context than the Organic principle provided.

This context is Milton's "universe of death," where Coleridge apprehended death-in-life as being "the wretchedness of *division*." If we stand in that universe, then "we think of ourselves as separated beings, and place nature in antithesis to the mind, as object to subject, thing to thought, death to life." To be so separated is to become, Coleridge says, "a soul-less fixed star, receiving no rays nor influences into my Being, *a Solitude which I so tremble at, that I cannot attribute it even to the Divine Nature.* "This, we can say, is Coleridge's Counter-Sublime, his answer to the anxiety of influence, in strong poets. The fear of solipsism is greater in him than the fear of not individuating his own imagination.

As with every other major Romantic, the prime precursor poet for Coleridge was Milton. There is a proviso to be entered here; for all these poets—Blake, Wordsworth, Shelley, Coleridge (only Keats is an exception)—there is a greater Sublime poetry behind Milton, but as its author is a people and not a single poet, and as it is far removed in time, its greatness does not inhibit a new imagination—not unless it is taken as the work of the Prime Precursor Himself, to whom all creation belongs. Only Coleridge, among these poets, acquired a double Sublime anxiety of influence. Beyond the beauty that has terror in it of Milton, was beauty more terrible. In a letter to Thelwall, December 17, 1796, Coleridge wrote: "Is not Milton a *sublimer* poet than Homer or Virgil? Are not his Personages more sublimely cloathed? And do you not know, that there is not perhaps *one* page in Milton's *Paradise Lost*, in which he has not borrowed his imagery from the Scriptures?—I allow, and rejoice that *Christ* appealed only to the understanding & the affections; but I affirm that, after reading Isaiah, or St. Paul's Epistle to the Hebrews, Homer & Virgil are disgustingly *tame* to me, & Milton himself barely tolerable." Yet these statements are rare in Coleridge. Frequently, Milton seems to blend with the ultimate influence, which I think is a normal enough procedure. In 1796, Coleridge also says, in his review of Burke's *Letter to a Noble Lord*: "It is lucky for poetry, that Milton did not live in our days...." Here Coleridge moves toward the center of his concern, and we should remember his formula: "Shakespeare was all men, potentially, except Milton." This leads to a more ambiguous formula, reported to us of a lecture that Coleridge gave on November 28, 1811: "Shakespeare became all things well into which he infused himself, while all forms, all things became Milton—the poet ever present to our minds and more than gratifying us for the loss of the distinct individuality of what he represents." Though Coleridge truly professes himself more than gratified, he admits loss. Milton's greatness is purchased at the cost of something dear to Coleridge, a principle of difference he knows may be flooded out by his monistic yearnings. For Milton, to Coleridge, is a mythic monad in himself. Commenting upon the apostrophe to light at the commencement of the third book of *Paradise Lost*, Coleridge notes: "In all modern poetry in Christendom there is an under consciousness of a sinful nature, a fleeting away of external things, the mind or subject greater than the object, the reflective character predominant. In the *Paradise Lost* the sublimest parts are the revelations of Milton's own mind, producing itself and evolving its own greatness; and this is truly so, that when that which is merely entertaining for its objective beauty is introduced, it at first seems a discord." This might be summarized as: where Milton is not, nature is barren, and its significance is that Milton is permitted just such a solitude as Coleridge trembles to imagine for the Divine Being.

Humphry House observed that "Coleridge was quite unbelievably modest about his own poems; and the modesty was of a curious kind, sometimes rather humble and over-elaborate." As House adds, Coleridge "dreaded publication" of his poetry, and until 1828, when he was fifty-six, there was nothing like an adequate gathering of his verse. Wordsworth's attitude was no help, of course, and the Hutchinson girls and Dorothy no doubt followed Wordsworth in his judgments. There was Wordsworth, and before him there had been Milton. Coleridge presumably knew what "Tintern Abbey" owed to "Frost at Midnight," but this knowledge nowhere found expression. Must we resort to psychological speculation in order to see what inhibited Coleridge, or are there more reliable aids available?

In the *Biographia Literaria* Coleridge is not very kind to his pre-Wordsworthian poetry, particularly to the "Religious Musings." Yet this is where we must seek what went wrong with Coleridge's ambitions—here, and if there were space, in "The Destiny of Nations" fragments (not its arbitrarily yoked-together form of 1817), and in the "Ode to the Departing Year," and in the "Monody on the Death of Chatterton" in its earlier versions. After Wordsworth had descended upon Coleridge, supposedly as a "know-thyself" admonition from heaven but really rather more like a new form of the Miltonic blight, then Coleridge's poetic ambitions sustained another kind of inhibition. The Miltonic shadow on early Coleridge needs to be studied first, before a view can be obtained of his maturer struggles with influence.

With characteristic self-destructiveness; Coleridge gave "Religious Musings" the definitive subtitle: "A Desultory Poem, Written on the Christmas Eve of 1794." The root-meaning of "desultory" is "vaulting," and though Coleridge consciously meant that his poem skipped about and wavered, his imagination meant "vaulting," for "Religious Musings" is a wildly ambitious poem. "This is the time ..." it begins, in direct recall of Milton's "Nativity" Hymn, yet it follows not the Hymn but the most sublime moments of *Paradise Lost*, particularly the invocation to Book III. As with the 1802 "Hymn before Sun-Rise," its great fault as a poem is that it never stops whooping; in its final version I count well over one hundred exclamation points in just over four hundred lines. Whether one finds this habit in Coleridge distressing or endearing hardly matters; he just never could stop doing it. He whoops because he vaults; he is a high jumper of the Sublime, and psychologically he could not avoid this. I quote the poem's final passage with relish and with puzzlement, for I am uncertain as to how good it may be, though it seems awful. Yet its awfulness is at least Sublime; it is not the drab, flat awfulness of Wordsworth at *his* common worst in *The Excursion* or even (heresy to admit this!) in so many passages of *The Prelude*—passages that we hastily skip by, feeling zeal and relief in getting at the great moments. Having just shouted out his odd version of Berkeley—that "life is a vision shadowy of truth"—Coleridge sees "the veiling clouds retire" and God appears in a blaze upon His Throne. Raised to a pitch of delirium by this vision, Coleridge soars aloft to join it:

> Contemplant Spirits! ye that hover o'er
> With untired gaze the immeasurable fount
> Ebullient with Creative Deity!
> And ye of plastic power, that interfused
> Roll through the grosser and material mass
> In organizing surge! Holies of God!
> (And what if Monads of the infinite mind?)
> I haply journeying my immortal course
> Shall sometime join your mystic choir! Till then

I discipline my young and novice thought
In ministeries of heart-stirring song,
And aye on Meditation's heaven-ward wing
Soaring aloft I breathe the empyreal air
Of Love, omnific, omnipresent Love,
Whose day-spring rises glorious in my soul
As the great Sun, when he his influence
Sheds on the frost-bound waters—The glad stream
Flows to the ray and warbles as it flows.

Scholars agree that this not terribly pellucid passage somehow combines an early Unitarianism with a later orthodox overlay, as well as quantities of Berkeley, Hartley, Newton, Neoplatonism, and possibly more esoteric matter. A mere reader will primarily be reminded of Milton and will be in the right, for Milton counts here and the rest do not. The Spirits Coleridge invokes are Miltonic angels, though their functions seem to be more complicated. Coleridge confidently assures himself and us that his course is immortal, that he may end up as a Miltonic angel and so perhaps also as a monad of the infinite mind. In the meantime, he will study Milton's "heart-stirring song." Otherwise, all he needs is love, which is literally the air he breathes, the sunrise radiating out of his soul in a stream of song, and the natural sun toward which he flows, a sun that is not distinct from God. If we reflect on how palpably sincere this is, how wholehearted, and consider what was to be Coleridge's actual poetic course, we will be moved. Moved to what? Well, perhaps to remember a remark of Coleridge's: "There are many men, especially at the outset of life, who, in their too eager desire for the end, overlook the difficulties in the way; there is another class, who see nothing else. The first class may sometimes fail; the latter rarely succeed." Whatever the truth of this for other men, no poet becomes a strong poet unless he starts out with a certain obliviousness of the difficulties in the way. He will soon enough meet those difficulties, however, and one of them will be that his precursor and inspirer threatens to subsume him, as Coleridge is subsumed by Milton in "Religious Musings" and in his other pre-Wordsworthian poems. And here I shall digress massively before returning to Coleridge's poetry, for my discourse enters now upon the enchanted and baleful ground of poetic influence, through which I am learning to find my way by a singular light—one that will bear a little explanation.

I do not believe that poetic influence is simply something that happens, that it is just the process by which ideas and images are transmitted from earlier to later poets. In that view, whether or not influence causes anxiety in the later poet is a matter of temperament and circumstance. Poetic influence thus reduces to source-study, of the kind performed upon Coleridge by Lowes and later scholars. Coleridge was properly scornful of such study, and I think most critics learn how barren an enterprise it turns out to be. I myself have no use for it as such, and what I mean by the study of poetic influence turns source-study inside out. The first principle of the proper study of poetic influence, as I conceive it, is that no strong poem has sources and no strong poem merely alludes to another poem. The meaning of a strong poem is another strong poem, a precursor's poem which is being misinterpreted, revised, corrected, evaded, twisted askew, made to suffer an inclination or bias which is the property of the later and not the earlier poet. Poetic influence, in this sense, is actually misprision, a poet's taking or doing amiss of a parent-poem that keeps *finding* him, to use a Coleridgean turn of phrase. Yet even this misprision is only the first step that a new poet takes when he advances from the early phase where his precursor floods him to a more Promethean phase where he quests for his own fire—which must nevertheless be stolen from his precursor.

I count some half-dozen steps in the life cycle of the strong poet as he attempts to convert his inheritance into what will aid him without inhibiting him by the anxiety of a failure in priority, a failure to have begotten himself. These steps are revisionary ratios, and for the convenience of a shorthand, I find myself giving them arbitrary names that are proving useful to me and perhaps can be of use to others. I list them herewith, with descriptions but not examples, as this can only be a brief sketch; I must get back to Coleridge's poetry, with this list helpfully in hand, to find my examples in Coleridge.

1. *Clinamen*, which is poetic misprision proper. I take the word from Lucretius, where it means a "swerve" of the atoms so as to make change possible in the universe. The later poet swerves away from the precursor by so reading the parent-poem as to execute a *clinamen* in relation to it. This appears as the corrective movement of his own poem, which implies that the precursor poem went accurately up to a certain point but then should have swerved, precisely in the direction that the new poem moves.

2. *Tessera*, which is completion and antithesis. I take the word not from mosaic-making, where it is still used, but from the ancient Mystery cults, where it meant a token of recognition—the fragment, say, of a small pot which with the other fragments would reconstitute the vessel. The later poet antithetically "completes" the precursor by so reading the parent-poem as to retain its teens but to mean them in an opposite sense, as

though the precursor had failed to go far enough.

3. *Kenosis*, which is a breaking device similar to the defense mechanisms our psyches employ against repetition-compulsions; *kenosis* then is a movement toward discontinuity with the precursor. I take the word from St. Paul, where it means the humbling or emptying out of Jesus by himself when he accepts reduction from Divine to human status. The later poet, apparently emptying himself of his own afflatus, his imaginative godhood, seems to humble himself as though he ceased to be a poet, but this ebbing is so performed in relation to a precursor's poem-of-ebbing that the precursor is emptied out also, and so the later poem of deflation is not as absolute as it seems.

4. *Daemonization*, or a movement toward a personalized Counter-Sublime in reaction to the precursor's Sublime. I take the term from general Neoplatonic usage, where an intermediary being, neither Divine nor human, enters into the adept to aid him. The later poet opens himself to what he believes to be a power in the parent-poem that does not belong to the parent proper but to a range of being just beyond that precursor. He does this, in his poem, by so stationing its relation to the parent-poem as to generalize away the uniqueness of the earlier work.

5. *Askesis*, or a movement of self-purgation which intends the attainment of a state of solitude. I take the term, general as it is, particularly from the practice of pre-Socratic shamans like Empedocles. The later poet does not, as in *kenosis*, undergo a revisionary movement of emptying but of curtailing: he yields up part of his own human and imaginative endowment so as to separate himself from others, including the precursor, and he does this in his poem by so stationing it in regard to the parent-poem as to make that poem undergo an *askesis* also; the precursor's endowment is also truncated.

6. *Apophrades*, or the return of the dead. I take the word from the Athenian dismal or unlucky days upon which the dead returned to reinhabit the houses in which they had lived. The later poet, in his own final phase, already burdened by an imaginative solitude that is almost a solipsism, holds his own poem so open again to the precursor's work that at first we might believe the wheel has come full circle and we are back in the later poet's flooded apprenticeship, before his strength began to assert itself in the revisionary ratios of *clinamen* and the others. But the poem is now held open to the precursor, where once it was open, and the uncanny effect is

that the new poem's achievement makes it seem to us not as though the precursor were writing it, but as though the later poet himself had written the precursor's characteristic work.

These then are six revisionary ratios, and I think they can be observed, usually in cyclic appearance, in the life's work of every post-Enlightenment strong poet—which in English means, for practical purposes, every post-Miltonic strong poet. Coleridge, to return now to where I began, had the potential of the strong poet but—unlike Blake, Wordsworth, and the major poets after them down to Yeats and Stevens in our time—declined the full process of developing into one. Yet his work, even in its fragmentary state, demonstrates this revisionary cycle in spite of himself. My ulterior purpose in this discussion is to use Coleridge as an instance because he is apparently so poor an example of the cycle I have sketched. But that makes him a sterner test for my theory of influence than any other poet I could have chosen.

I return to Coleridge's first mature poetry and to its *clinamen* away from Milton, the Cowperizing turn that gave Coleridge the Conversation Poems, particularly "Frost at Midnight." Hazlitt quotes Coleridge as having said to him in the spring of 1798 that Cowper was the best modern poet, meaning the best since Milton, which was also Blake's judgment. Humphry House demonstrated the relation between "Frost at Midnight" and *The Task*—a happy one, causing no anxieties, where a stronger poet appropriates from a weaker one. Coleridge used Cowper as he used Bowles, Akenside, and Collins, finding in all of them hints that could help him escape the Miltonic influx that had drowned out "Religious Musings." "Frost at Midnight," like *The Task*, swerves away from Milton by softening him, by domesticating his style in a context that excludes all Sublime terrors. When Coleridge rises to his blessing of his infant son at the poem's conclusion he is in some sense poetically "misinterpreting" the beautiful declaration of Adam to Eve: "With thee conversing I forget all time," gentling the darker overtones of the infatuated Adam's declaration of love. Or, more simply, like Cowper he is not so much humanizing Milton—that will take the strenuous, head-on struggles of Blake, Wordsworth, Shelley, Keats—as he is making Milton more childlike, or perhaps better, reading Milton as though Milton loved in a more childlike way.

The revisionary step beyond this, an antithetical completion or *tessera*, is ventured by Coleridge only in a few pantheistic passages that sneaked past his orthodox censor, like the later additions to "The Eolian Harp" or the veiled vision at the end of the second verse paragraph of "This Lime-Tree Bower My Prison." With his horror of division, his endless quest for unity, Coleridge could not sustain any revisionary impulse which involved his reversing Milton or daring to complete that sacred father.

But the next revisionary ratio, the *kenosis* or self-emptying, seems to me almost obsessive in Coleridge's poetry, for what is the total situation of the Ancient Mariner but a repetition-compulsion, which his poet breaks for himself only by the writing of the poem and then only momentarily? Coleridge had contemplated an Epic on the Origin of Evil, but we may ask, Where would Coleridge, if pressed, have located the origin of evil in himself? His Mariner is neither depraved in will nor even disobedient, but merely ignorant, and the spiritual machinery his crime sets into motion is so ambiguously presented as to be finally beyond analysis. I would ask the question, What was Coleridge trying (not necessarily consciously) to do for himself by writing the poem? And by this question I do not mean Kenneth Burke's notion of trying to do something for oneself as a person. Rather, what was Coleridge the poet trying to do for himself as poet? To which I would answer: trying to free himself from the inhibitions of Miltonic influence by humbling his poetic self and so humbling the Miltonic in the process. The Mariner does not empty himself out; he starts empty and acquires a Primary Imagination through his suffering. But for Coleridge the poem is a *kenosis*, and what is being humbled is the Miltonic Sublime's account of the origin of evil. There is a reduction from disobedience to ignorance, from the self-aggrandizing consciousness of Eve to the painful awakening of a minimal consciousness in the Mariner.

The next revisionary step in clearing an imaginative space for a maturing strong poet is the Counter-Sublime, the attaining of which I have termed *daemonization*, and this I take to be the relation of "Kubla Khan" and "Christabel" to *Paradise Lost*. Far more than "The Rime of the Ancient Mariner," these poems demonstrate a tracking by Coleridge with powers that are *daemonic*, even though the "Rime" explicitly invokes Neoplatonic daemons in its marginal glosses. Opium was the avenging *daemon* or *alastor* of Coleridge's life, his Dark or Fallen Angel, his experiential acquaintance with Milton's Satan. Opium was for him what wandering and moral tale-telling became for the Mariner—the personal shape of repetition-compulsion. The lust for paradise in "Kubla Khan," Geraldine's lust for Christabel—these are manifestations of Coleridge's revisionary daemonization of Milton, these are Coleridge's Counter-Sublime. Poetic Genius, the genial spirit itself, Coleridge must see as daemonic when it is his own rather than when it is Milton's.

It is at this point in the revisionary cycle that Coleridge begins to back away decisively from the ferocity necessary for the strong poet. He does not sustain his *daemonization*; he closes his eyes in holy dread, stands outside the circumference of the *daemonic* agent, and is startled by his own sexual daring out of finishing "Christabel." He moved on to the revisionary ratio I have called *askesis*, or the purgation into solitude, the curtailing of some imaginative powers in the name of others. In doing so, he prophesied the pattern for Keats in "The Fall of Hyperion," since in his *askesis* he struggles against the influence of a composite poetic father, Milton-Wordsworth. The great poems of this *askesis* are "Dejection: An Ode" and "To William Wordsworth," where criticism has demonstrated to us how acute the revision of Wordsworth's stance is, and how much of himself Coleridge purges away to make this revision justified. I would add only that both poems misread Milton as sensitively and desperately as they do Wordsworth; the meaning of "Dejection" is in its relation to "Lycidas" as much as in its relation to the "Intimations" ode, even as the poem "To William Wordsworth" assimilates *The Prelude* to *Paradise Lost*. Trapped in his own involuntary dualisms, longing for a monistic wholeness such as he believes is found in Milton and Wordsworth, Coleridge in his *askesis* declines to see how much of his composite parent-poet he has purged away also.

After that, sadly enough, we have only a very few occasional poems of any quality by Coleridge, and they are mostly not the poems of a strong poet—that is, of a man vaulting into the Sublime. Having refused the full exercise of a strong poet's misprisions, Coleridge ceased to have poetic ambitions. But there are significant exceptions—the late manuscript fragment "Limbo" and the evidently still-later fragment "Ne Plus Ultra." Here, and I think here only, Coleridge experiences the particular reward of the strong poet in his last phase—what I have called the *apophrades* or return of the dead: not a Counter-Sublime but a negative Sublime, like the *Last Poems* of Yeats or *The Rock* of Stevens. Indeed negative sublimity is the mode of these Coleridgean fragments and indicates to us what Coleridge might have become had he permitted himself enough of the perverse zeal that the great poet must exhibit in malforming his great precursor. "Limbo" and "Ne Plus Ultra" show that Coleridge could have become, at last, the poet of the Miltonic abyss, the bard of Demogorgon. Even as they stand, these fragments make us read Book II of *Paradise Lost* a little differently; they enable Coleridge to claim a corner of Milton's Chaos as his own.

Pater thought that Coleridge had succumbed to the Organic analogue because he hungered too intensively for eternity, as Lamb had said of his old school-friend. Pater also quoted De Quincey's summary of Coleridge: "He wanted better bread than can be made with wheat." I would add that Coleridge hungered also for an eternity of generosity between poets, as between people—a generosity that is not allowed in a world where each poet must struggle to individuate his own breath and this at the expense of his forebears as much as of his contemporaries. Perhaps also, to modify De Quincey, Coleridge wanted better poems than can be made without misprision.

I suggest then that the Organic analogue, with all its pragmatic neglect of the processes by which poems have to be produced, appealed so overwhelmingly to Coleridge because it seemed to preclude the anxiety of influence and to obviate the poet's necessity not just to unfold like a natural growth but to develop at the expense of others. Whatever the values of the Organic analogue for literary criticism—and I believe, with Pater, that it does more harm than good—it provided Coleridge with a rationale for a dangerous evasion of the inner steps he had to take for his own poetic development. As Blake might have said, Coleridge's imagination insisted upon slaying itself on the stems of generation—or, to invoke another Blakean image, Coleridge lay down to sleep upon the Organic analogue as though it were a Beulah-couch of soft, moony repose.

What was our loss in this? What poems might a stronger Coleridge have composed? The *Notebooks* list *The Origin of Evil, an Epic Poem*; *Hymns to the Sun, the Moon, and the Elements—six hymns*; and, more fascinating even than these, a scheme for an epic on "the destruction of Jerusalem" by the Romans. Still more compelling is a March 1802 entry in the *Notebooks*: "Milton, a Monody in the metres of Samson's Choruses—only with more rhymes/—poetical influences—political-moral-Dr. Johnson/." Consider the date of this entry—only a month before the first draft of "Dejection"— and some sense of what *Milton, a Monody* might have been begins to be generated. In March 1802, William Blake, in the midst of his sojourn at Hayley's Felpham, was deep in the composition of *Milton: a Poem in 2 Books, To Justify the Ways of God to Men*. In the brief, enigmatic notes for *Milton, a Monody* Coleridge sets down "—poetical influences—political-moral-Dr. Johnson," the last being, we can assume, a refutation of Johnson's vision of Milton in *The Lives of the Poets*, a refutation that Cowper and Blake would have endorsed. "Poetical influences," Coleridge says, and we may recall that this is one of the themes of Blake's *Milton*, where the Shadow of the Poet Milton is one with the Covering Cherub, the great blocking agent who inhibits fresh human creativity by embodying in himself all the sinister beauty of tradition. Blake's *Milton* is a kind of monody in places, not as a mourning for Milton, but as Milton's own, solitary utterance as he goes down from a premature Eternity (where he is unhappy) to struggle again in fallen time and space. I take it though that

*Milton, a Monody* would have been modeled upon Coleridge's early "Monody on the Death of Chatterton" and so would have been Coleridge's lamentation for his Great Original. Whether, as Blake was doing at precisely the same time, Coleridge would have dared to identify Milton as the Covering Cherub, as the angel or *daemon* blocking Coleridge himself out from the poet's paradise, I cannot surmise. I wish deeply that Coleridge had written the poem.

It is ungrateful, I suppose, as the best of Coleridge's recent scholars keep telling us, to feel that Coleridge did not give us the poems he had it in him to write. Yet we have, all apology aside, only a double handful of marvelous poems by him. I close therefore by attempting a description of the kind of poem I believe Coleridge's genius owed us and which we badly need, and always will need. I would maintain that the finest achievement of the High Romantic poets of England was their humanization of the Miltonic Sublime. But when we attend deeply to the works where this humanization is most strenuously accomplished—Blake's *Milton* and *Jerusalem*, Wordsworth's *Prelude*, Shelley's *Prometheus Unbound*, Keats's two *Hyperions*, even in a way Byron's *Don Juan*—we sense at last a quality lacking, a quality in which Milton abounds for all his severity. This quality, though not in itself a tenderness, made Milton's Eve possible, and we miss such a figure in all her Romanic descendants. More than the other five great Romantic poets, Coleridge was able, by temperament and by subtly shaded intellect, to have given us a High Romantic Eve, a total humanization of the tenderest and most appealing element in the Miltonic Sublime. Many anxieties blocked Coleridge from that rare accomplishment, and of these the anxiety of influence was not the least.

### The Rime of the Ancient Mariner

Poetry (and potentially its criticism) alone of all human talk need not be reductive. Coleridge in *The Ancient Mariner* tells a story that relates itself clearly to a major Romantic archetype, the Wanderer, the man with the mark of Cain, or the mocker of Christ, who must expiate in a perpetual cycle of guilt and suffering, and whose torment is in excess of its usually obscure object and source. This archetype figures in Blake and in Keats but is more basic to Wordsworth and Clare and Beddoes. In Coleridge, Byron, and Shelley it becomes something more, a personal myth so consuming that we hardly know whether to seek it first in the life or in the work.

*The Ancient Mariner* is in the tradition of the stories of Cain and of the Wandering Jew, but it does not reduce to them. It is a late manifestation of the Gothic Revival, and its first version is clearly to be related to the ballad of *The Wandering Jew* in Percy's *Reliques*, but its historical sources also tend to mislead us when we attempt to describe it in its own terms, which is the business of criticism.

The Ancient Mariner, bright-eyed and compulsive, is a haunter of wedding feasts, and in a grim way he is the chanter of a prothalamium. Yet he does not address himself to bride or groom but to a gallant who is the bridegroom's next of kin. His story means most, he implies, when it is juxtaposed with the special joy of the wedding celebration, but it is not relevant to those being joined by a sacrament. Its proper audience is an unwilling one; its function is monitory. The message can only be relayed from a lurker at the threshold to a prospective sharer of the feast.

The world of the Mariner's voyage is purely visionary; the ship is driven by a storm toward the South Pole and into a realm simpler and more drastic than the natural world of experience. Into a sea of ice, where no living thing was to be seen, through the snow fog there comes suddenly a great sea bird, the albatross. An albatross, with its wingspread of eleven feet and its length of some three and a half feet, and its white color, is a startling phenomenon in itself, and its great power of flight can easily betoken the generosity of nature. Whatever its source, and Coleridge leaves this mysterious, the poem's albatross comes to the mariners as a free gift. They hail it in God's name as if it were human; they domesticate it with their food, which it has never eaten before; they play with it as if it were child or pet. Very directly they associate it with their luck, for now the ice splits, a south wind springs up, and they start the journey northward back to the ordinary world. The poem's first great event is suddenly placed before us; without apparent premeditation or conscious motive, the narrator murders the albatross.

The murder is a gratuitous act, but then so is the initial appearance of the bird. There is a tradition of seemingly motiveless malevolence that goes from Shakespeare's Iago (whom Coleridge saw as a tragic poet, manipulating men rather than words) and Milton's Satan to the protagonists of Poe, Melville, and Dostoevsky, and that appears in Gide, Camus, and other recent writers. The tradition begins with the demonic (tinged with Prometheanism), moves (in the later nineteenth century) into a vitalism crossed by the social image of man in revolt, and climaxes (in our own time) in a violence that yet confirms individual existence and so averts an absolute despair of self. Coleridge's mariner belongs to this tradition whose dark ancestors include Cain, the Wandering Jew, and the Judas whose act of betrayal is portrayed as a desperate assertion of freedom by Wilde, Yeats, and D.H. Lawrence.

This tradition's common denominator is that of a desperate assertion of self and a craving for a heightened sense of identity. This is what the Mariner brings about for himself, in a death-in-life purgatorial fashion; for his companions he brings only a terrible death and a mechanical life-in-death following his own partial redemption.

Several influential modern readings of *The Ancient Mariner* have attempted to baptize the poem by importing into it the notion of Original Sin and the myth of the Fall. But the Mariner is neither disobedient in his dire action nor altered in nature by its first effects. There is nothing in him to suggest the depravity of the natural heart, nor is the slaying of an albatross at all an adequate symbol of a lapse that demands expression in the language of theology. Coleridge in his *Table Talk* (May 31, 1830) felt the poem was already too overtly moral (thinking of the pious conclusion) and said of it:

> It ought to have had no more moral than the Arabian Nights'
> tale of the merchant's sitting down to eat dates by the side of a
> well, and throwing the shells aside, and lo! a genie starts up,
> and says he *must* kill the aforesaid merchant because one of the
> date shells had, it seems, put out the eye of the genie's son.

*The Ancient Mariner* seems to have just this peculiar moral logic; you shoot an albatross quite casually, as you might throw aside a date shell. The tradition of the gratuitous crime also characterizes itself by its emphasis on the casual as opposed to the causal. Lafcadio in *Les Caves du Vatican*, just before performing his crime without a motive, says, "It's not so much about events that I'm curious, as about myself." Lafcadio and the Mariner are not (in advance) concerned about what ensues from an act; the act for each becomes a bracketed phenomenon, *pure act*, detached from motivation or consequences, and existent in itself. But the Mariner learns not to bracket, and the poem would have us learn, not where to throw our date shells, nor to love all creatures great and small, but to connect all phenomena, acts and things, in the fluid dissolve of the imagination:

> O! the one Life within us and abroad,
> Which meets all motion and becomes its soul

Frequently noted by critics is the extraordinary passivity of the Mariner. Wordsworth first said that the Mariner "does not act, but is continually acted upon." Not only does the Mariner rarely act (he shoots once, drinks his own blood once, so as to cry out that he has seen a sail, and blesses once), but usually he expresses no reaction to events. Most of the strong emotional and moral statements in the poem are in Coleridge's frequently beautiful marginal prose. The Mariner is merely an accurate observer, not a man of any sensibility. Despite the wonder and terror of what befalls him, he does not reach a height of emotional expression until part 4 of the poem, and then is driven to it, fittingly, by *solitude*. Alone with the dead men, and surrounded by the slime of subhuman life, he wakens first into agony of soul, then into a sense of contrast between the human and what is "beneath" it in the scale of being, and finally into a startled awareness of unexpected beauty. The crisis comes with moonrise on the seventh night of his lonely ordeal. The marginal prose meets the crisis with a beauty of expression which seems to touch at the limits of art:

> In his loneliness and fixedness he yearneth towards the jour-neying Moon, and the stars that still sojourn, yet still move onward; and every where the blue sky belongs to them, and is their appointed rest, and their native country and their own natural homes, which they enter unannounced, as lords that are certainly expected and yet there is a silent joy at their arrival.

He can be saved only by translating this yearning from the moon and stars to what envelops his own loneliness and fixedness, by naturalizing himself in his surroundings and finding a joy that will intimate the one life he shares with the creatures of the great deep. The finest stanzas in the poem trace his transference of love from the moon and stars to "God's creatures of the great calm":

> The moving Moon went up the sky,
> And no where did abide:
> Softly she was going up,
> And a star or two beside—
>
> Her beams bemocked the sultry main,
> Like April hoar-frost spread;
> But where the ship's huge shadow lay,
> The charmèd water burnt alway
> A still and awful red.
>
> Beyond the shadow of the ship,
> I watched the water-snakes:
> They moved in tracks of shining white,
> And when they reared, the elfish light
> Fell off in hoary flakes.

The moon's beams *bemock* the ocean, because upon that rotting and still torrid surface (the moon is just rising and the heat of the tropical sun yet abides) an appearance of "April hoar-frost" is now spread. The light given by the water snakes is called elfish and is said to fall off "in hoary flakes." Moonlight and hoarfrost are an imaginative unity at the close of "Frost at Midnight"; they give and take light, to and from one another, and the light, like the fair luminous mist in "Dejection," is emblematic both of creative joy and of the One Life of the phenomenal universe.

The Mariner now sees the beauty and happiness of what he had characterized, not inaccurately, as slime:

> O happy living things! no tongue
> Their beauty might declare:
> A spring of love gushed from my heart,
> And I blessed them unaware:
> Sure my kind saint took pity on me,
> And I blessed them unaware.
>
> The self-same moment I could pray;
> And from my neck so free
> The Albatross fell off, and sank
> Like lead into the sea.

His consciousness remains passive; he blesses them "unaware." As a sacramental moment this is unique, even in Romantic poetry. A less than ordinary man, never before alive to the sacramental vision of Nature as life, joy, love, suddenly declares the most elemental forms of life in Nature to be joyous and deserving of his affection. The slimy sea serpents are nearly as formless as the chaos Coleridge is to dread in his late poems of "Positive Negation," "Limbo," and "Ne Plus Ultra." Yet these creatures have color and beauty, they are alive, and "everything that lives is holy," as Blake insisted. At this, its climactic point, *The Ancient Mariner* is the most vital and imaginative achievement of Coleridge's poetry. Here, for once, he places complete trust in his Imagination, and it cannot fail him.

*The Ancient Mariner* is not, like "Kubla Khan," a poem about poetry. The shaping spirit, or Secondary Imagination, is not its theme, though recently critics have tried for such a reading. The Mariner's failure, and his subsequent salvation, is one of the Primary Imagination, "the repetition in the finite mind of the eternal act of creation in the infinite I AM." God looked upon His Creation and saw that it was good. The Mariner has now first learned to repeat in his very finite mind this eternal act of perception and creation. This awakening certainly does not bring the whole soul of this man into activity; the Mariner does not learn to order his experience so as first to balance and then be free of it. He falls victim to it, and its eternal verbal repetition becomes his obsession. Had the Mariner been a poet, he could have written the Rime he incarnates. He has seen the truth, but the truth does not set him free. He returns to life as a mere fundamentalist of the Primary Imagination, endlessly repeating the story of his own salvation and the one moral in it that he can understand:

> He prayeth best, who loveth best
> All things both great and small;
> For the dear God who loveth us,
> He made and loveth all.

The other moral is less simple but quite as elemental. Coleridge has written the poem as an alternative reaction to the Mariner's experience, for that experience of purgation through love of the One Life is his own. The higher Imagination shapes truth; the lower merely takes it, through Nature, from the Shaping Spirit of God. The poem celebrates the continued power of creative joy in its creator. But the poem also foreshadows the eventual fate of its creator, when the activity of the whole soul will yield to torpor. Coleridge as theologian and philosopher found more willing auditors than the Mariner did, but his quest came to duplicate that of his creation.

# Herman Melville

## (1819–1891)

*Moby-Dick*

"CANST THOU DRAW OUT LEVIATHAN WITH A HOOK?," GOD'S TAUNTING question to Job. Can be said to be answered by Captain Ahab with a "Yes!" in thunder. Job's God wins, Ahab loses, and the great white leviathan swims away, harpooned yet towing Ahab with him. But Ahab's extraordinary last speech denies that Moby-Dick is the conquerer:

> I turn my body from the sun. What ho, Tashtego! Let me hear thy hammer. Oh! Ye three unsurrendered spires of mine; thou uncracked keel; and only god-bullied hull; thou firm deck. And haughty helm, and Pole-pointed prow,—death-glorious ship! Must ye then perish, and without me? Am I cut off from the last fond pride of meanest shipwrecked captains? Oh, lonely death on lonely life! Oh, now I feel my topmost greatness lies in my topmost grief. Ho, ho! from all your furthest bounds, pour ye now in, ye bold billows of my whole foregone life, and top this one piled comber of my death! Towards thee I roll, thou all-destroying but unconquering whale; to the last I grapple with thee; from hell's heart I stab at thee; for hate's sake I spit my last breath at thee. Sink all coffins and all hearses to one common pool! and since neither can be mine, let me then tow to pieces, while still chasing thee, though tied to thee, thou damned whale! *Thus,* I give up the spear!

Beyond the allusions—Shakespearean, Miltonic, Byronic—what rings out here is Melville's own grand self-echoing, which is of Father Mapple's sermon as it concludes:

He drooped and fell away from himself for a moment; then lifting his face to them again, showed a deep joy in his eyes, as he cried out with a heavenly enthusiasm,—"But oh! shipmates! on the starboard hand of every woe, there is a sure delight; and higher the top of that delight, than the bottom of the woe is deep. Is not the main-truck higher than the kelson is low? Delight is to him—a far, far upward, and inward delight—who against the proud gods and commodores of this earth, ever stands forth his own inexorable self. Delight is to him whose strong arms yet support him, when the ship of this base treacherous world has gone down beneath him. Delight is to him, who gives no quarter in the truth, and kills, burns, and destroys all sin though he pluck it out from under the robes of Senators and Judges. Delight,—top-gallant delight is to him, who acknowledges no law or lord, but the Lord his God, and is only a patriot to heaven. Delight is to him, whom all the waves of the billows of the seas of the boisterous mob can never shake from this sure Keel of the Ages. And eternal delight and deliciousness will be his, who coming to lay him down, can say with his final breath—O Father!—chiefly known to me by Thy rod—mortal or immortal, here I die. I have striven to be Thine, more than to be this world's, or mine own. Yet this is nothing; I leave eternity to Thee; for what is man that he should live out the lifetime of his God?"

Father Mapple's intensity moves from "a sure delight, and higher the top of that delight" through "a far, far upward. And inward delight" on to "Delight,—top-gallant delight is to him," heaven's patriot. Ahab's equal but antithetical intensity proceeds from "unsurrendered spires of mine" through "my topmost greatness lies in my topmost grief" to end in "top this one piled comber of my death." After which the *Pequod* goes down with Tashtego hammering a hawk to the mainmast, an emblem not of being "only a patriot to heaven" but rather of a Satanic dragging of "a living part of heaven along with her." Admirable as Father Mapple is, Ahab is certainly the hero, more Promethean than Satanic, and we need not conclude (as so many critics do) that Melville chooses Mapple's stance over Ahab's. William Faulkner, in 1927, asserted that the book he most wished he had written was *Moby-Dick*, and called Ahab's fate "a sort of Golgotha of the heart become immutable as bronze in the sonority of its plunging ruin," characteristically adding: "There's a death for a man, now."

As Faulkner implied, there is a dark sense in which Ahab intends his

Golgotha, like Christ's, to be a vicarious atonement for all of staggering Adam's woes. When Melville famously wrote to Hawthorne: "I have written a wicked book," he was probably quite serious. The common reader does not come to love Ahab, and yet there is a serious disproportion between the reader's awe of, and admiration for, Ahab, and the moral dismissal of the monomaniacal hero by many scholarly critics. Ahab seems to provoke academic critics rather more even than Milton's Satan does. Ishmael, presumably speaking for Melville, consistently emphasizes Ahab's greatness. And so does Ahab himself, as when he confronts the corposants or St. Elmo's fire, in the superb Chapter 119, "The Candles":

> Oh! thou clear spirit of clear fire, whom on these seas I as Persian once did worship, till in the sacramental act so burned by thee, that to this hour I bear the scar; I now know thee, thou clear spirit, and I now know that thy right worship is defiance. To neither love nor reverence wilt thou be kind; and e'en for hate thou canst but kill; and all are killed. No fearless fool now fronts thee. I own thy speechless, placeless power; but to the last gasp of my earthquake life will dispute its unconditional, unintegral mastery in me. In the midst of the personified impersonal, a personality stands here. Though but a point at best; whencesoe'er I came; wheresoe'er I go; yet while I earthly live, the queenly personality lives in me, and feels her royal rights. But war is pain, and hate is woe. Come in thy lowest form of love, and I will kneel and kiss thee; but at thy highest, come as mere supernal power; and though thou launchest navies of full-freighted worlds, there's that in here that still remains indifferent. Oh, thou clear spirit, of thy fire thou madest me, and like a true child of fire, I breathe it back to thee.

If Ahab has a religion, it is Persian or rather Parsee, and so Zoroastrian, But Melville has not written a Zoroastrian hymn to the benign light for Ahab to chant. Ahab's invocation is clearly Gnostic in spirit and in substance, since the light is hailed as being both ambiguous and ambivalent. Ahab himself knows that the clear spirit of clear fire is not from the Alien God but from the Demiurge, and he seems to divide the Demiurge into both the "lowest form of love" and the "highest ... mere supernal power." Against this dialectical or even self-contradictory spirit, Ahab sets himself as personality rather than as moral character: "In the midst of the personified impersonal, a personality stands here." As a personality, Ahab confronts "the personified impersonal," which he astonishingly names as his father, and defies, as knowing less than he, Ahab, knows:

> I own thy speechless, placeless power; said I not so? Nor was it wrung from me; nor do I now drop these links. Thou canst blind; but I can then grope. Thou canst consume; but I can then be ashes. Take the homage of these poor eyes, and shutter-hands. I would not take it. The lightning flashes through my skull; mine eye-balls ache and ache; my whole beaten brain seems as beheaded, and rolling on some stunning ground. Oh, oh! Yet blindfold, yet will I talk to thee. Light though thou be, thou leapest out of darkness; but I am darkness leaping out of light, leaping out of thee! The javelins cease; open eyes; see, or not? There burn the flames! Oh, thou magnanimous! now I do glory in my genealogy. But thou art but my fiery father; my sweet mother, I know not. Oh, cruel! what hast thou done with her? There lies my puzzle; but thine is greater. Thou knowest not how came ye, hence callest thyself unbegotten; certainly knowest not thy beginning, hence callest thyself unbegun. I know that of me, which thou knowest not of thyself, oh, thou omnipotent. There is some unsuffusing thing beyond thee, thou clear spirit, to whom all thy eternity is but time, all thy creativeness mechanical. Through thee, thy flaming self, my scorched eyes do dimly see it. Oh, thou foundling fire, thou hermit immemorial, thou too hast thy incommunicable riddle, thy unparticipated grief. Here again with haughty agony, I read my sire. Leap! leap up, and lick the sky! I leap with thee; I burn with thee; would fain be welded with thee; defyingly I worship thee!

The visionary center of *Moby-Dick*, and so of all Melville, as critics always have recognized, is chapter 42, "The Whiteness of the Whale." It is Ishmael's meditation, and not Ahab's, and yet how far is it from Ahab? Ishmael is himself half a Gnostic:

> Though in many of its aspects this visible world seems formed in love, the invisible spheres were formed in fright.

Closer to Carlyle than to Emerson, this extraordinary sentence is the prelude to the final paragraph of Ishmael's reverie:

But not yet have we solved the incantation of this whiteness, and learned why it appeals with such power to the soul; and more strange and far more portentous—why, as we have seen, it is at once the most meaning symbol of spiritual things, nay, the very veil of the Christian's Deity; and yet should be as it is, the intensifying agent in things the most appalling to mankind.

Is it that by its indefiniteness it shadows forth the heartless voids and immensities of the universe, and thus stabs us from behind with the thought of annihilation, when beholding the white depths of the milky way? Or is it, that as in essence whiteness is not so much a color as the visible absence of color, and at the same time the concrete of all colors; is it for these reasons that there is such a dumb blankness, full of meaning, in a wide landscape of snows—a colorless, all-color of atheism from which we shrink? And when we consider that other theory of the natural philosophers, that all other earthly hues—every stately or lovely emblazoning—the sweet tinges of sunset skies and woods; yea, and the gilded velvets of butterflies, and the butterfly cheeks of young girls; all these are but subtile deceits, not actually inherent in substances, but only laid on from without; so that all deified Nature absolutely paints like the harlot, whose allurements cover nothing but the charnel-house within; and when we proceed further, and consider that the mystical cosmetic which produces every one of her hues, the great principle of light, for ever remains white or colorless in itself, and if operating without medium upon matter, would touch all objects, even tulips and roses, with its own blank tinge—pondering all this, the palsied universe lies before us a leper; and like wilful travellers in Lapland, who refuse to wear colored and coloring glasses upon their eyes, so the wretched infidel gazes himself blind at the monumental white shroud that wraps all the prospect around him. And of all these things the Albino whale was the symbol. Wonder ye then at the fiery hunt?

Ishmael's "visible absence of color" becomes the trope of whiteness, "a dumb blankness," similar to its descendant in the beach-scene of Wallace Stevens's "The Auroras of Autumn":

Here, being visible is being white,
Is being of the solid of white, the accomplishment
Of an extremist in an exercise ...

The season changes. A cold wind chills the beach.
The long lines of it grow longer, emptier,
A darkness gathers though it does not fall.

And the whiteness grows less vivid on the wall.
The man who is walking turns blankly on the sand.

Melville and Stevens alike shrink from "a colorless, all-color of atheism," not because they are theists, but precisely because they both believe
in and fear the Demiurge. When Ishmael cries out: "Wonder ye then at the
fiery hunt?" he refutes all those critics, moral and psychoanalytic, who
condemn Ahab as being immoral or insane. It was Melville, after all, who
wrote two memorable quatrains, in the mode of Blake, which he entitled
"Fragments of a lost Gnostic Poem of the 12th Century":

Found a family, build a state,
The pledged event is still the same:
Matter in end will never abate
His ancient brutal claim.

Indolence is heaven's ally here,
And energy the child of hell:
The Good Man pouring from his pitcher clear,
But brims the poisoned well.

There the Gnosticism is overt, and we are left a little cold, since even
a heretical doctrine strikes us as tendentious, as having too clear a design
upon us. Perhaps "The Bell-Tower" is a touch tendentious also. *Moby-
Dick*, despite its uneven rhetoric, despite its excessive debt to Shakespeare,
Milton, and Byron, is anything but tendentious. It remains the darker half
of our national epic, complementing *Leaves of Grass* and *Huckleberry Finn*,
works of more balance certainly, but they do not surpass or eclipse
Melville's version of darkness visible.

# Walt Whitman

## (1819–1892)

THE INFLUENCE OF WALT WHITMAN'S POETRY UPON HIS LIFE WAS absolute: a purer instance of the work in the writer hardly could be found. So disturbed was the household in which Whitman was raised, so dark the fates of his siblings, that Walt's self-creation appears a miracle.

At thirty, in 1849, Whitman returned to his family, abandoning his career as a journalist. He read and wrote, and worked at carpentering with his father and brothers. In the notebooks of 1854, we can see *Leaves of Grass* start to emerge, even as Walter Whitman, Sr. declined. In early July 1855, Whitman self-published the first edition of *Leaves of Grass*. On July 11, his father died. Ten days later, Ralph Waldo Emerson mailed Whitman his superb response to the poet's gift of *Leaves of Grass*.

Whitman and Emily Dickinson remain the greatest and most difficult of American poets. This is just as true now in the early twenty-first century as it was in the nineteenth. Dickinson is cognitively difficult: her mind is the strongest and most original among all poets in English since William Shakespeare and William Blake. Whitman did not have unusual conceptual powers, any more than Tennyson did. But, like Tennyson, Whitman is one of the geniuses of figurative language. His descendants among major American poets are very disparate: Wallace Stevens, W.C. Williams, Ezra Pound, T.S. Eliot, Hart Crane, John Ashbery, A.R. Ammons. Yet they share the legacy of Whitman's nuanced rhetoric, his "intricate evasions of as" [Wallace Stevens].

There is a clear relation between Whitman's biography and his elaborate command of all the resources of trope. An auto-didact, Whitman's formal education ceased at eleven. He then was apprenticed as a printer's devil to newspapers, and progressed to printer and to editor. Whitman's pages of poetry in the 1855 *Leaves of Grass* have more the look of a nineteenth century American newspaper page than of a coventionally printed page of verse. William Blake, also self-educated, was apprenticed early to an engraver, and Blake's model always remained the engraved, illuminated page. Whitman did not read Blake until late in life, and then was intrigued both by the apparent similarities and by their more profound differences. The superbly multivalent title, *Leaves of Grass*, in the first place reflects nineteenth century printers' lingo. Leaves are pages, but also bundles of paper sheets, while grass is throwaway printers' stuff filling up pages. Whitman, though he sometimes pretends to literalism, is never more bewilderingly metaphorical than in the phrase "Leaves of Grass." Leaves are a major poetic fiction throughout Western tradition: they represent the fragility of individual lives, in an unbroken sequence from Homer, Virgil, Dante, Milton, and Shelley on to what Wallace Stevens calls "the fiction of the leaves." Grass is flesh in Isaiah and the Psalms: "Leaves of Grass" thus might mean a doubling of our most characteristic images of mortality.

For Whitman, grass is the more important fiction, beautifully elaborated in section 6 of *Song of Myself*. Beyond the large composite metaphor of "leaves of grass," Whitman's dominant trope is what he calls the "tally," a twig or cutting, like the sprig of lilac in the Lincoln elegy, or the calamus, aromatic underground stem of sweetflag, and the prime phallic emblem in the overtly homoerotic poems gathered together in the *Calamus* section of the third edition of *Leaves of Grass* in 1860.

These days, when the "discipline" of Queer Studies has taken its place on faculties next to Feminist Criticism, Multiculturalism, and all the other allied Resentments, it is of some importance to note that Whitman is rather more an autoerotic poet than a homoerotic one. He tallies by masturbating, and accumulates his poems by self-fulfillment. *Song of Myself*, sections 28–30, and "Spontaneous Me" are crucial instances.

Whitman's yearnings indubitably were homoerotic, but they were rarely (if ever) realized. The inhibition was not social but intensely personal: "To touch my person to some one else's is about as much as I can stand." Though the second-oldest of the eight siblings, Whitman early on became the father and mother to the seven others, four of whom were borderline or psychotic. That helped produce the characteristic Whitmanian stance: generously open to others, but quick to close up when the integrity of his single self might suffer vastation.

The relation between Whitman the person and Walt Whitman, one of the roughs, archetypal American poet, is astonishingly complex and still defies criticism. It inspires the greatest originality in Whitman's poetry, an astonishing psychic cartography which he divides into three components: "my soul," "myself" and "the real me," also called "the me myself." The Whitmanian soul is his unknown nature, ethos or character, and derives from the Emersonian Oversoul. Rough Walt, an American bard at last, is the "myself" of *Song of Myself*:

> Walt Whitman, a kosmos, of Manhattan the son,
> turbulent, fleshy, sensual, eating, drinking and breeding,
> No sentimentalist, no stander above men and women or apart
>     from them,
> No more modest than immodest.

That self or outered personality is a fiction, that is, the mythic Walt who is inspired to sum us all up: "Through me the afflatus emerging and surging, through me the current and index." But the true, personal self is quite otherwise:

> Apart from the pulling and hauling stands what I am,
> Stands amused, complacent, compassionating, idle, unitary,
> Looks down, is erect, or bends an arm on an impalpable certain
>     rest,
> Looking with side-curved head curious what will come next,
> Both in and out of the game and watching and wondering at it.

It is that real Me that mocks the poet Walt on the beach in "As I Ebb'd with the Ocean of Life." Dark demon or dusky brother, the Me Myself is at home wit the great trope of origins in Whitman's poetry: the fourfold of Night, Death, the Mother, and the Sea. That enormous, fused metaphor haunts American poetry since, and is particularly central in Wallace Stevens and Hart Crane. It has been crucial also in poets elsewhere, who are Whitman's inheritors: D.H. Lawrence in England, Fernando Pessoa in Portugal, Federico García Lorca in Spain, Pablo Neruda in Chile, Jorge Luis Borges in Argentina, Octavio Paz in Mexico.

Whitman's poetry formed his life, from 1855 on. *Song of Myself* engendered *Crossing Brooklyn Ferry*, which in turn helped stimulate the great *Sea-Drift* elegies and the "Lilacs" lament for Abraham Lincoln. After the great decade 1855-1865, Whitman burned out. His last twenty-seven years, down to his death two-months short of turning seventy-three, sadly show him depleted by the sublime strength of his earlier poetry.

## Song of Myself

Wordsworth celebrated the continuities of hearing, and dreaded the discontinuities of seeing. Emerson, in the defensive discontinuities of seeing, found a path to a more drastic, immediate, and total Sublime than European tradition wished or needed to discover. His greatest disciple, Whitman, an American bard at last, illustrates better than his master, the seer, both the splendor and the disaster of so aboriginal a repression.

My proof-text in Whitman is inevitably *Song of Myself*, but of its fifty-two sections I will concentrate only upon some Sublime centers, though I want to give a mapping-out of the revisionary pattern of the entire poem, for Whitman's romance of the self does follow essentially the model of the British Romantic crisis-poem, though with revealing, Emersonian, further distortions of the model. Employing my own shorthand, this is the pattern of ratios in *Song of Myself*:

| Sections: | 1–6 | *Clinamen*, irony of presence and absence |
|---|---|---|
| | 7–27 | *Tessera*, synecdoche of part for whole |
| | 28–30 | *Kenosis*, metonymy of emptying out |
| | 31–38 | *Daemonization*, hyperbole of high and low |
| | 39–49 | *Askesis*, metaphor of inside vs. outside |
| | 50–52 | *Apophrades*, metalepsis reversing early and late |

To adumbrate this pattern fully would take too long, but the principal contours can be sketched. The opening six sections are overtly a celebration, and what they celebrate presumably is a return of the repressed, an ecstatic union of soul and self, of primary and antithetical, or, more simply, they celebrate the American Sublime of influx, of Emersonian self-recognition and consequent self-reliance. What ought to be overwhelmingly present in the first six sections is what Whitman, criticizing Keats, referred to as the great poet's "powerful press of himself." But in these opening sections, the reader confronts instead images of absence rather than of presence; indeed, the reader is led inevitably to the bewildered observation that the poet's absence is so sacred a void that his presence never could hope to fill it. Defensively, Whitman opens with a reaction-formation against his precursor Emerson, which rhetorically becomes not the digressiveness or "permanent parabasis" of German Romantic irony, but the sharper, simpler irony of saying one thing while meaning another. Whitman says "I celebrate" and he cunningly means: "I contract and withdraw while asserting that I expand." Thus in section 2, he evades being intoxicated by all outward fragrance, narcissistically preferring "the smoke of my own breath." This characteristic and beautiful evasiveness intensifies in section 4, where the true self, "the Me myself," takes up a stance in total contradiction to the embracings and urgings that the poet only ostensibly celebrates:

Apart from the pulling and hauling stands what I am,
Stands amused, complacent, compassionating, idle, unitary,
Looks down, is erect, or bends an arm on an impalpable certain
    rest,
Looking with side-curved head curious what will come next,
Both in and out of the game and watching and wondering at it.

If this dialectical evasion is a *clinamen* away from Emerson, then precisely what sort of guilt of indebtedness does it seek to void? Is there a crucial enough difference between the Emersonian and Whitmanian versions
of an American Sublime so as to allow Whitman enough breathing-space?
I need to digress again, upon antithetical theory and the American
Sublime, if I am to answer this question and thus be able to get back to
mapping *Song of Myself*. What I want to be able to explain is why Whitman,
in section 5, resorts to the image of transparency when he describes the
embrace between his self and his soul, and why in section 6 he writes so
firmly within the materialist tradition of Epicurus and Lucretius. Epicurus
said: "The what is unknowable," and Whitman says he cannot answer the
child's question: *What is the grass?* Poetically, he does answer, in a magnificent series of tropes, much admired by the hesitant Hopkins, and pro-
gressing from the Homeric: "And now it seems to me the beautiful uncut
hair of graves" until we are given the astonishing and very American: "This
grass is very dark to be from the white heads of old mothers."

In the 1856, Second Edition of *Leaves of Grass*, Whitman addressed
Emerson directly, acknowledging that "it is yours to have been the original true Captain who put to sea, intuitive, positive, rendering the first
report, to be told less by any report, and more by the mariners of a thousand bays, in each tack of their arriving and departing, many years after
this." But Whitman aspired after strength, and so could not abide in this
perfectly accurate tribute. In 1863, in a private notation, full of veneration
for the precursor, he subtly described Emerson, perhaps better than even
Nietzsche was to describe him:

America in the future, in her long train of poets and writers,
while knowing more vehement and luxurious ones, will, I
think, acknowledge nothing nearer [than] this man, the actual
beginner of the whole procession—and certainly nothing
purer, cleaner, sweeter, more canny, none, after all, more thoroughly her own and native. The most exquisite taste and cau-
tion are in him, always saving his feet from passing beyond the
limits, for he is transcendental of limits, and you see

underneath the rest a secret proclivity, American maybe, to dare and violate and make escapades.

By the time he wrote *Specimen Days* (1882), the consequences of misprision had triumphed in Whitman. Emerson was then condemned as having only a gentleman's admiration of power, and as having been an influence upon Whitman just "for a month or so." Five years later, Whitman lied outright, saying: "It is of no importance whether I had read Emerson before starting *L. of G.* or not. The fact happens to be positively that I had *not*." Rather desperately, Whitman went on to say: "*L of G.*'s word is *the body, including all*, including the intellect and soul; E's word is mind (or intellect or soul)." Though I will return to this last remark of Whitman's later, in studying his opening swerve away from Emerson, I wish to end these citations from Whitman-on-Emerson by quoting the truest of them, again from *Specimen Days*:

> The best part of Emersonianism is, it breeds the giant that destroys itself. Who wants to be any man's mere follower? lurks behind every page. No teacher ever taught, that has so provided for his pupil's setting up independently—no truer evolutionist.

Here, Whitman has provided antithetical theory with the inevitable trope for Emersonianism or the American Sublime: "it breeds the giant that destroys itself." We need not be surprised to discover that the trope was, however, Emerson's own invention, crucial in the essay *Self-Reliance* (which Whitman certainly *had* read before he wrote *Song of Myself*):

> I affect to be intoxicated with sights and suggestions, but I am not intoxicated. My giant goes with me wherever I go. (...)

I return finally to the opening six sections of *Song of Myself*, with their defensive swerve away from Emerson, even as they appear to celebrate an Emersonian realization of the self. Whitman, not a poet-of-ideas like Emerson, but more traditionally a poet (however odd that sounds), seems to have known implicitly that a poetic representation of a desire tends to be stronger (that is, less limiting) than a poetic representation of an act. *Song of Myself*, in its beginnings, therefore substitutes the desires for union between split parts of the self, and between self and soul, for the acts of union proper, whatever those might be. Whitman wishes to originate his own mode, but he cannot do so without some discontinuity with Emerson, a prophet of discontinuity, and how do you cast off an influence that itself denounces all influence? Emersonianism urges itself to breed a giant that will destroy itself, but this most gigantic of its giants painfully found himself anticipated in nearly every trope, and in every movement of the spirit, a pain that Whitman shared with Thoreau.

It is evident, both from the opening emphases in *Song of Myself* and from Whitman's comments in *Specimen Days*, on the rival words of precursor and ephebe, that Whitman's intended swerve from Emerson is to deny Emerson's distinction between the Soul and Nature, in which Nature includes all of the NOT ME, "both nature and art, all other men and my own body." Whitman's ME must include his own body, or so he would persuade us. He writes what in 1881 he would title at last *Song of Myself*, and not *Song of the Soul* or even *Song of My Soul*. But the embrace between his soul and his self in section 5, which makes the axis of things appear not opaque but transparent, oddly makes "you my soul" the active partner, and the self, "the other I am," wholly passive in this courtship. If we translate soul as "character" and self as "personality," then we would find it difficult to identify so passive a personality with "Walt Whitman, a kosmos, of Manhattan the son, / Turbulent, fleshy, sensual, eating, drinking and breeding" of section 24. Clearly, there is a division in Whitman between two elements in the self, as well as between self and soul, and it is the first of these divisions that matters, humanly and poetically. Indeed, it was from the first of these divisions that I believe Emerson initially rescued Whitman, thus making it possible for Whitman to become a poet. The "real me" or "me myself" in Whitman could not bear to be touched, ever, except by the maternal trinity of night, death, and the sea, while Walt Whitman, one of the roughs, learned from Emerson to cry: "Contact!" There is a sublime pathos in Whitman making his Epicurean *clinamen* away from Emerson by overproclaiming the body. Emerson had nothing to say about two subjects and two subjects only, sex and death, because he was too healthy-minded to believe that there was much to say about either. Emerson had no sexual problems, and was a Stoic about death.

I return to mapping *Song of Myself*, with its implicit contrast that Whitman, gloriously and plangently, always had much too much to say about sex and death, being in this the ancestor not only of Hart Crane and, perhaps surprisingly, of Wallace Stevens and, these days, of Ammons and Ashbery, but also of such prose obfuscators of sex and death as Hemingway and his egregious ephebe, Norman Mailer. Whitman, surpassing all his descendants, makes of a linked sex-and-death a noble synecdoche for all of existence, which is the figurative design of sections 7–27 of *Song of Myself*. A universalizing flood tide of reversals-into-the-opposite reaches a great climax in section 24, which is an antithetical completion of the self without rival in American poetry, astonishing both for its dignity and its pathos, and transcending any other modern poet's attempt to think and represent by synecdoche. The reader cannot know whether to admire this proclamation more for its power or for its precision:

> Unscrew the locks from the doors!
> Unscrew the doors themselves from their jambs!
>
> Whoever degrades another degrades me,
> And whatever is done or said returns at last to me.
>
> Through me the afflatus surging and surging, through me the
> current and index.
>
> I speak the pass-word primeval, I give the sign of democracy,
> By God! I will accept nothing which all cannot have their
> counterpart of on the same terms.
>
> Through me many long dumb voices,
> Voices of the interminable generations of prisoners and slaves,
> Voices of the diseas'd and despairing and of thieves and
> dwarfs,
> Voices of the threads that connect the stars, and of wombs
> and of the father-stuff,
> And of the rights of them the others are down upon,
> Of the deform'd, trivial, flat, foolish, despised,
> Fog in the air, beetles rolling balls of dung.

We can say of this astonishing chant that as completing synecdoche it verges on emptying-out metonymy, reminding us of the instability of all tropes and of all psychic defenses. Primarily, Whitman's defense in this passage is a fantasy reversal, in which his own fear of contact with other selves is so turned that no outward overthrow of his separateness is possible. It is as though he were denying denial, negating negation, by absorbing every outward self, every outcast of society, history, and even of nature. To say that one will accept nothing which all cannot have their counterpart of on the same terms is indeed to say that one will accept no overthrow from outside oneself, no negation or denial. Whitman, with the genius of his enormous drive towards antithetical completion, can be judged to end the *tessera* phase of his poem in the remarkable triad of sections 25–27. For

in section 25, nature strikes back against the poet, yet he is strong enough
to sustain himself, but in 26–27 hie exhaustedly begins to undergo a kind
of passive slide-down of spirit that precludes the fierce *kenosis* or emptying-
out of his poethood in sections 28–30. At the end of 27, Whitman confesses: "To touch my person to some one else's is about as much as I can
stand." The Whitmanian *kenosis*, in 28–30, appears to make of masturbation a metonymic reduction of the self, where touch substitutes for the
whole being, and a pathetic salvation is sought through an exaltation of the
earth that the poet has moistened:

> A minute and a drop of me settle my brain,
> I believe the soggy clods shall become lovers and lamps,
> And a compend of compends is the meat of a man or woman,
> And a summit and flower there is the feeling they have for
>      each other,
> And they are to branch boundlessly out of that lesson
>      until it becomes omnific,
> And until one and all shall delight us, and we them.

This is the prelude to the most awesome repression in our literature,
the greatest instance yet of the American Sublime, sections 31–38. Rather
than map the glories of this Sublime, I will examine instead the violent
descent into the abyss that culminates it in section 38. Having merged both
the fathering force and the universal brotherhood into himself, with terrifying eloquence ("I am the man, I suffer'd, I was there"; and "Agonies are
one of my changes of garments"), Whitman pays the fearful price of
Emersonian Compensation. Nothing indeed is gotten for nothing:

> Enough! enough! enough!
> Somehow I have been stunn'd. Stand back!
> Give me a little time beyond my cuff'd head, slumbers,
> dreams,
>      gaping,
> I discover myself on the verge of a usual mistake.
> That I could forget the mockers and insults!
> That I could forget the trickling tears and the blows of the
>      bludgeons and hammers!
> That I could look with a separate look on my own crucifixion
>      and bloody crossing.
> I remember now,
> I resume the overstaid fraction,

The grave of rock multiplies what has been confided to it, or to
     any graves,
Corpses rise, gashes heal, fastenings roll from me.

Emerson had prophesied a Central Man who would reverse the
"great Defeat" of Christ, insisting that "we demand Victory." Whitman,
more audacious even than his precursor, dares to present himself both as
a repetition of the great Defeat and as the Victory of a Resurrection: "I
troop forth replenish'd with supreme power, one of an average unending
procession." What are we to do with a hyperbolical Sublime this outrageous? Whitman too is saying: "*I and the Abyss*," despite the self-deception
of that "average unending procession." But Whitman's repression is
greater, as it has to be, since a crucial part of its anteriority is a primal fixation upon Emerson, a fixation that I want to explore in the conclusion of
this chapter once I have concluded my sketchy mapping of the later ratios
in *Song of Myself*.

Sections 39–49 are an attempt at a sublimating consolidation of the
self, in which Whitman presents us with his version of the most characteristic of High Romantic metaphors, his self as inside reciprocally address-
ing the natural world as a supposedly answering outside. The final or
reductive form of this perspectivizing is summed up in an appropriately
entitled poem of Wallace Stevens, *The American Sublime*:

But how does one feel?
One grows used to the weather,

The landscape and that;
And the sublime comes down
To the spirit itself,

The spirit and space,
The empty spirit
In vacant space.

That is to say: the Sublime comes down to the Abyss in me inhabit-
ing the Abyss of space. Whitman's version of this coming down completes
his great *askesis*, in section 49:

I hear you whispering there O stars of heaven,
O suns—O grass of graves—O perpetual transfers and
     promotions,

If you do not say any thing how can I say any thing?
. . . . . . . . . . . . . . . . . . . . . . . . . . . . . . . .
Of the turbid pool that lies in the autumn forest,
Of the moon that descends the steeps of the soughing twilight,
Toss, sparkles of day and dusk—toss on the black stems that
    decay in the muck,
Toss to the moaning gibberish of the dry limbs.

I ascend from the moon, I ascend from the night,
I perceive that the ghastly glimmer is noonday sunbeams
    reflected,
And debouch to the steady and central from the offspring
    great or small.

The steadiness of the central is reached here only through the rhetorical equivalent of sublimation, which is metaphor, the metaphor of two lights, sun and moon, with the sun necessarily dominating, and taking as its tenor the Emersonian "steady and central." I return to the formula for poetic sublimation ventured earlier in this discourse. The sublimating ratio is a limitation because what it concentrates is being evaded, that is, is remembered only in order not to be presented, with something else substituted in the presentation. Whitman does not present what he is remembering, his dream of divination, of being a dazzling sunrise greater than the merely natural sun. Instead of this autonomous splendor, he accepts now a perspectivizing, a balancing of "sparkles of day and dusk." His restitution For this *askesis* comes in his great poem's close, in sections 50–52, which form a miraculous transumption of all that has gone before. Yet the Whitmanian metaleptic reversal differs crucially from the Wordsworthian–Tennysonian model, in that it places the burden upon the reader, rather than upon the poet. It is the reader, and not the poet, who is challenged directly to make his belatedness into an earliness. Whitman was to perfect this challenge in *Crossing Brooklyn Ferry*, appropriately called *Sun-Down Poem* when it first appeared in the second *Leaves of Grass*, in 1856. Here, in *Song of Myself*, the challenge is made explicit at the close of section 51: "Will you speak before I am gone? will you prove already too late?" Nowhere in Emerson (and I concede to no reader in my fanatical love of Emerson) is there so strong a representation of the Central Man who is coming as there is in Whitman's self-presentation in section 52. I would select this as the greatest of Emerson's prophecies of the Central Man, from the journals, April 1846:

He or That which in despair of naming aright, some have called the *Newness*,—as the Hebrews did not like to pronounce the word,—he lurks, he hides, he who is success, reality, joy, power,—that which constitutes Heaven, which reconciles impossibilities, atones for shortcomings, expiates sins or makes them virtues, buries in oblivion the crowded historical past, sinks religions, philosophies, nations, persons to legends; reverses the scale of opinion, of fame; reduces sciences to opinion, and makes the thought of the moment the key to the universe, and the egg of history to come.

... 'Tis all alike,—astronomy, metaphysics, sword, spade, pencil, or instruments and arts yet to be invented,—this is the inventor, the worth-giver, the worth. This is He that shall come; or, if He come not, nothing comes: He that disappears in the moment when we go to celebrate Him. If we go to burn those that blame our celebration, He appears in them. The Divine Newness. Hoe and spade, sword and pen, cities, pictures, gardens, laws, bibles, are prized only because they were means he sometimes used. So with astronomy, music, arithmetic, castes, feudalism,—we kiss with devotion these hems of his garment,—we mistake them for Him; they crumble to ashes on our lips.

The Newness is Influx, or fresh repression, lurking and hiding, imaged in depth, in burying and in sinking. This daemonic force then projects the past and introjects the future, and yet *not now*, but only in the realm of what *shall come*: "He ... disappears in the moment when we go to celebrate Him," and more than his garment would crumble to ashes on our lips. Whitman, as this Newness, is even more splendidly elusive:

The spotted hawk swoops by and accuses me, he complains of my gab and my loitering.

I too am not a bit tamed, I too am untranslatable,
I sound my barbaric yawp over the roofs of the world.

The last scud of day holds back for me,
It flings my likeness after the rest and true as any on the
    shadow'd wilds,
It coaxes me to the vapor and the dusk.

I depart as air, I shake my white locks at the runaway sun,
I effuse my flesh in eddies, and drift it in lacy jags.

I bequeath myself to the dirt to grow from the grass I love,
If you want me again look for me under your boot-soles.

You will hardly know who I am or what I mean,
But I shall be good health to you nevertheless,
And filter and fibre your blood.

Failing to fetch me at first keep encouraged,
Missing me one place search another,
I stop somewhere waiting for you.

The hawk accuses Whitman of belatedness, of "loitering," but the poet is one with the hawk, "untranslatable" in that his desire is perpetual, always transcending act. There, in the twilight, Whitman arrests the lateness of the day, dissolving the presentness of the present, and effusing his own presence until it is air and earth. As the atmosphere we are to breathe, the ground we are to walk, the poet introjects our future, and is somewhere up ahead, waiting for us to catch up. So far ahead is he on our mutual quest, that he can afford to stop, though he will not tell us precisely where. His dominant trope remains the grass, but this trope is now transumptive, for it is grass not yet grown but "to grow." Implicit in such a trope is the more-than-Emersonian promise that this Central Man will not disappear "in the moment when we go to celebrate him."

I end by returning to Whitman's American Sublime of sections 31–38, with specific reference to the grand march of section 33, where the poet says: "I am afoot with my vision." Here is a part of this audacious mounting into the Sublime:

Solitary at midnight in my back yard, my thoughts gone from
    me a long while,
Walking the old hills of Judaea with the beautiful, gentle God
    by my side,
Speeding through space, speeding through heaven and the
    stars,
Speeding amid the seven satellites and the broad ring, and the
    diameter of eighty thousands miles,
Speeding with tail'd meteors, throwing fire-balls like the rest,

Carrying the crescent child that carries its own full mother in
    its belly,

Storming, enjoying, planning, loving, cautioning,
Backing and filling, appearing and disappearing,
I tread day and night such roads.

I visit the orchards of spheres and look at the product,
And look at quintillions ripen'd and look at quintillions green.

I fly those flights of a fluid and swallowing soul,
My course runs below the soundings of plummets.

I help myself to material and immaterial,
No guard can shut me off, no law prevent me.

As an hyperbolical progression, this sequence is matched only by its
misprision or sublime parody, the flight of the Canon Aspirin in *Notes
toward a Supreme Fiction*. Whitman's angelic flight breaks down the distinction between material and immaterial, because his soul, as he precisely
says, is "fluid and swallowing." Similarly, the Canon's angelic flight breaks
down the limits between fact and thought, but the Canon's soul being
more limited, the later angelic flight fails exactly where Whitman's cannot
fail. The Canon imposes orders upon reality, but Whitman discovers or
uncovers orders, because he is discovering himself (even though he does
not uncover himself, despite his constant assertions that he is about to do
so). I vary an earlier question in order to conclude this discourse. Why is
Whitman's American Sublime larger and stronger than either the Sublime
of his precursor, Emerson, or the Sublime of his ephebe, Stevens? In the
language of misprision, this means: why and how is Whitman's poetic
repression greater and more forceful than that of the other major figures
in his own tradition?

Whitman's ego, in his most Sublime transformations, wholly absorbs
and thus pragmatically forgets the fathering force, and presents instead the
force of the son, of his own self or, in Whitman's case, perhaps we should
say of his own selves. Where Emerson *urges* forgetfulness of anteriority,
Whitman more strenuously *does* forget it, though at a considerable cost.
Emerson says: "*I and the Abyss*"; Whitman says: "*The Abyss of Myself*." The
second statement is necessarily more Sublime and, alas, even more
American.

# Leo Tolstoy

## (1828–1910)

*War and Peace*

TOLSTOY, AS BEFITS THE WRITER SINCE SHAKESPEARE WHO MOST HAS THE art of the actual, combines in his representational praxis the incompatible powers of the two strongest ancient authors, the poet of the *Iliad* and the original teller of the stories of Abraham, Jacob, Joseph, and Moses in *Genesis* and *Exodus*. Perhaps it was because he was closer both to Homer and the Yahwist that Tolstoy was so outrageous a critic of Shakespeare. Surely no other reader of Shakespeare ever has found *Hamlet*, *Macbeth*, and *King Lear* tedious and offensive. Why Tolstoy could accept the *Iliad*'s morality, and not *Hamlet*'s, is a profound puzzle, since Hamlet has more in common with Joseph or with the David of 2 Samuel than he does with Achilles or Hector. I surmise that Tolstoy, despite himself, owed too much to Shakespearean representation, and could not bear to acknowledge the inevitable debt. Prince Andrew has more of Hotspur than of Lord Byron in him, and even Pierre, in his comic aspects, reflects the Shakespearean rather than the Homeric or biblical naturalism. If your characters change less because of experience than by listening to themselves reflect upon their relation to experience, then you are another heir of Shakespeare's innovations in mimesis, even if you insist passionately that your sense of reality is morally centered while Shakespeare's was not.

Shakespeare and Tolstoy had the Bible rather than the *Iliad* in common, and the Shakespearean drama that most should have offended Tolstoy was *Troilus and Cressida*. Alas, *King Lear* achieved that bad eminence, while only Falstaff, rather surprisingly, convinced Tolstoy. But then the effect of the greatest writers upon one another can be very odd. Writing in 1908, Henry James associated *War and Peace* with Thackeray's *The Newcomes* and

Dumas's *The Three Musketeers*, since all these were "large loose baggy monsters, with ... queer elements of the accidental and the arbitrary." Twenty years earlier, James had a vision of Tolstoy as "a monster harnessed to his great subject—all human life!—as an elephant might be harnessed, for purposes of traction, not to a carriage, but to a coach-house."

James's demand for "an absolutely premeditated art" might seem to collide with Tolstoy's notorious polemic, *What is Art?*, but that is merely an illusion. Even in translation, Tolstoy is clearly a writer who transcends James *as an artist*, even as Homer overgoes Virgil and Shakespeare dwarfs Ben Jonson. The representation of persons in *War and Peace* has the authority and the mastery of what we are compelled to call the real that Tolstoy shares with only a few: Homer, the Bible, Dante, Chaucer, Shakespeare, Cervantes, perhaps Proust. Philip Rahv remarked memorably upon "the critic's euphoria in the Tolstoyan weather." The best word there is "weather." *War and Peace*, like our cosmos, has weather, but no one would want to say that Tolstoy, like the High Romantics or Dostoevsky, had created a heterocosm. You suffer and die, or joy and live, on our earth in Tolstoy, and not in a visionary realm.

The Marxist critic Lukács reluctantly conceded that in certain moments Tolstoy broke through to "a clearly differentiated, concrete and existent world, which, if it could spread out into a totality, would be completely inaccessible to the categories of the novel and would require a new form of artistic creation: the form of the renewed epic." Lukács denied that Tolstoy could accomplish this as a totality, but his ideology made him less than generous towards Tolstoy. A short novel like *Hadji Murad* certainly is such a totality, but the thirteen hundred pages of *War and Peace*, granted the impossibility of an absolute totality at such a length, also gives us "a clearly differentiated, concrete and existent world." Tolstoy does what a nineteenth-century novelist ought not to be able to do: he reveals aspects of our ordinary reality that we could never see if he had not seen them first. Dickens and Balzac render an extraordinary phantasmagoria that we are eager to absorb into reality, but Tolstoy, more like Shakespeare than he could bear to know, persuades us that the imitation of what seems to be essential nature is more than enough.

Shakespeare is inexhaustible to analysis, partly because his rhetorical art is nearly infinite. Tolstoy scarcely yields to analysis at all, because his rhetoric evidently also gives the effect of the natural. You have to brood on the balance of determinism and free will in Tolstoy's personages because he insists that this is your proper work, but you are too carried along by the force of his narrative and the inevitability of his characters' modes of speaking and thinking to question either the structure of plot or the individual images of voice that inhabit the story. If James and Flaubert and Joyce, the three together, are to be considered archetypes of the novelist, then Tolstoy seems something else, larger and more vital, for which we may lack a name, since Lukács was doubtless correct when he insisted that "the great epic is a form bound to the historical moment," and that moment was neither Tolstoy's nor ours.

## II

W. Gareth Jones emphasizes that *War and Peace* is not so much a single narrative related by Tolstoy but a network of many narratives, addressed to us as though each of us were Prince Andrew, receptive and dispassionate. Perhaps that is Andrew's prime function in the novel, to serve as an ideal model for the Tolstoyan reader, even as Pierre perhaps becomes at last the ideal Tolstoyan storyteller. Isaiah Berlin and Martin Price both have illuminated the way that Tolstoy's heroes win through to serenity by coming to accept "the permanent relationships of things and the universal texture of human life," as Berlin phrases it. If that seems not wholly adequate to describe the changed Pierre of book fifteen, the cause is Tolstoy's preternaturally natural strength and not the weakness of his best critics. How can a critic convey either the cognitive wisdom or the restrained yet overwhelming pathos that is manifested in Tolstoy's account of the meeting between Pierre and Natásha at Princess Mary's when Pierre returns to Moscow after his liberation and imprisonment, and subsequent illness and recovery? It is difficult to conceive of an art subtler than Tolstoy exercises in Pierre's realisation that Princess Mary's mourning companion is Natásha, and that he is in love with Natásha:

> In a rather low room lit by one candle sat the princess and with her another person dressed in black. Pierre remembered that the princess always had lady companions, but who they were and what they were like he never knew or remembered. "This must be one of her companions," he thought, glancing at the lady in the black dress.
>
> The princess rose quickly to meet him and held out her hand. "Yes," she said, looking at his altered face after he had kissed her hand, "so this is how we meet again. He often spoke of you even at the very last," she went on, turning her eyes from Pierre to her companion with a shyness that surprised him for an instant.
>
> "I was so glad to hear of your safety. It was the first piece of good news we had received for a long time."

Again the princess glanced round at her companion with even more uneasiness in her manner and was about to add something, but Pierre interrupted her.

"Just imagine—I knew nothing about him!" said he. "I thought he had been killed. All I know I heard at second hand from others. I only know that he fell in with the Rostóvs.... What a strange coincidence!"

Pierre spoke rapidly and with animation. He glanced once at the companion's face, saw her attentive and kindly gaze fixed on him, and, as often happens when one is talking, felt somehow that this companion in the black dress was a good, kind, excellent creature who would not hinder his conversing freely with Princess Mary.

But when he mentioned the Rostóvs, Princess Mary's face expressed still greater embarrassment. She again glanced rapidly from Pierre's face to that of the lady in the black dress and said: "Do you really not recognize her?"

Pierre looked again at the companion's pale, delicate face with its black eyes and peculiar mouth, and something near to him, long forgotten and more than sweet, looked at him from those attentive eyes.

"But no, it can't be!" he thought. "This stern, thin, pale face that looks so much older! It cannot be she. It merely reminds me of her. But at that moment Princess Mary said, "Natásha!" And with difficulty, effort, and stress, like the opening of a door grown rusty on its hinges, a smile appeared on the face with the attentive eyes, and from that opening door came a breath of fragrance which suffused Pierre with a happiness he had long forgotten and of which he had not even been thinking—especially at that moment. It suffused him, seized him, and enveloped him completely. When she smiled doubt was no longer possible, it was Natásha and he loved her.

Massively simple, direct, realistic, as this is, it is also, in its full context, with the strength of the vast novel behind it, an absolutely premeditated art. Henry James is not one of the great literary critics, despite the idolatry of his admirers. Tolstoy, Dickens, and Walt Whitman bear not the slightest resemblance to what James saw them as being, though the old James repented on the question of Whitman. If the highest art after all catches us unaware, even as we and Pierre together learn the secret and meaning of his life in this central moment, then no novelistic art, not even that of Proust, can surpass Tolstoy's. "Great works of art are only great because they are accessible and comprehensible to everyone." That rugged Tolstoyan principle is certainly supported by this moment, but we cannot forget that Lear and Gloucester conversing, one mad and the other blind, is not accessible and comprehensible to everyone, and touches the limits of art as even Tolstoy does not. It is a sadness that Tolstoy could not or would not accommodate the transcendental and extraordinary in *King Lear*, *Macbeth*, and *Hamlet*, and yet did not resist the biblical story of Joseph and his brothers, or the strife of Achilles and Hector. The Tolstoyan rejection of Shakespeare may be, however twisted askew, the most formidable tribute that Shakespeare's powers of representation have ever received.

# Marcel Proust

## (1871-1922)

*In Search of Lost Time*

SEXUAL JEALOUSY IS THE MOST NOVELISTIC OF CIRCUMSTANCES, JUST AS incest, according to Shelley, is the most poetical of circumstances. Proust is the novelist of our era, even as Freud is our moralist. Both are speculative thinkers, who divide between them the eminence of being the prime wisdom writers of the age.

Proust died in 1922, the year of Freud's grim and splendid essay, "Certain Neurotic Mechanisms in Jealousy, Paranoia, and Homosexuality." Both of them great ironists, tragic celebrants of the comic spirit, Proust and Freud are not much in agreement on jealousy, paranoia, and homosexuality, though both start with the realization that all of us are bisexual in nature.

Freud charmingly begins his essay by remarking that jealousy, like grief, is normal and comes in three stages: *competitive*, or normal, *projected*, *delusional*. The *competitive*, or garden variety, is compounded of grief, due to the loss of the loved object, and of the reactivation of the narcissistic scar, the tragic first loss, by the infant, of the parent of the other sex to the parent of the same sex. As normal, *competitive* jealousy is really normal Hell, Freud genially throws into the compound such delights as enmity against the successful rival, some self-blaming, self-criticism, and a generous portion of bisexuality.

*Projected* jealousy attributes to the erotic partner one's own actual unfaithfulness or repressed impulses, and is cheerfully regarded by Freud as being relatively innocuous, since its almost delusional character is highly amenable to analytic exposure of unconscious fantasies. But *delusional* jealousy proper is more serious; it also takes its origin in repressed impulses towards infidelity, but the object of those impulses is of one's own sex, and this, for Freud, moves one across the border into paranoia.

What the three stages of jealousy have in common is a bisexual component, since even *projected* jealousy trades in repressed impulses, and these include homosexual desires. Proust, our other authority on jealousy, preferred to call homosexuality "inversion," and in a brilliant mythological fantasia traced the sons of Sodom and the daughters of Gomorrah to the surviving exiles from the Cities of the Plain. Inversion and jealousy, so intimately related in Freud, become in Proust a dialectical pairing, with the aesthetic sensibility linked to both as a third term in a complex series.

On the topos of jealousy, Proust is fecund and generous; no writer has devoted himself so lovingly and brilliantly to expounding and illustrating the emotion, except of course Shakespeare in *Othello* and Hawthorne in *The Scarlet Letter*. Proust's jealous lovers—Swann, Saint-Loup, above all Marcel himself—suffer so intensely that we sometimes need to make an effort not to empathize too closely. It is difficult to determine just what Proust's stance towards their suffering is, partly because Proust's ironies are both pervasive and cunning. Comedy hovers nearby, but even tragicomedy seems an inadequate term for the compulsive sorrows of Proust's protagonists. Swann, after complimenting himself that he has not, by his jealousy, proved to Odette that he loves her too much, falls into the mouth of Hell:

> He never spoke to her of this misadventure, and ceased even to think of it himself. But now and then his thoughts in their wandering course would come upon this memory where it lay unobserved, would startle it into life, thrust it forward into his consciousness, and leave him aching with a sharp, deep-rooted pain. As though it were a bodily pain, Swann's mind was powerless to alleviate it; but at least, in the case of bodily pain, since it is independent of the mind, the mind can dwell upon it, can note that it has diminished, that it has momentarily ceased. But in this case the mind, merely by recalling the pain, created it afresh. To determine not to think of it was to think of it still, to suffer from it still. And when, in conversation with his friends, he forgot about it, suddenly a word casually uttered would make him change countenance like a wounded man when a clumsy hand has touched his aching limb. When he came away from Odette he was happy, he felt calm, he recalled her smiles, of gentle mockery when speaking of this or that other person, of tenderness for himself; he recalled the gravity of her head which she seemed to have lifted from its axis to let it droop and fall, as though in spite of herself, upon his lips, as she had done on the first evening in the carriage, the languishing looks she

had given him as she lay in his arms, nestling her head against her shoulder as though shrinking from the cold.

But then at once his jealousy, as though it were the shadow of his love, presented him with the complement, with the converse of that new smile with which she had greeted him that very evening—and which now, perversely, mocked Swann and shone with love for another—of that droop of the head, now sinking on to other lips, of all the marks of affection (now given to another) that she had shown to him. And all the voluptuous memories which he bore away from her house were, so to speak, but so many sketches, rough plans like those which a decorator submits to one, enabling Swann to form an idea of the various attitudes, aflame or faint with passion, which she might adopt for others. With the result that he came to regret every pleasure that he tasted in her company, every new caress of which he had been so imprudent as to point out to her the delights, every fresh charm that he found in her, for he knew that, a moment later, they would go to enrich the collection of instruments in his secret torture-chamber.

Jealousy here is a pain experienced by Freud's bodily ego, on the frontier between psyche and body: "To determine not to think of it was to think of it still, to suffer from it still." As the shadow of love, jealousy resembles the shadow cast by the earth up into the heavens, where by tradition it ought to end at the sphere of Venus. Instead, it darkens there, and since the shadow is Freud's reality principle, or our consciousness of our own mortality, Proust's dreadfully persuasive irony is that jealousy exposes not only the arbitrariness of every erotic object-choice but also marks the passage of the loved person into a teleological overdetermination, in which the supposed inevitability of the person is simply a mask for the inevitability of the lover's death. Proust's jealousy thus becomes peculiarly akin to Freud's death drive, since it, too, quests beyond the pleasure/unpleasure principle. Our secret torture-chamber is furnished anew by every recollection of the beloved's erotic prowess, since what delighted us has delighted others.

Swann experiences the terrible conversion of the jealous lover into a parody of the scholar, a conversion to an intellectual pleasure that is more a deviation than an achievement, since no thought can be emancipated from the sexual past of all thought (Freud), if the search for truth is nothing but a search for the sexual past:

Certainly he suffered as he watched that light, in whose golden atmosphere, behind the closed sash, stirred the unseen and detested pair, as he
listened to that murmur which revealed the presence of the man who had
crept in after his own departure, the perfidy of Odette, and the pleasures
which she was at that moment enjoying with the stranger. And yet he was
not sorry he had come; the torment which had forced him to leave his own
house had become less acute now that it had become less vague, now that
Odette's other life, of which he had had, at that first moment, a sudden
helpless suspicion, was definitely there, in the full glare of the lamp-light,
almost within his grasp, an unwitting prisoner in that room into which,
when he chose, he would force his way to seize it unawares; or rather he
would knock on the shutters, as he often did when he came very late, and
by that signal Odette would at least learn that he knew, that he had seen
the light and had heard the voices, and he himself, who a moment ago had
been picturing her as laughing with the other at his illusions, now it was he
who saw them, confident in their error, tricked by none other than himself, whom they believed to be far away but who was there, in person, there
with a plan, there with the knowledge that he was going, in another
minute, to knock on the shutter. And perhaps the almost pleasurable sensation he felt at that moment was something more than the assuagement
of a doubt, and of a pain: was an intellectual pleasure. If, since he had fall-
en in love, things had recovered a little of the delightful interest that they
had had for him long ago—though only in so far as they were illuminated
by the thought or the memory of Odette—now it was another of the faculties of his studious youth that his jealousy revived, the passion for truth,
but for a truth which, too, was interposed between himself and his mistress, receiving its light from her alone, a private and personal truth the
sole object of which (an infinitely precious object, and one almost disinterested in its beauty) was Odette's life, her actions, her environment, her
plans, her past. At every other period in his life, the little everyday activi-
ties of another person had always seemed meaningless to Swann; if gossip
about such things was repeated to him, he would dismiss it as insignificant,
and while he listened it was only the lowest, the most commonplace part
of his mind that was engaged; these were the moments when he felt at his
most inglorious. But in this strange phase of love the personality of another person becomes so enlarged, so deepened, that the curiosity which he
now felt stirring inside him with regard to the smallest details of a woman's
daily life, was the same thirst for knowledge with which he had once studied history. And all manner of actions from which hitherto he would have
recoiled in shame, such as spying, to-night, outside a window, to-morrow
perhaps, for all he knew, putting adroitly provocative questions to casual

witnesses, bribing servants, listening at doors, seemed to him now to be precisely on a level with the deciphering of manuscripts, the weighing of evidence, the interpretation of old monuments—so many different methods of scientific investigation with a genuine intellectual value and legitimately employable in the search for truth.

In fact, poor Swann is at the wrong window, and the entire pasage is therefore as exquisitely painful as it is comic. What Freud ironically called the overevaluation of the object, the enlargement or deepening of the beloved's personality, begins to work not as one of the enlargements of life (like Proust's own novel) but as the deepening of a personal Hell. Swann plunges downwards and outwards, as he leans "in impotent, blind, dizzy anguish over the bottomless abyss" and reconstructs the petty details of Odette's past life with "as much passion as the aesthete who ransacks the extant documents of fifteenth-century Florence in order to penetrate further into the soul of the Primavera, the fair Vanna or the Venus of Botticelli."

The historicizing aesthete, John Ruskin, say, or Walter Pater, becomes the archetype of the jealous lover, who searches into lost time not for a person, but for an epiphany or moment-of-moments, a privileged fiction of duration:

> When he had been paying social calls Swann would often come home with little time to spare before dinner. At that point in the evening, around six o'clock, when in the old days he used to feel so wretched, he no longer asked himself what Odette might be about, and was hardly at all concerned to hear that she had people with her or had gone out. He recalled at times that he had once, years ago, tried to read through its envelope a letter addressed by Odette to Forcheville. But this memory was not pleasing to him, and rather than plumb the depths of shame that he felt in it he preferred to indulge in a little grimace, twisting up the corners of his mouth and adding, if need be, a shake of the head which signified "What do I care about it?" True, he considered now that the hypothesis on which he had often dwelt at that time, according to which it was his jealous imagination alone that blackened what was in reality the innocent life of Odette—that this hypothesis (which after all was beneficent, since, so long as his amorous malady had lasted, it had diminished his sufferings by making them seem imaginary) was not the correct one, that it was his jealousy that had seen

things in the correct light, and that if Odette had loved him more than he supposed, she had also deceived him more. Formerly, while his sufferings were still keen, he had vowed that, as soon as he had ceased to love Odette and was no longer afraid either of vexing her or of making her believe that he loved her too much, he would give himself the satisfaction of elucidating with her, simply from his love of truth and as a point of historical interest, whether or not Forcheville had been in bed with her that day when he had rung her bell and rapped on her window in vain, and she had written to Forcheville that it was an uncle of hers who had called. But this so interesting problem, which he was only waiting for his jealousy to subside before clearing up, had precisely lost all interest in Swann's eyes when he had ceased to be jealous. Not immediately, however. Long after he had ceased to feel any jealousy with regard to Odette, the memory of that day, that afternoon spent knocking vainly at the little house in the Rue La Pérouse, had continued to torment him. It was as though his jealousy, not dissimilar in that respect from those maladies which appear to have their seat, their centre of contagion, less in certain persons than in certain places, in certain houses, had had for its object not so much Odette herself as that day, that hour in the irrevocable past when Swann had knocked at every entrance to her house in turn, as though that day, that hour alone had caught and preserved a few last fragments of the amorous personality which had once been Swann's, that there alone could he now recapture them. For a long time now it had been a matter of indifference to him whether Odette had been, or was being, unfaithful to him. And yet he had continued for some years to seek out old servants of hers, to such an extent had the painful curiosity persisted in him to know whether on that day, so long ago, at six o'clock, Odette had been in bed with Forcheville. Then that curiosity itself had disappeared, without, however, his abandoning his investigations. He went on trying to discover what no longer interested him, because his old self, though it had shrivelled to extreme decrepitude, still acted mechanically, in accordance with preoccupations so utterly abandoned that Swann could not now succeed even in picturing to himself that anguish—so compelling once that he had been unable to imagine that he would ever be delivered from it, that only the death of the woman he loved (though death, as will be shown later on in this story by a cruel corroboration, in no way diminishes the sufferings caused by jealousy) seemed to him capable of smoothing the path of his life which then seemed impassably obstructed.

Jealousy dies with love, but only with respect to the former beloved. Horribly a life-in-death, jealousy renews itself like the moon, perpetually trying to discover what no longer interests it, even after the object of desire has been literally buried. Its true object is "that day, that hour in the irrevocable past," and even that time was less an actual time than a temporal fiction, an episode in the evanescence of one's own self. Paul de Man's perspective that Proust's deepest insight is the nonexistence of the self founds itself upon this temporal irony of unweaving, this permanent parabasis of meaning. One can remember that even this deconstructive perspective is no more or less privileged than any other Proustian trope, and so cannot give us a truth that Proust himself evades.

## II

The bridge between Swann's jealousy and Marcel's is Saint-Loup's jealousy of Rachel, summed up by Proust in one of his magnificently long, baroque paragraphs:

Saint-Loup's letter had come as no surprise to me, even though I had had no news of him since, at the time of my grandmother's illness, he had accused me of perfidy and treachery. I had grasped at once what must have happened. Rachel, who liked to provoke his jealousy (she also had other causes for resentment against me), had persuaded her lover that I had made sly attempts to have relations with her in his absence. It is probable that he continued to believe in the truth of this allegation, but he had ceased to be in love with her, which meant that its truth or falsehood had become a matter of complete indifference to him, and our friendship alone remained. When, on meeting him again, I tried to talk to him about his accusations, he merely gave me a benign and affectionate smile which seemed to be a sort of apology, and then changed the subject. All this was not to say that he did not, a little later, see Rachel occasionally when he was in Paris. Those who have played a big part in one's life very rarely disappear from it suddenly for good. They return to it at odd moments (so much so that people suspect a renewal of old love) before leaving it for ever. Saint-Loup's breach with Rachel had very soon become less painful to him, thanks to the soothing pleasure that was given him by her incessant demands for money. Jealousy, which prolongs the course of love, is not capable of containing many more ingredients than the other products of the imagination. If one takes with one, when one starts on a journey, three or four images which incidentally one is sure to lose on the way (such as the lilies and anemones heaped on the Ponte Vecchio, or the Persian church shrouded in mist), one's trunk is already pretty full. When one leaves a mistress, one would be just as glad, until one had begun to forget her, that she should not become the property of three or four potential protectors whom one pictures in one's mind's eye, of whom, that is to say, one is jealous: all those whom one does not so picture count for nothing. Now frequent demands for money from a cast-off mistress no more give one a complete idea of her life than charts showing a high temperature would of her illness. But the latter would at any rate be an indication that she was ill, and the former furnish a presumption, vague enough it is true, that the forsaken one or forsaker (whichever she be) cannot have found anything very remarkable in the way of rich protectors. And so each demand is welcomed with the joy which a lull produces in the jealous one's sufferings, and answered with the immediate dispatch of money, for naturally one does not like to think of her being in want of anything except lovers (one of the three lovers one has in one's mind's eye), until time has enabled one to regain one's composure and to learn one's successor's name without wilting. Sometimes Rachel came in so late at night that she could ask her former lover's permission to lie down beside him until the morning. This was a great comfort to Robert, for it reminded him how intimately, after all, they had lived together, simply to see that even if he took the greater part of the bed for himself it did not in the least interfere with her sleep. He realised that she was more comfortable, lying close to his familiar body, than she would have been elsewhere, that she felt herself by his side—even in an hotel—to be in a bedroom known of old in which one has one's habits, in which one sleeps better. He felt that his shoulders, his limbs, all of him, were for her, even when he was unduly restless from insomnia or thinking of the things he had to do, so entirely usual that they could not disturb her and that the perception of them added still further to her sense of repose.

The heart of this comes in the grandly ironic sentence: "Jealousy, which prolongs the course of love, is not capable of containing many more ingredients than the other products of the imagination." That is hardly a compliment to the capaciousness of the imagination, which scarcely can hold on for long to even three or four images. Saint-Loup, almost on the farthest shore of jealousy, has the obscure comfort of having become, for Rachel, one of those images not quite faded away, when "he felt that his shoulders, his limbs, all of him, were for her," even when he has ceased to be there, or anywhere, for her, or she for him. Outliving love, jealousy has become love's last stand, the final basis for a continuity between two former lovers.

Saint-Loup's bittersweet evanescence as a lover contrasts both with Swann's massive historicism and with the novel's triumphant representation of jealousy, Marcel's monumental search after lost time in the long aftermath of Albertine's death. Another grand link between magnificent jealousies is provided by Swann's observations to Marcel, aesthetic reflections somewhat removed from the pain of earlier realities:

> It occurred to me that Swann must be getting tired of waiting for me. Moreover I did not wish to be too late in returning home because of Albertine, and, taking leave of Mme de Surgis and M. de Charlus, I went in search of my invalid in the cardroom. I asked him whether what he had said to the Prince in their conversation in the garden was really what M. de Bréauté (whom I did not name) had reported to us, about a little play by Bergotte. He burst out laughing: "There's not a word of truth in it, not one, it's a complete fabrication and would have been an utterly stupid thing to say. It's really incredible, this spontaneous generation of falsehood. I won't ask who it was that told you, but it would be really interesting, in a field as limited as this, to work back from one person to another and find out how the story arose. Anyhow, what concern can it be of other people, what the Prince said to me? People are very inquisitive. I've never been inquisitive, except when I was in love, and when I was jealous. And a lot I ever learned! Are you jealous?" I told Swann that I had never experienced jealousy, that I did not even know what it was. "Well, you can count yourself lucky. A little jealousy is not too unpleasant, for two reasons. In the first

place, it enables people who are not inquisitive to take an interest in the lives of others, or of one other at any rate. And then it makes one feel the pleasure of possession, of getting into a carriage with a woman, of not allowing her to go about by herself. But that's only in the very first stages of the disease, or when the cure is almost complete. In between, it's the most agonising torment. However, I must confess that I haven't had much experience even of the two pleasures I've mentioned— the first because of my own nature, which is incapable of sustained reflexion; the second because of circumstances, because of the woman, I should say the women, of whom I've been jealous. But that makes no difference. Even when one is no longer attached to things, it's still something to have been attached to them; because it was always for reasons which other people didn't grasp. The memory of those feelings is something that's to be found only in ourselves; we must go back into ourselves to look at it. You mustn't laugh at this idealistic jargon, but what I mean to say is that I've been very fond of life and very fond of art. Well, now that I'm a little too weary to live with other people, those old feelings, so personal and individual, that I had in the past, seem to me—it's the mania of all collectors—very precious. I open my heart to myself like a sort of showcase, and examine one by one all those love affairs of which the rest of the world can have known nothing. And of this collection, to which I'm now even more attached than to my others, I say to myself, rather as Mazarin said of his books, but in fact without the least distress, that it will be very tiresome to have to leave it all. But, to come back to my conversation with the Prince, I shall tell one person only, and that person is going to be you.

We are in the elegy season, ironically balanced between the death of jealousy in Swann and its birth in poor Marcel, who literally does not know that the descent into Avernus beckons. When the vigor of an affirmation has more power than its probability, clearly we are living in a fiction, the metaphor or transference that we call love, and might call jealousy. Into that metaphor, Marcel moves like a sleepwalker, with his obsessions central to *The Captive* and insanely pervasive in *The Fugitive*. A great passage in *The Captive*, which seems a diatribe against jealousy, instead is a passionately ironic celebration of jealousy's aesthetic victory over our merely temporal happiness:

However, I was still at the first stage of enlightenment with regard to Léa. I was not even aware whether Albertine knew her. No matter, it came to the same thing. I must at all costs prevent her from renewing this acquaintance or making the acquaintance of this stranger at the Trocadéro. I say that I did not know whether she knew Léa or not; yet I must in fact have learned this at Balbec, from Albertine herself. For amnesia obliterated from my mind as well as from Albertine's a great many of the statements that she had made to me. Memory, instead of being a duplicate, always present before one's eyes, of the various events of one's life, is rather a void from which at odd moments a chance resemblance enables one to resuscitate dead recollections; but even then there are innumerable little details which have not fallen into that potential reservoir of memory, and which will remain forever unverifiable. One pays no attention to anything that one does not connect with the real life of the woman one loves; one forgets immediately what she has said to one about such and such an incident or such and such people one does not know, and her expression while she was saying it. And so when, in due course, one's jealousy is aroused by these same people, and seeks to ascertain whether or not it is mistaken, whether it is indeed they who are responsible for one's mistress's impatience to go out, and her annoyance when one has prevented her from doing so by returning earlier than usual, one's jealousy, ransacking the past in search of a clue, can find nothing; always retrospective, it is like a historian who has to write the history of a period for which he has no documents; always belated, it dashes like an enraged bull to the spot where it will not find the dazzling, arrogant creature who is tormenting it and whom the crowd admire for his splendour and cunning. Jealousy thrashes around in the void, uncertain as we are in those dreams in which we are distressed because we cannot find in his empty house a person whom we have known well in life, but who here perhaps is another person and has merely borrowed the features of our friend, uncertain as we are even more after we awake when we seek to identify this or that detail of our dream. What was one's mistress's expression when she told one that? Did she not look happy, was she not actually whistling, a thing that she never does unless she has some amorous thought in her mind and finds one's presence importunate and irritating? Did she not tell one something that is contradicted by what she now affirms, that she knows or does not know such and such a person? One does not know, and one will never know; one searches desperately among the unsubstantial fragments of a dream, and all the time one's life with one's mistress goes on, a life that is oblivious of what may well be of importance to one, and attentive to what is perhaps of none, a life hagridden by people who have no real connexion with one, full of lapses of memory, gaps, vain anxieties, a life as illusory as a dream.

Thrashing about in the void of a dream in which a good friend perhaps is another person, jealousy becomes Spenser's Malbecco: "who quite / Forgot he was a man, and jealousy is hight." Yet making life "as illusory as a dream," hagridden by lapses and gaps, is Marcel's accomplishment, and Proust's art. One does not write an other-than-ironic diatribe against one's own art. Proust warily, but with the sureness of a great beast descending upon its helpless prey, approaches the heart of his vision of jealousy, his sense that the emotion is akin to what Freud named as the defense of isolation, in which all context is burned away and a dangerous present replaces all past and all future.

Sexual jealousy in Proust is accompanied by a singular obsessiveness in regard to questions of space and of time. The jealous lover, who, as Proust says, conducts researches comparable to those of the scholar, seeks in his inquiries every detail he can find as to the location and duration of each betrayal and infidelity. Why? Proust has a marvelous passage in *The Fugitive* volume of *Remembrance*:

> It is one of the faculties of jealousy to reveal to us the extent to which the reality of external facts and the sentiments of the heart are an unknown element which lends itself to endless suppositions. We imagine that we know exactly what things are and what people think, for the simple reason that we do not care about them. But as soon as we have a desire to know, as the jealous man has, then it becomes a dizzy kaleidoscope in which we can no longer distinguish anything. Had Albertine been unfaithful to me? With whom? In what house? On what day? On the day when she had said this or that to me, when I remembered that I had in the course of it said this or that? I could not tell. Nor did I know what her feelings were for me, whether they were inspired by self-interest or by affection. And all of a sudden I remembered some trivial incident, for instance

that Albertine had wished to go to Saint-Martin-le-Vêtu, saying that the name interested her, and perhaps simply because
she had made the acquaintance of some peasant girl who lived
there. But it was useless that Aimé should have informed me of
what he had learned from the woman at the baths, since
Albertine must remain eternally unaware that he had informed
me, the need to know having always been exceeded, in my love
for Albertine, by the need to show her that I knew; for this
broke down the partition of different illusions that stood
between us, without having ever had the result of making her
love me more, far from it. And now, since she was dead, the second of these needs had been amalgamated with the effect of the
first: the need to picture to myself the conversation in which I
would have informed her of what I had learned, as vividly as the
conversation in which I would have asked her to tell me what I
did not know; that is to say, to see her by my side, to hear her
answering me kindly, to see her cheeks become plump again,
her eyes shed their malice and assume an air of melancholy;
that is to say, to love her still and to forget the fury of my jealousy in the despair of my loneliness. The painful mystery of
this impossibility of ever making known to her what I had
learned and of establishing our relations upon the truth of what
I had only just discovered (and would not have been able, perhaps, to discover but for her death) substituted its sadness for
the more painful mystery of her conduct. What? To have so
desperately desired that Albertine—who no longer existed—
should know that I had heard the story of the baths! This again
was one of the consequences of our inability, when we have to
consider the fact of death, to picture to ourselves anything but
life. Albertine no longer existed; but to me she was the person
who had concealed from me that she had assignations with
women at Balbec, who imagined that she had succeeded in
keeping me in ignorance of them. When we try to consider
what will happen to us after our own death, is it not still our living self which we mistakenly project at that moment? And is it
much more absurd, when all is said, to regret that a woman
who no longer exists is unaware that we have learned what she
was doing six years ago than to desire that of ourselves, who
will be dead, the public shall still speak with approval a century hence? If there is more real foundation in the latter than in
the former case, the regrets of my retrospective jealousy

proceeded none the less from the same optical error as in other men the desire for posthumous fame. And yet, if this impression of the solemn finality of my separation from Albertine had momentarily supplanted my idea of her misdeeds, it only succeeded in aggravating them by bestowing upon them an irremediable character. I saw myself astray in life as on an endless beach where I was alone and where, in whatever direction I might turn, I would never meet her.

"The regrets of my retrospective jealousy proceeded none the less from the same optical error as in other men the desire for posthumous fame"—is that not as much Proust's negative credo as it is Marcel's? Those "other men" include the indubitable precursors, Flaubert and Baudelaire, and Proust himself as well. The aesthetic agon for immortality is an optical error, yet this is one of those errors about life that are necessary for life, as Nietzsche remarked, and is also one of those errors about art that is art. Proust has swerved away from Flaubert into a radical confession of error; the novel is creative envy, love is jealousy, jealousy is the terrible fear that there will not be enough space for oneself (including literary space), and that there never can be enough time for oneself, because death is the reality of one's life. A friend once remarked to me, at the very height of her own jealousy, that jealousy was nothing but a vision of two bodies on a bed, neither of which was one's own, where the hurt resided in the realization that one body ought to have been one's own. Bitter as the remark may have been, it usefully reduces the trope of jealousy to literal fears: where was one's body, where will it be, when will it not be? Our ego is always a bodily ego, Freud insisted, and jealousy joins the bodily ego and the drive as another frontier concept, another vertigo whirling between a desperate inwardness and the injustice of outwardness. Proust, like Freud, goes back after all to the prophet Jeremiah, that uncomfortable sage who proclaimed a new inwardness for his mother's people. The law is written upon our inward parts for Proust also, and the law is justice, but the god of law is a jealous god, though he is certainly not the god of jealousy.

Freud, in "The Passing of the Oedipus Complex," writing two years after Proust's death, set forth a powerful speculation as to the difference between the sexes, a speculation that Proust neither evades nor supports, and yet illuminates, by working out of the world that Freud knows only in the pure good of theory. Freud is properly tentative, but also adroitly forceful:

Here our material—for some reason we do not understand—becomes far more shadowy and incomplete. The female sex develops an Oedipus-complex, too, a super-ego and a latency period. May one ascribe to it also a phallic organization and a castration complex? The answer is in the affirmative, but it cannot be the same as in the boy. The feministic demand for equal rights between the sexes does not carry far here; the morphological difference must express itself in differences in the development of the mind. "Anatomy is Destiny," to vary a saying of Napoleon's. The little girl's clitoris behaves at first just like a penis, but by comparing herself with a boy playfellow the child perceives that she has "come off short," and takes this fact as ill-treatment and as a reason for feeling inferior. For a time she still consoles herself with the expectation that later, when she grows up, she will acquire just as big an appendage as a boy. Here the woman's "masculine complex" branches off. The female child does not understand her actual loss as a sex characteristic, but explains it by assuming that at some earlier date she had possessed a member which was just as big and which had later been lost by castration. She does not seem to extend this conclusion about herself to other grown women, but in complete accordance with the phallic phase she ascribes to them large and complete, that is, male, genitalia. The result is an essential difference between her and the boy, namely, that she accepts castration as an established fact, an operation already performed, whereas the boy dreads the possibility of its being performed.

The castration-dread being thus excluded in her case, there falls away a powerful motive towards forming the super-ego and breaking up the infantile genital organization. These changes seem to be due in the girl far more than in the boy to the results of educative influences, of external intimidation threatening the loss of love. The Oedipus-complex in the girl is far simpler, less equivocal, than that of the little possessor of a penis; in my experience it seldom goes beyond the wish to take the mother's place, the feminine attitude towards the father. Acceptance of the loss of a penis is not endured without some attempt at compensation. The girl passes over—by way of a symbolic analogy, one may say—from the penis to a child; her Oedipus-complex culminates in the desire, which is long cherished, to be given a child by her father as a present, to bear him a child. One has the impression that the Oedipus-complex is later gradually abandoned because this wish is never fulfilled.

The two desires, to possess a penis and to bear a child, remain powerfully charged with libido in the unconscious and help to prepare the woman's nature for its subsequent sex rôle. The comparative weakness of the sadistic component of the sexual instinct, which may probably be related to the penis-deficiency, facilitates the transformation of directly sexual trends into those inhibited in aim, feelings of tenderness. It must be confessed, however, that on the whole our insight into these processes of development in the girl is unsatisfying, shadowy and incomplete.

Anatomy is destiny in Proust also, but this is anatomy taken up into the mind, as it were. The exiles of Sodom and Gomorrah, more jealous even than other mortals, become monsters of time, yet heroes and heroines of time also. The Oedipus complex never quite passes, in Freud's sense of passing, either in Proust or in his major figures. Freud's castration complex, ultimately the dread of dying, is a metaphor for the same shadowed desire that Proust represents by the complex metaphor of jealousy. The jealous lover fears that he has been castrated, that his place in life has been taken, that true time is over for him. His only recourse is to search for lost time, in the hopeless hope that the aesthetic recovery of illusion and of experience alike, will deceive him in a higher mode than he fears to have been deceived in already.

# Thomas Mann

## (1875–1955)

THE GREATEST OF MODERN GERMAN LITERARY SCHOLARS, ERNST ROBERT Curtius, observed that European literature was a continuous tradition from Homer through Goethe, and became something else afterwards. Thomas Mann is part of that something else, which begins with Wordsworth and has not yet ended. Mann, too ironic to study the nostalgias, nevertheless was highly conscious of his lifelong agon with his true precursor, Goethe. It was a loving agon, though necessarily not lacking in dialectical and indeed ambivalent elements. From his essay on "Goethe and Tolstoy" (1922) through his remarkable triad of Goethe essays in the 1930s (on the man of letters, the "representative of the Bourgeois Age," and *Faust*) on to the "Fantasy on Goethe" of the 1950s, Mann never wearied of reimagining his great original. The finest of these reimaginings, the novel, *Lotte in Weimar*, was published in Stockholm in 1939. We know it in English as *The Beloved Returns*, and it is surely the most neglected of Mann's major fictions. Mann is renowned as the author of *The Magic Mountain*, the tetralogy *Joseph and His Brothers*, *Doctor Faustus*, *Death in Venice*, and *Felix Krull*, while even the early *Buddenbrooks* remains widely read. But *Lotte in Weimar*, after some initial success, seems to have become a story for specialists, at least in English-speaking countries. Perhaps this is because Goethe, who exported splendidly to Britain and America in the time of Carlyle and Emerson, now seems an untranslatable author. Or it may be that Goethe's spirit has not survived what happened in and through Germany from 1933 until 1945.

In his essay on *Faust*, Mann remarks that the poem depicts love as a devil's holiday. The meditation upon Goethe's career as a man of letters centers itself in a remarkable paragraph that is as much on Mann as on Goethe:

But this business of reproducing the outer world through the inner, which it re-creates after its own form and in its own way, never does, however much charm and fascination may emanate from it, quite satisfy or please the outer world. The reason is that the author's real attitude always has something of opposition in it, which is quite inseparable from his character. It is the attitude of the man of intellect towards the ponderous, stubborn, evil-minded human race, which always places the poet and writer in this particular position, moulding his character and temperament and so conditioning his destiny. "Viewed from the heights of reason," Goethe wrote, "all life looks like some malignant disease and the world like a madhouse." This is a characteristic utterance of the kind of man who writes: the expression of his smarting impatience with mankind. More of the same thing than one would suppose is to be found in Goethe's works: phrases about the "human pack" in general and his "dear Germans" in particular, typical of the specific irritability and aloofness I mean. For what are the factors that condition the life of the writer? They are twofold: perception and a feeling for form; both of these simultaneously. The strange thing is that for the poet they are one organic unity, in which the one implies, challenges, and draws out the other. This unity is, for him, mind, beauty, freedom—everything. Where it is not, there is vulgar human stupidity, expressing itself in lack of perception and imperviousness to beauty of form—nor can he tell you which of the two he finds the more irritating.

We would hardly know that this aesthetic stance is that of Goethe rather than Flaubert, of Mann rather than T.S. Eliot. It seems Mann's shrewd warning to us is that the true man or woman of letters always exists in opposition to the formlessness of daily life, even when the writer is as socially amiable and spiritually healthy as Goethe and his disciple, Thomas Mann. That spiritual health is the subject of the grand essay by Mann on "Goethe as Representative of the Bourgeois Age," which nevertheless makes clear how heroically Goethe (and Mann) had to struggle in order to achieve and maintain such health:

As for Goethe, I may make an observation here having to do with certain human and personal effects and symptoms of the anti-ideal constitution; an observation which, indeed, leads me so far into intimate and individual psychology that only indications are possible. There can be no doubt that ideal faith, although it must be prepared for martyrdom, makes one happier in spirit than belief in a lofty and completely ironic sense of poetic achievement without values and opinions, entirely objective, mirroring everything with the same love and the same indifference. There are in Goethe, on closer examination, as soon as the innocence of the youthful period is past, signs of profound maladjustment and ill humour, a hampering depression, which must certainly have a deep-lying uncanny connection with his mistrust of ideas, his child-of-nature dilettantism. There is a peculiar coldness, ill will, *médisance*, a devil-may-care mood, an inhuman, elfish irresponsibility—which one cannot indulge enough, but must love along with him if one loves him. If one peers into this region of his character one understands that happiness and harmony are much more the affair of the children of spirit than of the children of nature. Clarity, harmony within oneself, strength of purpose, a positive believing and decided aim—in short, peace in the soul—all this is much more easily achieved by these than by the children of nature. Nature does net confer peace of mind, simplicity, single-mindedness; she is a questionable element, she is a contradiction, denial, thorough-going doubt. She endows with no benevolence, not being benevolent herself. She permits no decided judgments, for she is neutral. She endows her children with indifference; with a complex of problems, which have more to do with torment and ill will than with joy and mirth.

Goethe, Mann, and nature are everywhere the same; their happiness and harmony are aesthetic constructs, and never part of the given. Contradictory, skeptical, and full of the spirit that denies, Goethe and Mann triumph by transferring "liberal economic principles to the intellectual life"; they practice what Goethe called a "free trade of conceptions and feelings." The late "Fantasy on Goethe" has a delicious paragraph on the matter of Goethe's free trade in feelings:

Goethe's love life is a strange chapter. The list of his love affairs has become a requirement of education; in respectable German society one has to be able to rattle off the ladies like the loves of Zeus. Those Friederikes, Lottes, Minnas, and Mariannes have become statues installed in niches in the cathedral of humanity; and perhaps this makes amends to them for their disappointments. For the fickle genius who for short whiles lay at their feet was never prepared to take the consequences, to bear the restriction upon his life and liberty that these charming adventures might have involved. Perhaps the fame of the ladies is compensation to them for his recurrent flights, for the aimlessness of his wooing, the faithlessness of his sincerity, and the fact that his loving was a means to an end, a means to further his work. Where work and life are one, as was the case with him, those who know only how to take life seriously are left with all the sorrows in their laps. But he always reproved them for taking life seriously. "Werther must—must be?" he wrote to Lotte Buff and her fiancé. "You two do not feel *him*, you feel only *me* and *yourselves*.... If only you could feel the thousandth part of what Werther means to a thousand hearts, you would not reckon the cost to you." All his women bore the cost, whether they liked it or not.

It is to this aspect of Goethe as "fickle genius" that Mann returned in *The Beloved Returns*, which can serve here as representative both of the strength and limitation of Mann's art of irony.

## II

After forty-four years, the model for the heroine of Goethe's notorious *The Sorrows of Young Werther* goes to Weimar on pilgrimage, not to be reunited with her lover, now sixty-seven to her sixty-one, but rather in the hopeless quest to be made one both with their mutual past, and with his immortal idea of what she once had been, or could have been. For four hundred pages, Mann plays out the all but endless ironies of poor Lotte's fame, as the widowed and respectable lady, who has her limitations but is nobody's fool, both enjoys and endures her status and function as a living mythology. Mann's supreme irony, grotesque in its excruciating banalities, is the account of the dinner that the stiff, old Goethe gives in honor of the object of his passion, some forty-four years after the event. Poor Lotte, after being treated as a kind of amalgam of cultural relic and youthful indiscretion shrived by temporal decay, is dismissed by the great man with a palpably insincere: "Life has held us sundered far too long a time for me not to ask of it that we may meet often during your sojourn."

But Mann was too cunning to conclude his book there. A marvelous final meeting is arranged by Goethe himself, who hears Lotte's gentle question, "So meeting again is a short chapter, a fragment?" and replies in the same high aesthetic mode:

"Dear soul, let me answer you from my heart, in expiation and farewell. You speak of sacrifice. But it is a mystery, indivisible, like all else in the world and one's person, one's life, and one's work. Conversion, transformation, is all. They sacrificed to the god, and in the end the sacrifice was God. You used a figure dear and familiar to me; long since, it took possession of my soul. I mean the parable of the moth and the fatal, luring flame. Say, if you will, that I am the flame, and into me the poor moth flings itself. Yet in the chance and change of things I am the candle too, giving my body that the light may burn. And finally, I am the drunken butterfly that falls to the flame—figure of the eternal sacrifice, body transmuted into soul, and life to spirit. Dear soul, dear child, dear childlike old soul, I, first and last, am the sacrifice, and he that offers it. Once I burned you, ever I burn you, into spirit and light. Know that metamorphosis is the dearest and most inward of thy friend, his great hope, his deepest craving: the play of transformation, changing face, greybeard to youth, to youth the boy, yet ever the human countenance with traits of its proper stage, youth like a miracle shining out in age, age out of youth. Thus mayst thou rest content, beloved, as I am, with having thought it out and come to me, decking thine ancient form with signs of youth. Unity in change and flux, conversion constant out of and into oneself, transmutation of all things, life showing now its natural, now its cultural face, past turning to present, present pointing back to past, both preluding future and with her dim foreshadowings already full. Past feeling, future feeling—feeling is all. Let its open wide eyes upon the unity of the world—eyes wide, serene, and wise. Wouldst thou ask of me repentance? Only wait. I see her ride towards me, in a mantle grey. Then once more the hour of Werther and Tasso will strike, as at midnight already midday strikes, and God give me to say what I suffer—only this first and last will then remain to me. Then forsaking will be only leave-taking, leave-taking for ever, death-struggle of feeling and the hour full of frightful pangs, pangs such as probably for some time precede the hour of death, pangs which are dying if not yet death. Death, final flight into the flame—the All-in-one—why should it too be aught but transformation? In

thy quiet heart, dear visions, may you rest—and what a pleasant moment that will be, when we anon awake together!"

In some complex sense, part of the irony here is Mann's revenge upon
his precursor, since it is Mann who burns Goethe into spirit and light, into
the metamorphosis of hope and craving that is *The Beloved Returns*. Mann
and Goethe die each other's life, live each other's death, in the pre-socratic
formulation that so obsessed W.B. Yeats. But for Mann, unlike the occult
Yeats, the movement through death into transformation is a complex
metaphor for the influence relationship between Goethe and his twentieth-
century descendant. What Mann, in his "Fantasy on Goethe," delineated in
his precursor is charmingly accurate when applied to Mann himself:

> We have here a kind of splendid narcissism, a contentment with
> self far too serious and far too concerned to the very end with
> self-perfection, heightening, and distillation of personal
> endowment, for a petty-minded word like "vanity" to be appli-
> cable. Here is that profound delight in that self and its growth
> to which we owe *Poetry and Truth*, the best, at any rate the most
> charming autobiography the world has seen—essentially a
> novel in the first person which informs us, in the most won-
> derfully winning tone, how a genius is formed, how luck and
> merit are indissolubly linked by an unknown decree of grace
> and how a personality grows and flourishes under the sun of a
> higher dispensation. Personality! Goethe called it "the supreme
> bliss of mortal man"—but what it really is, in what its inner
> nature consists, wherein its mystery lies—for there is a mystery
> about it—not even he ever explained. For that matter, for all his
> love for the telling word, for the word that strikes to the heart
> of life, he never thought that everything must be explained.
> Certainly this phenomenon known as "personality" takes us
> beyond the sphere of purely intellectual, rational, analyzable
> matters into the realm of nature, where dwell those elemental
> and daemonic things which "astound the world" without being
> amenable to further elucidation.

The splendid narcissism of Mann, at his strongest, is precisely daemonic, is that profound delight in the self without which works as various
as *The Magic Mountain* and *Doctor Faustus* would collapse into the weari-
ness of the irony of irony.

## III

In his remarkable essay, "Freud and the Future" (1936), Mann wrote the pattern for his own imitation of Goethe:

> The ego of antiquity and its consciousness of itself were different from our own, less exclusive, less sharply defined. It was, as it were, open behind; it received much from the past and by repeating it gave it presentness again. The Spanish scholar Ortega y Gasset puts it that the man of antiquity, before he did anything, took a step backwards, like the bull-fighter who leaps back to deliver the mortal thrust. He searched the past for a pattern into which he might slip as into a diving-bell, and being thus at once disguised and protected might rush upon his present problem. Thus his life was in a sense a reanimation, an archaizing attitude. But it is just this life as reanimation that is the life as myth. Alexander walked in the footsteps of Miltiades; the ancient biographers of Caesar were convinced, rightly or wrongly, that he took Alexander as his prototype. But such "imitation" meant far more than we mean by the word today. It was mythical identification, peculiarly familiar to antiquity; but it is operative far into modern times, and at all times is psychically possible. How often have we not been told that the figure of Napoleon was cast in the antique mould! He regretted that the mentality of the time forbade him to give himself out for the son of Jupiter Ammon, in imitation of Alexander. But we need not doubt that—at least at the period of his Eastern exploits—he mythically confounded himself with Alexander; while after he turned his face westwards he is said to have declared: "I am Charlemagne." Note that: not "I am like Charlemagne" or "My situation is like Charlemagne's," but quite simply "I am he." That is the formulation of the myth. Life, then—at any rate, significant life—was in ancient times the reconstitution of the myth in flesh and blood; it referred to and appealed to the myth; only through it, through reference to the past, could it approve itself as genuine and significant. The myth is the legitimization of life; only through and in it does life find self-awareness, sanction, consecration. Cleopatra fulfilled her Aphrodite character even unto death—and can one live and die more significantly or worthily than in the celebration of the myth? We have only to think of Jesus and His life,

which was lived in order that that which was written might he fulfilled. It is not easy to distinguish between his own consciousness and the conventionizations of the Evangelists. But His word on the Cross, about the ninth hour, that "*Eli, Eli, lama sabachthani?*" was evidently not in the least an outburst of despair and disillusionment; but on the contrary a lofty messianic sense of self. For the phrase is not original, not a spontaneous outcry. It stands at the beginning of the Twenty-second Psalm, which from one end to the other is an announcement of the Messiah. Jesus was quoting, and the quotation meant: "Yes, it is I!" Precisely thus did Cleopatra quote when she took the asp to her breast to die; and again the quotation meant: "Yes, it is I!"

In effect, Mann quotes Goethe, and thus proclaims "Yes, it is I." The ego of antiquity is simply the artist's ego, appropriating the precursor in order to overcome the belatedness of the influence process. Mann reveals the true subject of his essay on Freud just two paragraphs further on:

> Infantilism—in other words, regression to childhood—what a role this genuinely psychoanalytic element plays in all our lives! What a large share it has in shaping the life of a human being; operating, indeed, in just the way I have described: as mythical identification, as survival, as a treading in footprints already made! The bond with the father, and the transference to father-substitute pictures of a higher and more developed type—how these infantile traits work upon the life of the individual to mark and shape it! I use the word "shape," for to me in all seriousness the happiest, most pleasurable element of what we call education (*Bildung*), the shaping of the human being, is just this powerful influence of admiration and love, this childish identification with a father-image elected out of profound affinity. The artist in particular, a passionately childlike and play-possessed being, can tell us of the mysterious yet after all obvious effect of such infantile imitation upon his own life, his productive conduct of a career which after all is often nothing but a reanimation of the hero under very different temporal and personal conditions and with very different, shall we say childish means. The *imitatio* Goethe, with its Werther and Wilhelm Meister stages, its old-age period of *Faust* and *Diwan*, can still shape and mythically mould the life of an artist—rising out of

his unconscious, yet playing over—as is the artist way—into a smiling, childlike, and profound awareness.

The profound awareness is Mann's own, and concerns his own enactment of the imitatio Goethe. Subtly echoed and reversed here is Goethe's observation in his *Theory of Color* to the effect that "even perfect models have a disturbing effect in that they lead us to skip necessary stages in our *Bildung*, with the result, for the most part, that we are carried wide of the mark into limitless error." This is also the Goethe who celebrated his own originality as well as his power of appropriating from others. Thus he could say that: "Only by making the riches of the others our own do we bring anything great into being," but also insist: "What can we in fact call our own except the energy, the force, the will!" Mann, acutely sensing his own belatedness, liked to quote the old Goethe's question: "Does a man live when others also live?"

The Goethe of *The Beloved Returns* is not Goethe, but Mann himself, the world parodist prophesied and celebrated by Nietzsche as the artist of the future. E.R. Curtius doubtless was accurate in seeing Goethe as an ending and not as a fresh beginning of the cultural tradition. Mann too now seems archaic, not a modernist or post-Romantic, but a belated Goethe, a humanist triumphing through the mystery of his own personality and the ironic playfulness of his art. Like his vision of Goethe, Mann now seems a child of nature rather than of the spirit, but laboring eloquently to burn through nature into the transformation that converts deathliness into a superb dialectical art.

## The Magic Mountain

I always feel a bit bored when critics assign my own work so definitely and completely to the realm of irony and consider me an ironist through and through, without also taking account of the concept of humor.

—Thomas Mann (1953)

The author of *The Magic Mountain* insisted that he wished to draw laughter from his reader's heart, rather than an intellectual smile. He has provoked so many intellectual smiles in his exegetes that they have bored us all more than a bit. The irony of irony is that finally it defeats not meaning (as deconstructionist critics insist) but interest, without which we cannot go on reading. Thomas Mann doubtless was what Erich Heller called him, "the ironic German," but rereading *The Magic Mountain* is much more than an experience in irony. Not that the book ever provokes me to laughter. Mann is hardly S.J. Perelman or Philip Roth. Yet it is now more than sixty years since the novel first was published, and the book clearly has mellowed. The irony of one age is never the irony of another, and *The Magic Mountain* seems now a work of gentle high seriousness; as earnest, affectionate, and solid as its admirable hero, Hans Castorp.

That *The Magic Mountain* parodies a host of literary genres and conventions is finely obvious. The effect of Nietzsche upon Mann was very strong, and parody was Nietzsche's answer to the anxieties of influence. Mann evidently did believe that what remained to be done was for art to become its own parody. Presumably that would have redeemed an irony that at bottom may have been mere indecisiveness. Reading the novel now, the common reader scarcely will recognize the parody of romantic convention, and can afford to bypass the endless ambiguities of Mann's late version of romantic irony.

This is not to agree with Erich Heller's ironic conclusion: "Such is our world that sense and meaning have to be disguised—as irony, or as literature, or as both come together: for instance in *The Magic Mountain*." Mann's story now primarily offers neither "meaning" nor irony, but rather a loving representation of past realities, of a European culture forever gone, the culture of Goethe and Freud. A reader in 1985 must experience the book as a historical novel, the cairn of a humanism forever lost, forever longed for. Mann's superb workmanship fashioned the most vivid version we have of a Europe before the catastrophe of the Nazi horror. Where Mann intended parody, the counter-ironies of time and change have produced instead a transformation that today makes *The Magic Mountain* into an immensely poignant study of the nostalgias.

## II

Hans Castorp himself now seems to me both a subtler and a more likable representation than he did when I first read the novel, nearly forty years ago. Despite Mann's endorsement of the notion, Castorp is no quester, and pursues no grail or ideal. He is a character of considerable detachment, who will listen with almost equal contentment to the enlightened Settembrini, the terroristic Naphta, or the heroically vitalistic Peeperkorn. His erotic detachment is extraordinary; after seven months he makes love to Clavdia just once, and then avoids any other sexual experience for the rest of his seven-year stay at the sanatorium. If he has a high passion for Clavdia, it nevertheless carries few of the traditional signs of love's torments. Whether his detachment has some root in his having been an orphan since the age of seven is unclear, but essentially he is content to see, to be taught, to absorb.

We do not think of Castorp as weak, and yet his nature seems almost totally free of aggressivity. It is as though the death drive in him does not take its origin in a wounded narcissism. Castorp bears no psychic scars, and probably never will acquire any. Whatever his maker's intentions, he is not in himself ironic, nor does he seem anymore to be a parody of anything or anyone whatsoever. The common reader becomes very fond of Castorp, and even begins to regard him as a kind of Everyman, which he most certainly is not. His true drive is towards self-education, education sought for its own sake alone. Castorp is that ideal student the universities always proclaim yet never find. He is intensely interested in everything, in all possible knowledge, and yet that knowledge is an end in itself. Knowledge is not power for him, whether over himself or over others; it is in no way Faustian.

Despite his passion for hermeticism, Castorp is not striving to become an esoteric adept, whether rationalist like Settembrini or antirationalist like Naphta. And though he is fascinated by Peeperkorn as a grand personality and an apostle of vitalism, Castorp is more than content with his own apparent colorlessness, and with his own evasions of his only once-fulfilled desire for Clavdia, representative as she is of the dark eros that mingles sexual love and death. Castorp is a survivor, and I do not believe that we are to foresee him as dying upon the battlefields of World War I. Naphta kills himself, in frustration at lacking the courage to kill Settembrini; Settembrini is broken by his contemplation of Naphta's desperate act; Peeperkorn too is a suicide, unable to bear the onset of impotence. Only Castorp will go on, strengthened and resolute, and possibly will complete his self-transformation from engineer to artist, so as to write a novel not unlike *The Magic Mountain*.

### III

What kind of magic is it—what enchantment does the mountain sanatorium possess? At one extreme limit, the book admits the occult, when Castorp's dead cousin, Joachim, appears at the séance:

> There was one more person in the room than before. There in the background, where the red rays lost themselves in gloom, so that the eye scarcely reached thither, between writing-desk and screen, in the doctor's consulting-chair, where in the intermission Elly had been sitting, Joachim sat. It was the Joachim

of the last days, with hollow, shadowy cheeks, warrior's beard
and full, curling lips. He sat leaning back, one leg crossed over
the other. On his wasted face, shaded though it was by his
head-covering, was plainly seen the stamp of suffering, the
expression of gravity and austerity which had beautified it. Two
folds stood on his brow, between the eyes, that lay deep in their
bony cavities; but there was no change in the mildness of the
great dark orbs, whose quiet friendly gaze sought out Hans
Castorp, and him alone. That ancient grievance of the out-
standing ears was still to be seen under the head-covering, his
extraordinary head-covering, which they could not make out.
Cousin Joachim was not in mufti. His sabre seemed to be leaning against his leg, he held the handle, one thought to distinguish something like a pistol-case in his belt. But that was no
proper uniform he wore. No colour, no decorations; it had a
collar like a *litewka* jacket, and side pockets. Somewhere low
down on the breast was a cross. His feet looked large, his legs
very thin, they seemed to be bound or wound as for the business of sport more than war. And what was it, this headgear? It
seemed as though Joachim had turned an army cook-pot
upside-down on his head, and fastened it under his chin with a
band. Yet it looked quite properly warlike, like an old-fashioned
foot-soldier, perhaps.

By thus making the occult prophetic of what was to come—the uniform and helmet are of World War I—Mann essentially chose, all ironies
aside, a mystical theory of time. Many exegetes have noted the book's
obsession with the number seven, in all its variants. Others have noted that
after Joachim dies, all temporal references disappear from the novel.
Castorp forgets his own age, and the length of his own stay on the Magic
Mountain. He passes into timelessness:

How long Joachim had lived here with his cousin, up to the
time of his fateful departure, or taken all in all; what had been
the date of his going, how long he had been gone, when he had
come back; how long Hans Castorp himself had been up here
when his cousin returned and then bade time farewell; how
long—dismissing Joachim from our calculations—Frau
Chauchat had been absent; how long, since what date, she had
been back again (for she did come back); how much mortal
time Hans Castorp himself had spent in House Berghof by the

time she returned; no one asked him all these questions, and he probably shrank from asking himself. If they had been put to him, he would have tapped his forehead with the tips of his fingers, and most certainly not have known—a phenomenon as disquieting as his incapacity to answer Herr Settembrini, that long-ago first evening, when the latter had asked him his age.

The opening words of the novel describe Castorp as "an unassuming young man," but this fellow who seems the apotheosis of the average is of course hermetic and daemonic, marked from birth for singular visions of eternity. *Bildung*, the supposed thematic pattern that the book inherits from Goethe, Stifter, Keller, and others, hardly is possible for Castorp, who does not require the endless cultural instruction nearly everyone else wishes to inflict upon him. He need not develop; he simply unfolds. For he is Primal Man, the Ur-Adam of the Gnostic myth that Mann lovingly expounds in the "Prelude" of his Joseph tetralogy. Indeed, he already is Mann's Joseph, the favored of Heaven.

IV

Much of what Mann intended as memorable value in *The Magic Mountain* paradoxically has been lost to time. The social satire, intellectual irony, and sense of cultural crisis are all now quite archaic. Settembrini, Naphta, Peeperkorn, Clavdia, and Joachim all possess an antique charm, a kind of faded aesthetic dignity, parodies of parodies, period pieces, old photographs uncannily right and yet altogether odd. Hans Castorp, as colorless now as he was in 1924, retains his immediacy, his relevance, his disturbing claim upon us. He is not the Nietzschean new man, without a superego, but the Nietzschean will-to-interpretation: receptive rather than rapacious, plural rather than unitary, affective rather than indifferent, distanced from rather than abandoned to desire. In some sense, Castorp knows that he himself is an interpretation, knows that he represents neither Schopenhauer's will to live, nor Freud's mingled drives of love and death, but Nietzsche's will to power over the text of life. The implicit questions Castorp is always putting to everyone else in the book are: Who exactly are you, the interpreter, and what power do you seek to gain over my life? Because he puts these questions to us also, with cumulative force, Castorp becomes a representation we cannot evade. Mann, taking leave of his hero, said that Castorp mattered because of his "dream of love," presumably the vision of the chapter "Snow." It was fortunate that Mann, a miraculous artisan, had wrought better than even he himself knew. Castorp is one of those rare fictions who acquire the authority to call our versions of reality into some doubt. The reader, interpreting Castorp, must come to ask herself or himself: What is my dream of love, my erotic illusion, and how does that dream or illusion qualify my own possibilities of unfolding?

# James Joyce

## (1882-1941)

HOW DO YOU CHRONICLE THE PRINCIPAL DATES IN THE LIFE OF THE PREMIER writer in English of the twentieth century? Dublin's James Joyce might have mentioned February 2, 1882, when he was born, or June 16, 1904, when he took his first walk with Nora Barnacle, a date that became "Bloomsday," when all of *Ulysses* is enacted. Doubtless, he would have added July 26, 1907, when their daugther Lucia was born, and the earlier birth of their son, Giorgio, on July 27, 1905. We must record Joyce's death on January 13, 1941, not yet fifty-nine, and the death of Nora Barnacle Joyce on April 10, 1951.

From a reader's perspective, the crucial dates are the publication of Joyce's major works: *Dubliners* (1914), *A Portrait of the Artist as a Young Man* (1916), *Ulysses* (1922), *Finnegans Wake* (1939). No narrative prose fiction in English since Charles Dickens could be judged to equal that sequence in aesthetic eminence, though partisans of Henry James might dispute the point, I suppose. I myself would turn to Dante and to Shakespeare as Joyce's true precursors, and masters. Certainly only they, Cervantes, and Chaucer transcend Joyce in the arts of representation. Blind Milton, and Jonathan Swift, might be brought forward also, but no others, I think, in English.

Only the authentic though mostly surface difficulties of *Finnegans Wake*, which have prevented a general readership, pragmatically result in the solitary eminence of *Ulysses* among all writings in English, possibly since the seventeenth century. How can we describe the influence of *Ulysses* upon James Joyce himself, except to say that, to surpass himself, Joyce had to compose *Finnegans Wake*.

Samuel Beckett, writing about *Work in Progress* a decade before it was published as *Finnegans Wake*, charmingly compared the earthly paradises of Dante and Joyce:

> Dante's Terrestrial Paradise is the carriage entrance to a
> Paradise that is not celestial: Mr. Joyce's Terrestrial Paradise is
> the tradesmen's entrance on to the sea-shore.

Beckett, who began as Joyce's most eminent disciple, favors neither Dante
nor Joyce over the other. *Ulysses* is too comprehensive to be primarily an
*Inferno*, and the *Wake* is too cheerful to be a *Purgatorio*. Had Joyce lived,
his old age would have been given to an epic on the sea, presumably not a
*Paradiso*.

   Mary T. Reynolds, writing about Joyce and Dante, wisely remarked
that: "Art, for Joyce, is fatherhood." Leopold Bloom's son, Rudy, is dead,
and Stephen, whatever the scheme of *Ulysses*, is not an apt substitute.
Fatherhood, in Joyce and in Shakespeare, is a mystery: the image of cuck-
oldry haunts both. Shakespeare wisely gives us not the slightest clue
whether he himself personally was Catholic, Protestant, skeptic, nihilist, or
Hermetist. Joyce, we need doubt, was a *totally* lapsed Catholic. For Joyce,
God is a hangman, as he is in José Saramago's *The Gospel According to Jesus
Christ*. I bring this forward only to point out that "God the Father" is the
least Joycean of all possible phrases.

   I propose instead: *Ulysses* the father, which returns us to the fatherhood of the marvelous Poldy Bloom. Poldy is Joyce, Shakespeare, and a
God purged of the hangman's stigma. That also makes Poldy the Ghost in
*Hamlet*, and we should remember that Stephen quotes the subtle Sabellian
heresy that the Father was Himself His Own Son.

   The effect of Joyce's masterworks upon his own life was uncanny:
*Ulysses* and the *Wake* reject Dante's attempt to reconcile poetry and religion. In turn, they rendered Joyce yet more himself. More than any other
modern writer, Joyce fathered himself through his own work.

*Ulysses*

It is an odd sensation to begin writing an introduction to a volume of Joyce
criticism on June 16, 1985, particularly if one's name is Bloom. Poldy is, as
Joyce intended, the most *complete* figure in modern fiction, if not indeed in
all Western fiction, and so it is appropriate that he have a saint's day in the
literary calendar: Bloomsday. He is, thankfully, no saint, but a mild, gentle
sinner; in short, a good man. So good a man is he that even the critic Hugh
Kenner, who in his earlier commentary saw Poldy as an instance of modern depravity, an Eliotic Jew as it were, in 1980 could call Joyce's hero "fit
to live in Ireland without malice, without violence, without hate." How
many are fit to live, in fact or fiction, in Ireland or America, without

malice, without violence, without hate? Kenner, no sentimentalist, now finds in Poldy what the reader must find: a better person than oneself.

Richard Ellmann, Joyce's biographer, shrewdly says of Poldy that "he is not afraid that he will compromise his selfhood." Currently fashionable criticism, calling itself "Post-Structuralist Joyce," oddly assimilates Joyce to Barthes, Lacan, Derrida; producing a Poldy without a self, another floating signifier. But Joyce's Poldy, as Ellmann insists, is heroic and imaginative; his mimetic force allies him to the Wife of Bath, Falstaff and Sancho Panza, and like them his presence is overwhelming. Joyce's precursors were Dante and Shakespeare, and Poldy has a comprehensiveness and immediacy worthy of his ancestry. It is good to remember that, after Dante and Shakespeare, Joyce cared most for Wordsworth and Shelley among the poets. Wordsworth's heroic naturalism and Shelley's visionary skepticism find their way into Poldy also.

How Jewish is Poldy? Here I must dissent a touch from Ellmann, who says that when Poldy confronts the Citizen, he states an ethical view "more Christian than Judaic." Poldy has been unbelieving Jew, Protestant and Catholic, but his ethical affirmations are normative Jewish, as Joyce seems to have known better than Ellmann does. When Poldy gazes upon existence, he finds it good. The commonplace needs no hallowing for Poldy. Frank Budgen, taking the hint from Joyce, emphasizes how much older Poldy seems than all the other inhabitants of Joyce's visionary Dublin. We do not think of Poldy as being thirty-eight, prematurely middle-aged, but rather as living in what the Hebrew Bible called *olam*: time without boundaries. Presumably, that is partly why Joyce chose to make his Ulysses Jewish rather than Greek. Unlike a modern Greek, Poldy is in surprising continuity with a lineage of which he has little overt knowledge. How different would the book have been if Joyce had centered on a Greek living in Dublin? The aura of exile would not be there. Joyce, the Dubliner in exile, tasting his own stoic version of a Dantesque bitterness, found in Poldy as wandering Jew what now seems his inevitable surrogate. Poldy, not Stephen, is Joyce's true image.

Yet Poldy is certainly more like Homer's Ulysses than like the Yahwist's Jacob. We see Poldy surviving the Cyclops, but not wrestling with one among the Elohim in order to win a new name for himself. Truly Jewgreek, Poldy has forsworn the Covenant, even if he cannot escape from having been chosen. Joyce, too, has abandoned the Church, but cannot escape the intellectual discipline of the Jesuits. Poldy's sense of election is a little more mysterious, or perhaps it is Joyce's sense of his hero's election that is the true mystery of the book. At the end of the Cyclops episode, Joyce evidently felt the necessity of distancing himself from Poldy, if only because literary irony fails when confronted by the heroic pathos of a creation that defies even Joyce's control.

> —Are you talking about the new Jerusalem? says the citizen.
> —I'm talking about injustice, says Bloom.
> —Right, says John Wyse. Stand up to it then with force like men.

But that is of course not Poldy's way. No interpolated sarcasm, however dramatically wrought, is able to modify the dignity of Poldy's rejoinder:

> —But it's no use, says he. Force, hatred, history, all that. That's not life for men and women, insult and hatred. And everybody knows that it's the very opposite of that that is really life.
> —What, says Alf.
> —Love, says Bloom. I mean the opposite of hatred.

Twelve delirious pages of hyperbole and phantasmagoria follow, detailing the forced exit of the noble Poldy from the pub, and ending in a grand send-up indeed:

> When, lo, there came about them all a great brightness and they beheld the chariot wherein He stood ascend to heaven. And they beheld Him in the chariot, clothed upon in the glory of the brightness, having raiment as of the sun, fair as the moon and terrible that for awe they durst not look upon Him. And there came a voice out of heaven, calling: *Elijah! Elijah!* And he answered with a main cry: *Abba! Adonai!* And they beheld Him even Him, ben Bloom Elijah, amid clouds of angels ascend to the glory of the brightness at an angle of forty-five degrees over Donohoe's in Little Green Street like a shot off a shovel.

It is all in the juxtaposition of "ben Bloom Elijah" and "like a shot off a shovel," at once a majestic deflation and a complex apotropaic gesture on Joyce's own part. Like Falstaff and Sancho Panza, Poldy runs off with the book, and Joyce's strenuous ironies, dwarfing the wit of nearly all other authors, essentially are so many reaction-formations against his love for (and identity with) his extraordinary hero. Homer's Ulysses may be as complete as Poldy, but you wouldn't want to be in one boat with him (you would drown, he would survive). Poldy would comfort you in every sorrow, even as he empathizes so movingly with the pangs of women in childbirth.

Joyce was not Flaubert, who at once was Madame Bovary and yet was wholly detached from her, at least in aesthetic stance. But how do you maintain a fixed stance toward Poldy? Falstaff is the monarch of wit, and Sancho Panza the Pope of innocent cunning. Poldy's strength, as Joyce evidently intended, is in his completeness. "The complete man" is necessarily a trope, but for what? On one side, for range of affect, like Tennyson's Ulysses, Poldy is a part of all that he has met. His curiosity, his susceptibility, his compassion, his potential interest these are infinite. On another side, for cognitive activity, Poldy, unlike Stephen, is certainly not brilliant, and yet he has a never-resting mind, as Ulysses must have. He can be said to have a Shakespearean mind, though he resembles no one in Shakespeare (a comparison of Poldy and Shylock is instructive). Poldy is neither Hamlet nor Falstaff, but perhaps he is Shakespeare, or Shakespeare reborn as James Joyce, even as Stephen is the younger Dante reincarnated as Joyce. We can think of Poldy as Horatio to Stephen's Hamlet, since Horatio represents us, the audience, and we represent Shakespeare. Poldy is our representative, and it is Joyce's greatest triumph that increasingly we represent him, as we always have and will represent Shakespeare.

Post-Structuralist Joyce never wearies of reminding us that Poldy is a trope, but it is truer to say that we are tropes for Poldy, who as a super-mimesis of essential nature is beyond us. I may never recover from a walk through a German park with a dear friend who is the most distinguished of post-Structuralists. When I remarked to him, in my innocent cunning, that Poldy was the most lovable person in Western fiction, I provoked him to the annoyed response that Poldy was not a person, but only language, and that Joyce, unlike myself, knew this very well. Joyce knew very well that Poldy was more than a person, but only in the sense that Poldy was a humane and humanized God, a God who had become truly a bereft father, anguishing for his lost Rudy. Poldy is not a person only if God is not a person, and the God of the Jews, for all his transcendental sublimities, is also very much a person and a personality, as befits his immanent sublimities. Surely the uniqueness of Yahweh, among all the rival godlings, is that Yahweh is complete. Yahweh is the complete God, even as Poldy is the complete man, and God, after all, like Poldy, is Jewish.

## II

French post-Structuralism is of course only a belated modernism, since everything from abroad is absorbed so slowly in xenophobic Paris. French Hegel, French Freud, French Joyce are all after the event, as it were, just as French romanticism was a rather delayed phenomenon.

French Joyce is about as close to the text of *Ulysses* and *Finnegans Wake* as Lacan is to the text of *Three Essays on the Theory of Sexuality* or Derrida to Hegel and Heidegger. Nor should they be, since cultural belatedness or Alexandrianism demands the remedy of misprision, or creative misreading. To say that "meaning" keeps its distance from Poldy is both to forget that Poldy is the Messiah (though which Messiah is not clear) and that one name (Kabbalistic) for Yahweh is "language." The difference between Joyce and French Joyce is that Joyce tropes God as language and the belated Parisians (and their agents) trope the Demiurge as language, which is to say that Joyce, heroic naturalist, was not a Gnostic and Lacan was (perhaps unknowingly).

As a knowing Gnostic, I lament the loss of Joycean heroic naturalism and of Poldy's natural heroism. Let them deconstruct Don Quixote; the results will be as sorrowful. Literary criticism is a mode which teaches us not only to read Poldy as Sancho Panza and Stephen as the Don, but more amiably takes us back to Cervantes, to read Sancho as Poldy. By a Borgesian blessing in the art of mistaken attribution, we then will learn to read not only *Hamlet* and the *Inferno* as written by Joyce, but *Don Quixote* as well, with the divine Sancho as an Irish Jew!

Joyce necessarily is closer to Shakespeare than to Cervantes, and Joyce's obsession with *Hamlet* is crucial in *Ulysses*. His famous reading of Hamlet, as expounded by Stephen, can be regarded as a subtle coming-to-terms with Shakespeare as his most imposing literary father in the English language. Ellmann, certainly the most reliable of all Joyce scholars, insisted that Joyce "exhibits none of that anxiety of influence which has been attributed to modern writers.... If Joyce had any anxiety, it was over not incorporating influences enough." This matter is perhaps more dialectical than Ellmann realized. Not Dante, but Shakespeare is Joyce's Virgil, as Ellmann also notes, and just as Dante's poetic voice matures even as Virgil fades out of the *Commedia*, so Shakespeare had to fade out of *Ulysses* even as Joyce's voice matured.

In Stephen's theory, Shakespeare is the dead king, rather than the young Hamlet, who becomes the type of the Romantic artist, Stephen himself. Shakespeare, like the ghost, has been betrayed, except; than Anne Hathaway went Gertrude one better, and cuckolded the Bard with both his brothers. This sexual defeat has been intensified by Shakespeare's loss of the dark lady of the sonnets, and to his best friend, a kind of third brother. Shakespeare's revenge is to resurrect his own dead son, Hamnet, who enters the play as Prince Hamlet, with the purpose of vindicating his father's honor. Such a resurrected son appears to be free of the Oedipal ambivalences, and in Joyce's view does not lust after Gertrude or feel any jealousy, however repressed, for the dead father. So Stephen and Poldy, as two aspects of Shakespeare/Joyce, during the "Circe" episode gaze into a mirror and behold a transformed Shakespeare, beardless and frozen-faced ("rigid in facial paralysis"). I do not interpret this either as the view that Poldy and Stephen "amount only to a paralytic travesty of a Shakespeare" (W.M. Schutte) or that "Joyce warns us that he is working with near-identities, not perfect ones" (Ellmann). Rather, I take it as a sign of influence-anxiety, as the precursor Shakespeare mocking the ephebe Joyce: "Be like me, but you presume in attempting to be too much like me. You are merely a beardless version, rigid in facial paralysis, lacking my potency and my ease of countenance."

The obscene Buck Mulligan, Joyce's black beast, weakly misreads *Hamlet* as masturbation and Poldy as a pederast. Joyce himself, through Stephen, strongly misreads *Hamlet* as the cuckold's revenge, a play presumably likelier to have been written by Poldy than by Stephen. In a stronger misreading still, I would suggest that Joyce rewrites *Hamlet* so as to destroy the element in the play that most menaces him, which is the very different, uncannily disinterested Hamlet of Act V. Stephen quotes the subtle Sabellian heresy that the Father was Himself His Own Son. But what we may call the even subtler Shakespearean heresy (which is also Freudian) holds rather that the Son was Himself His Own Father. This is the Hamlet of Act V, who refers to his dead father only once, and then only as the king. Joyce's Hamlet has no Oedipus complex. Shakespeare's Hamlet may have had one, but it passes away in the interval between Acts IV and V.

Stephen as the Prince does not convince me; Poldy as the ghost of the dead king, and so as Shakespeare/Joyce, is rather more troublesome. One wishes the ghost could be exorcised, leaving us with the fine trinity of Shakespeare/Poldy/Joyce, with Poldy as the transitional figure reconciling forerunner and latecomer, a sort of Messiah perhaps. Shakespeare is the original Testament or old aesthetic Law, while Joyce is the belated Testament or new aesthetic dispensation. Poldy is the inter-Testamentary figure, apocryphal and apocalyptic, and yet overwhelmingly a representation of life in the here and now. Joyce went on to write *Finnegans Wake*, the only legitimate rival to Proust's vast novel in the Western literature of our time. More than the difficulties, both real and imaginary, of the *Wake* have kept Joyce's common readers centered upon *Ulysses*. Earwicker is a giant hieroglyph; Poldy is a person, complete and loving, self-reliant, larger and more evocative even than his book.

# T.S. Eliot

## (1888–1965)

I

THOMAS STEARNS ELIOT IS A CENTRAL FIGURE IN THE WESTERN LITERARY culture of this century. His undoubted achievement as a lyric and elegiac poet in itself would suffice to establish him in the main Romantic tradition of British and American poetry that moves from Wordsworth and Whitman on to Geoffrey Hill and John Ashbery, poets of our moment. There is an obvious irony in such a judgment. Eliot's professed sense of *the* tradition, *his* tradition, was rather different, tracing as it did the true line of poetry in English from its origins in medieval Provence and Italy through its later developments in France. I borrow that remark from Northrop Frye, whose sympathetic but dissenting analysis of Eliot's cultural polemic is reprinted in this collection. Eliot's polemical stance as a literary critic can be distinguished from his rhetorical stance as a poet, and both postures of the spirit are fortunately quite distinct from his cultural position, self-proclaimed as Anglo-Catholic, Royalist and Classical.

An obsessive reader of poetry growing up in the nineteen thirties and forties entered a critical world dominated by the opinions and example of Eliot. To speak out of even narrower personal experience, anyone adopting the profession of teaching literature in the early nineteen fifties entered a discipline virtually enslaved not only by Eliot's insights but by the entire span of his preferences and prejudices. If one's cultural position was Jewish, Liberal and Romantic, one was likely to start out with a certain lack of affection for Eliot's predominance, however much (against the will) the subtle force of the poetry was felt. If a young critic particularly loved Shelley, Milton, Emerson, Pater, and if that same critic did not believe that Blake was a naive and eccentric genius, then regard for Eliot seemed

unnecessary. Whatever he actually represented, a neochristian and neo-
classic Academy had exalted him, by merit raised, to what was pragmatically rather a bad eminence. In *that* critical climate, Hopkins was considered the only valid Victorian poet, greatly superior to Browning and
Tennyson, while Whitman seemed an American nightmare and Wallace
Stevens, if he passed at all, had to be salvaged as a Late Augustan. Thirty
years on, these views have a kind of antique charm, but in 1954 they were
at least annoying, and if one cared enough, they had some capacity for
infuriating.

I resume these matters not to stir up waning rancors, but to explain
why, for some critics of my own generation, Eliot only recently has ceased
to represent the spiritual enemy. His disdain for Freud, his flair for demon-
strating the authenticity of his Christianity by exhibiting a judicious anti-
Semitism, his refined contempt for human sexuality—somehow these did
not seem to be the inevitable foundations for contemporary culture.
Granted that he refrained from the rhetorical excesses of his ally Ezra
Pound; there is nothing in him resembling the Poundian apothegm: "All
the jew part of the Bible is black evil." Still, an Academy that found its ideology in Eliot was not a place where one could teach comfortably, or where
one could have remained, had the Age of Eliot not begun to wane. The
ascendancy of Eliot, as a fact of cultural politics, is something many among
us could not wish to see return.

## II

Eliot asserted for his poetry a seventeenth century ancestry, out of
Jacobean dramatists and Metaphysical lyricists. Its actual forerunners are
Whitman and Tennyson, and Eliot's strength is felt now when we read
"When Lilacs Last in the Dooryard Bloom'd" and "Maud: A
Monodrama," and find ourselves believing that they are influenced by *The
Waste Land*. It is a neglected truth of American poetic history that Eliot and
Stevens are more Whitmanian than Hart Crane, whose allegiance to
Whitman was overt. Though Eliot and Stevens consciously did not feel or
know it, their poetry is obsessed with Whitman's poetry. By this I mean
Whitman's tropes and Whitman's curious transitions between topics, and
not at all the example of Whitman, far more crucial for Crane and many
others.

It is the pattern of Eliot's figurations that is most High Romantic, a
pattern that I suspect he learned from Tennyson and Whitman, who
derived it from Keats and Shelley, who in turn had been instructed by
Wordsworth's crisis lyrics and odes, which go back yet further to

Spenserian and Miltonic models. Consider Eliot's "Ash-Wednesday," his conversion-sequence of 1930. The poem's six movements are not a Dantesque *Vita Nuova*, despite Eliot's desires, but a rather strict reenactment of the Wordsworthian drama of experiential loss and compensatory imaginative gain:

(I) This is an ironic movement that says "I rejoice" but means "I despair," which is the limited irony that Freud terms a "reaction formation," or an emotion masking ambivalently as its opposite. Despite the deliberate allusions to Cavalcanti and Dante, Ezekiel and the Mass, that throng the poem, the presumably unintended echoes of Wordsworth's "Intimations of Immortality" Ode carry the reader closer to the center of the poet's partially repressed anxieties and to his poetic anxieties in particular. "The infirm glory" and the "one veritable transitory power" are stigmata of the visionary gleam in its flight from the poet, and if what is lost here is more-than-natural, we remember that the loss in Wordsworth also transcends nature. Though Eliot employs the language of mysticism and Wordsworth the language of nature, the crisis for each is poetic rather than mystical or natural. Eliot's renunciation of voice, however ironical, leads directly to what for many readers has been the most memorable and poignant realization in the sequence: "Consequently I rejoice, having to construct something / Upon which to rejoice." No more illuminating epigraph could be assigned to Wordsworth's "Intimations" Ode, or to "Tintern Abbey" or "Resolution and Independence." The absence lamented in the first part of "Ash-Wednesday" is a once-present poetic strength, whatever else it represented experientially. In the Shakespearean rejection of the desire for "this man's gift and that man's scope," we need not doubt that the men are precursor poets, nor ought we to forget that not hoping to turn again is also an ironic farewell to troping, and so to one's own quest for poetic voice.

(II) The question that haunts the transition between the first two sections, pragmatically considered, is: "Am I, Eliot, still a poet?" "Shall these bones live?" is a synecdochal question, whole for part, since the immortality involved is the figurative survival of one's poetry: "As I am forgotten / And would be forgotten, so I would forget." Turning around against himself, this poet, in the mode of Browning's Childe Roland, asks only to be numbered among the scattered precursors, to fail as they have failed: "We have our inheritance."

(III) After such self-wounding, the poet seeks a kind of Pauline *kenosis*, akin to Christ's emptying himself of his own Divinity, which here can only mean the undoing of one's poetic gift. As inspiration fades away willfully, the gift wonderfully declares itself nevertheless, in that enchanted lyricism Eliot never ceased to share with the elegiac Whitman and the Virgilian Tennyson: "Lilac and brown hair; / Distraction, music of the flute, stops and steps of the mind over the third stair." The figurative movement is metonymic, as in the displacement of poetic power from the speaker to the curiously Pre-Raphaelite "broadbacked figure drest in blue and green," who is anything but a possible representation of Eliot's own poetic self.

(IV) This is the daemonic vision proper, allowing a sequence that denies sublimity, to re-attain a Romantic Sublime. In the transition between sections III and IV, Eliot appears to surmount the temptations of solipsism, so as to ask and answer the question: "Am I capable of loving another?" The unnamed other or "silent sister" is akin to shadowy images of desire in Tennyson and Whitman, narcissistic emblems certainly, but pointing beyond the self's passion for the self. Hugh Kenner, indubitably Eliot's best and most Eliotic critic, suggestively compares "Ash-Wednesday" to Tennyson's "The Holy Grail," and particularly to the fearful death-march of Percivale's quest in that most ornate portion of *The Idylls of the King*. Kenner of course awards the palm to Eliot over what he dismisses as a crude "Victorian ceremony of iterations" as compared to Eliot's "austere gestures of withdrawal and submission." A quarter of a century after he made them, Kenner's judgments seem eminently reversible, since Tennyson's gestures are, in this case, palpably more austere than his inheritor's. Tennyson has, after all, nothing quite so gaudy as: "Redeem / The unread vision in the higher dream / While jewelled unicorns draw by the guilded hearse."

(V) Percivale's desert, and the wasteland of Browning's Childe Roland, join the Biblical wildernesses in this extraordinary *askesis*, a self-curtailing rhapsody that truncates Romantic tradition as much as it does Eliot's individual talent. One could assert that this section affirms all the possibilities of sublimation, from Plato through Nietzsche to Freud, except that the inside/outside metaphor of dualism confines itself here only to "The Word without a word, the Word within." Eliot, like all his Romantic ancestors from Wordsworth to Pater, seeks a crossing to a subtle identification with an innocent earliness, while fearing to introject instead the belatedness of a world without imagination, the death-in-life of the poet who has outlasted his gift.

(VI) This is one of Eliot's triumphs, as an earliness is recovered under the sign of contrition. The "unbroken wings" still flying seaward are a beautiful metalepsis of the wings of section I, which were "merely vans to beat the air." A characteristic pattern of the Romantic crisis lyric is extended as the precursors return from the dead, but in Eliot's own colors, the "lost lilac" of Whitman and the "lost sea voices" of Tennyson joining Eliot's "lost heart" in the labor of rejoicing, having indeed constructed something upon which to rejoice.

### III

Eliot is hardly unique among the poets in having misrepresented either his actual tradition or his involuntary place in that tradition. His cultural influence, rather than his polemic, was closer to being an unique phenomenon. To have been born in 1888, and to have died in 1965, is to have flourished in the Age of Freud, hardly a time when Anglo-Catholic theology, social thought, and morality were central to the main movement of mind. Even a few sentences of Eliotic polemic, chosen at random, seem unreal in the world of 1984:

> It would perhaps be more natural, as well as in better conformity with the Will of God, if there were more celibates and if those who were married had larger families ...

> If you will not have God (and He is a jealous God) you should pay your respects to Hitler or Stalin.

> ... a positive culture must have a positive set of values, and the dissentients must remain marginal, tending to make only marginal contributions.

These are excerpts from *The Idea of a Christian Society* and were written in 1939. Frank Kermode, a distinguished authority on Eliot, writing in 1975, insisted "that Eliot profoundly changed our thinking about poetry and criticism without trying to impose as a condition of his gift the acceptance of consequences which, for him, followed as a matter of reason, as well as of belief and personal vocation." It may well be that the largest difference between Kermode's critical generation, in England, and the next generation, in America, is that we changed our thinking about poetry and criticism in reaction against Eliot's thinking, precisely because Eliot's followers had imposed upon us consequences peculiar to his belief and his personal vocation. Whether Eliot's discriminations were so fine as Kermode asserts is yet another matter. Shelley's skeptical yet passionate beliefs, according to Eliot, were not coherent, not mature, not founded upon the facts of experience. Eliot once gave thanks that Walter Pater never wrote about *Hamlet*; would that Eliot never had done so. We would have been spared the influential but unfortunate judgment "that here Shakespeare tackled a problem which proved too much for him." Eliot doubtless is in the line of poet-critics: Ben Jonson, Dryden, Dr. Samuel Johnson, Coleridge, Poe and Arnold are among those who precede him. As a critic, he does not approach the first four, but surely equals Poe and Arnold, equivocal praise, though he certainly surpassed Poe and Arnold as poets. It is difficult to prophesy that Eliot's criticism will prove to be of permanent value, but perhaps we need to await the arrival of a generation neither formed by him nor rebelling against him, before we justly can place him.

## IV

That Eliot, in retrospect, will seem the Matthew Arnold rather than the Abraham Cowley of his age, is the sympathetic judgment of A. Walton Litz. For motives admitted already, one might prefer to see Eliot as the Cowley, and some celebrated passages in *Four Quartets* are worthy of comparison with long-ago-admired Pindarics of that forgotten wit, but Arnold's burden as involuntary belated Romantic is indeed close to Eliot's. A direct comparison of Eliot's elegiac achievement to Whitman's or Tennyson's seems to me both more problematical and more inevitable. "Gerontion" contrasts unfavorably to "Tithonus" or "Ulysses," while *The Waste Land*, despite its critical high priests, lacks the coherence, maturity and experiential authenticity of "When Lilacs Last in the Dooryard Bloom'd." And yet it must be admitted that Eliot is what the closing lines of *The Waste Land* assert him to be: a shorer of fragments against his (and our) ruins. The phantasmagoric intensity of his best poems and passages can be matched only in the greatest visionaries and poets of Western literature. It is another paradox that the Anglo-Catholic, Royalist, Classical spokesperson should excel in the mode of fictive hallucination and lyric derangement, in the fashioning of nightmare images perfectly expressive of his age.

Eliot's influence as a poet is by no means spent, yet it seems likely that Robert Penn Warren's later poetry, the most distinguished now being written among us, will be the final stand of Eliot's extraordinary effort to establish an anti-Romantic counter-Sublime sense of *the* tradition to replace the continuity of Romantic tradition. That the continuity now has absorbed him is hardly a defeat; absorption is not rejection, and Eliot's poetry is securely in the canon. Eliot's strength, manifested in the many poets indebted to him, is probably most authentically commemorated by the poetry of Hart Crane, which engages Eliot's poetry in an agon without which Crane could not have achieved his difficult greatness. One can prefer Crane to Eliot, as I do, and yet be forced to concede that Eliot, more than Whitman, made Crane possible.

## V

The essays in this collection chronicle the agon that criticism has entered into with Eliot, primarily with Eliot's major poems. I have arranged them in the order of their publication, with only the first two, by Kenner and Frye, representing the literary climate while Eliot was still alive. Kenner, then and now, is Eliot's champion, to the extent of apparently preferring Eliot's verse dramas to Shakespeare's:

> None of the actors, deprived of fine lines to mouth, is allowed to affirm a vision centered on himself, as Othello does, as Hamlet does. And if they are deprived of that satisfaction, it is because the plays are about privacy, not affirmation. Shakespeare's is for better or worse a universe of actors, strutting and fretting; and so is the universe of *The Waste Land*; but the universe of Eliot's dramatic comedies is a universe of persons who learn to discard the satisfactions of the imprisoning role.

That is Kenner in 1962; reading him again after more than twenty years is to team that "modernism" is only another defensive antiquarianism. Northrop Frye, a year later, began the Romantic counter-offensive by noting that Eliot rather disapproved of Shakespeare because "Shakespeare does not always take a maturely dim view of human nature." The remaining critics in this volume wrote during the 1970s and the early 1980s, and are none of them Eliotics, like Kenner or such allied figures as F.R. Leavis, R.P. Blackmur, and Cleanth Brooks, all of whom placed Eliot with the sages as well as with the poets. But the critics whom I reprint here are, like Frye, in a more benign relation to Eliot than I can achieve. Olney, Goldman, Donoghue, Ellmann, Gordon, Nevo and Jay do not read Eliot as a cultural prophet or as a secular saint. They study him, with sympathy and insight, as one of the representative poets of his time, and each of them adds to our increasingly accurate sense of his authentic relation to poetic history.

Eliot, writing in 1948, ended his *Notes Towards the Definition of Culture* by affirming that the culture of Europe could not survive the disappearance of the Christian faith, because: "It is in Christianity that our arts have developed ... It is against a background of Christianity that all our thought has significance." That seems to be the center of Eliot's polemic, and each reader must make of it what she or he can or will. The Age of Freud, Kafka and Proust, of Yeats, Wallace Stevens, Beckett: somehow these thoughts and visions suggest a very different definition of culture than the Eliotic one. Perhaps it was fortunate for Eliot that he was a Late Romantic poet long before he became, for a time, the cultural oracle of the academies.

## The Waste Land

### I

Eliot's *Ara Vos Prec* (London: The Ovid Press, 1920) contained a curious, rather flat poem, oddly titled "Ode," which he sensibly never reprinted. It appears to lament or commemorate his failed sexual relationship with his first wife, and strangely connects the failure with two Whitmanian allusions ("Misunderstood / The accents of the now retired / Profession of the calamus" and "Io Hymen, Hymenae / Succuba eviscerate"). Manifestly, "Ode" mocks Whitman's erotic declarations, but the mockery is equivocal. Eliot's declared precursors form a celebrated company: Virgil, Dante, the English Metaphysicals and Jacobean dramatists, Pascal, Baudelaire, the French Symbolists, and Ezra Pound. His actual poetry derives from Tennyson and Whitman, with Whitman as the larger, indeed the dominant influence. Indeed, Shelley and Browning are more embedded in Eliot's verse than are Donne and Webster. English and American Romantic tradition is certainly not the tradition that Eliot chose, but the poetic family romance, like its human analogue, is not exactly an arena where the will dominates.

The Waste Land is an American self-elegy masking as a mythological romance, a Romantic crisis poem pretending to be an exercise in Christian irony. Mask and pretence, like the invention of more congenial fathers and ancestors, are customary poetic tropes, and certainly not to be censured. They are part of any poet's magic, or personal superstition, and they help to get authentic poems written. *The Waste Land*, rather than *Four Quartets* or the verse dramas, is Eliot's major achievement, a grand gathering of great fragments, and indisputably the most influential poem written in English in our century. I read it, on evidence internal and external, as being essentially a revision of Whitman's final great achievement, "When Lilacs Last in the Dooryard Bloom'd," ostensibly an elegy for Lincoln, but more truly the poet's lament for his own poethood. Elegy rather than brief epic or quest-romance, *The Waste Land* thus enters the domain of mourning and melancholia, rather than that of civilization and its discontents.

Many of the links between Eliot's and Whitman's elegies for the poetic self have been noted by a series of exegetes starting with S. Musgrove, and continuing with John Hollander and myself, and younger critics, including Gregory S. Jay and Cleo McNelly Kearns, whose definitive observations conclude the book I am now introducing. Rather than repeat Cleo Kearns, I intend to speculate here upon the place of *The Waste Land* in Romantic tradition, particularly in regard to its inescapable precursor, Whitman.

## II

In his essay, "The *Pensées* of Pascal" (1931), Eliot remarked upon Pascal's adversarial relation to his true precursor, Montaigne:

> One cannot destroy Pascal, certainly; but of all authors Montaigne is one of the least destructible. You could as well dissipate a fog by flinging hand-grenades into it. For Montaigne is a fog, a gas, a fluid, insidious element. He does not reason, he insinuates, charms, and influences.

Walt Whitman, too, is "a fluid, insidious element," a poet who "insinuates, charms, and influences." And he is the darkest of poets, despite his brazen self-advertisements, and his passionate hopes for his nation. *Song of Myself*, for all its joyous epiphanies, chants also of the waste places:

> Of the turbid pool that lies in the autumn forest,
> Of the moon that descends the steeps of the
>      soughing twilight,
> Toss, sparkles of day and dusk—toss on the
>      black stems that decay in the muck,
> Toss to the moaning gibberish of the dry limbs.

No deep reader of Whitman could forget the vision of total self-rejection that is the short poem, "A Hand-Mirror":

> Hold it up sternly—see this it sends back, (who is
>      it? is it you?)
> Outside fair costume, within ashes and filth,

No more a flashing eye, no more a sonorous voice
    or springy step,
Now some slave's eye, voice, hands, step,
A drunkard's breath, unwholesome eater's face,
    venerealee's flesh,
Lungs rotting away piecemeal, stomach sour and
    cankerous,
Joints rheumatic, bowels clogged with abomination,
Blood circulating dark and poisonous streams,
Words babble, hearing and touch callous,
No brain, no heart left, no magnetism of sex;
Such from one look in this looking-glass ere you go
    hence,
Such a result so soon—and from such a beginning!

Rather than multiply images of despair in Whitman, I turn to the most rugged of his self-accusations, in the astonishing "Crossing Brooklyn Ferry":

It is not upon you alone the dark patches fall,
The dark threw its patches down upon me also,
The best I had done seem'd to me blank and suspicious,
My great thoughts as I supposed them, were they not
    in reality meagre?
Nor is it you alone who know what it is to be evil,
I am he who knew what it was to be evil,
I too knotted the old knot of contrariety,
Blabb'd, blush'd, resented, lied, stole, grudg'd,
Had guile, anger, lust, hot wishes I dared not speak,
Was wayward, vain, greedy, shallow, sly, cowardly,
    malignant,
The wolf, the snake, the hog, not wanting in me,
The cheating look, the frivolous word, the adulterous
    wish, not wanting,
Refusals, hates, postponements, meanness, laziness,
    none of these wanting,
Was one with the rest, the days and haps of the rest,
Was call'd by my nighest name by clear loud voices of young
    men as they saw me approaching or passing,
Felt their arms on my neck as I stood, or the negligent
    leaning of their flesh against me as I sat,

Saw many I loved in the street or ferry-boat or public
      assembly, yet never told them a word,
Lived the same life with the rest, the same old
      laughing, gnawing, sleeping,
Play'd the part that still looks back on the actor or
      actress,
The same old role, the role that is what we make it, as
      great as we like,
Or as small as we like, or both great and small.

The barely concealed allusions to Milton's Satan and to *King Lear* strengthen Whitman's catalog of vices and evasions, preparing the poet and his readers for the darker intensities of the great *Sea-Drift* elegies and "Lilacs," poems that are echoed everywhere in Eliot's verse, but particularly in "The Death of Saint Narcissus," *The Waste Land*, and "The Dry Salvages." Many critics have charted these allusions, but I would turn consideration of Eliot's agon with Whitman to the question: "Why Whitman?" It is poetically unwise to go down to the waterline, or go to the headland with Walt Whitman, for then the struggle takes place in an arena where the poet who found his identifying trope in the sea-drift cannot lose.

An answer must be that the belated poet does not choose his trial by landscape or seascape. It is chosen for him by his precursor. Browning's quester in "Childe Roland to the Dark Tower Came" is as overdetermined by Shelley as Eliot is overdetermined by Whitman in *The Waste Land*, which is indeed Eliot's version of "Childe Roland," as it is Eliot's version of Percivale's quest in Tennyson's "The Holy Grail," a poem haunted by Keats in the image of Galahad. "Lilacs" is everywhere in *The Waste Land*: in the very lilacs bred out of the dead land, in the song of the hermit thrush in the pine trees, and most remarkably in the transumption of Whitman walking down to where the hermit thrush sings, accompanied by two companions walking beside him, the thought of death and the knowledge of death:

Then with the knowledge of death as walking one
      side of me,
And the thought of death close-walking the other
      side of me,
And I in the middle as with companions, and as
      holding the hands of companions,
I fled forth to the hiding receiving night that talks
      not,

Down to the shores of the water, the path by the
    swamp in the dimness,
To the solemn shadowy cedars and ghostly pines so
    still.

The "crape-veil'd women" singing their dirges through the night for
Lincoln are hardly to be distinguished from Eliot's "murmur of maternal
lamentation," and Whitman's "tolling tolling bells' perpetual clang" goes
on tolling reminiscent bells in *The Waste Land* as it does in "The Dry
Salvages." Yet all this is only a first-level working of the influence process,
of interest mostly as a return of the repressed. Deeper, almost beyond analytical modes as yet available to criticism, is Eliot's troubled introjection of
his nation's greatest and inescapable elegiac poet. "Lilacs" has little to do
with the death of Lincoln but everything to do with Whitman's ultimate
poetic crisis, beyond which his strongest poetry will cease. *The Waste Land*
has little to do with neo-Christian polemics concerning the decline of
Western culture, and everything to do with a poetic crisis that Eliot could
not quite surmount, in my judgment, since I do not believe that time will
confirm the estimate that most contemporary critics have made of *Four
Quartets*.

The decisive moment or negative epiphany of Whitman's elegy centers upon his giving up of the tally, the sprig of lilac that is the synecdoche
for his image of poetic voice, which he yields up to death and to the hermit thrush's song of death. Eliot's parallel surrender in "What the Thunder
Said" is to ask "what have we given?," where the implicit answer is "a
moment's surrender," a negative moment in which the image of poetic
voice is achieved only as one of Whitman's "retrievements out of the
night."

In his essay on Pascal, Eliot says of Montaigne, a little resentfully but
with full accuracy, that "he succeeded in giving expression to the skepticism of *every* human being," presumably including Pascal, and
Shakespeare, and even T.S. Eliot. What did Whitman succeed in expressing with equal universality? Division between "myself" and "the real me"
is surely the answer. Walt Whitman, one of the roughs, an American, is
hardly identical with "the Me myself" who:

Looks with its sidecurved head curious what will come
    next,
Both in and out of the game, and watching and
    wondering at it.

Thomas Stearns Eliot, looking with side-curved head, both in and out of the game, has little in common with Walt Whitman, one of the roughs, an American, yet almost can be identified with that American "Me myself."

## III

The line of descent from Shelley and Keats through Browning and Tennyson to Pound and Eliot would be direct, were it not for the intervention of the genius of the shores of America, the poet of *Leaves of Grass*. Whitman enforces upon Pound and Eliot the American difference, which he had inherited from Emerson, the fountain of our eloquence and of our pragmatism. Most reductively defined, the American poetic difference ensues from a sense of acute isolation, both from an overwhelming space of natural reality, and from an oppressive temporal conviction of belatedness, of having arrived after the event. The inevitable defense against nature is the Gnostic conviction that one is no part of the creation, that one's freedom is invested in the primal abyss. Against belatedness, defense involves an immersion in allusiveness, hardly for its own sake, but in order to reverse the priority of the cultural, pre-American past. American poets from Whitman and Dickinson onwards are more like Milton than Milton is, and so necessarily they are more profoundly Miltonic than even Keats or Tennyson was compelled to be.

What has wasted the land of Eliot's elegiac poem is neither the malady of the Fisher King nor the decline of Christianity, and Eliot's own psychosexual sorrows are not very relevant either. The precursors' strength is the illness of *The Waste Land*; Eliot after all can promise to show us "fear in a handful of dust" only because the monologist of Tennyson's *Maud* already has cried out: "Dead, long dead, / Long dead! / And my heart is a handful of dust." Even more poignantly, Eliot is able to sum up all of Whitman's extraordinary "As I Ebb'd with the Ocean of Life" in the single line: "These fragments I have shored against my ruins," where the fragments are not only the verse paragraphs that constitute the text of *The Waste Land*, but crucially are also Whitman's floating sea-drift:

Me and mine, loose windrows, little corpses,
Froth, snowy white, and bubbles,
(See, from my dead lips the ooze exuding at last,
See, the prismatic colors glistening and rolling,)
Tufts of straw, sands, fragments,
Buoy'd hither from many moods, one contradicting
      another.

From the storm, the long calm, the darkness, the swell,
Musing, pondering, a breath, a briny tear, a dab of
      liquid or soil,
Up just as much out of fathomless workings fermented
      and thrown,
A limp blossom or two, torn, just as much over waves
      floating, drifted at random,
Just as much for us that sobbing dirge of Nature,
Just as much whence we come that blare of the cloud—
      trumpets,
We, capricious, brought hither we know not whence,
      spread out before you,
You up there walking or sitting,
Whoever you are, we too lie in drifts at your feet.

"Tufts of straw, sands, fragments" are literally "shored" against Whitman's ruins, as he wends "the shores I know," the shores of America to which, Whitman said, Emerson had led all of us, Eliot included. Emerson's essays, Eliot pugnaciously remarked, "are already an encumbrance," and so they were, and are, and evermore must be for an American writer, but inescapable encumbrances are also stimuli, as Pascal learned in regard to the overwhelming Montaigne.

# Hart Crane

## (1899–1932)

O Thou steeled Cognizance whose leap commits
The agile precincts of the lark's return ...

I REMEMBER READING THESE LINES WHEN I WAS TEN YEARS OLD, CROUCHED
over Crane's book in a Bronx library. They, and much else in the book,
cathected me onto poetry, a conversion or investment fairly typical of many
in my generation. I still have the volume of Crane that I persuaded my
older sister to give me on my twelfth birthday, the first book I ever owned.
Among my friends there are a few others who owned Crane before any
other book. Growing up in the thirties, we found by Crane's poetry, and
though other poets followed (I went from Crane to Blake), the strength of
first love still hovers whenever they, or I, read Crane.

The Marlovian rhetoric swept us in, but as with Marlowe himself the
rhetoric was also a psychology and a knowing, rather than knowledge, a
knowing that precisely can be called Gnosis, transcending the epistemology of tropes. What the Australian poet Alec Hope, echoing Tamburlaine,
perceptively called the "The Argument of Arms" is as much Crane's knowing and language as it was Marlowe's. "Know ye not the argument of
arms?" Tamburlaine calls out to his protesting generals before he stabs his
own son to death for cowardice. As Hope expounds it, "the argument of
arms" is poetic warfare, the agnostic interplay of the Sublime mode:

There is no middle way and no compromise in such a world.
Beauty is the rival of beauty as force of force, and only the
supreme and perfect survives. Defeat, like victory, is total,
absolute, final.

This is indeed Marlowe's knowing, and it would be pointless for a humanist critic to complain that such a vision is human—all-too-human. *Power* is the central poetic concept in Marlowe as it will be in Milton, Emerson (a prose Milton, granted), and in Crane as a kind of American Marlowe. Hope rightly points to Hazlitt on *Coriolanus* as the proper theorist of the union of the Argument of Arms and the Argument of Poetry. Hazlitt also would not gain the approval of the natural supernaturalist kind of critical humanist:

> The principle of poetry is a very anti-leveling principle. It aims at effect, it exists by contrast. It admits of no medium. It is everything by excess. It rises above the ordinary standard of suffering and crimes.

But Crane is a prophet of American Orphism, of the Emersonian and Whitmanian Native Strain in our national literature. His poetic of power is therefore best caught by the American theorist proper:

> ... though Fate is immense, so is Power, which is the other fact in the dual world, immense. If Fate follows and limits Power, Power attends and antagonizes Fate. We must respect Fate as natural history. For who and what is this criticism that pries into the matter? Man not order of nature, sack and sack, belly and members, link in a chain, nor any ignominious baggage; but a stupendous antagonism, a dragging together of the poles of the Universe ...

This might be Melville, meditating upon his own Ahab, but of course it is the uncanny Sage of Concord, satirized by Melville as Plotinus Plinlimmon and as Confidence Man; yet the satire was uneasy. Crane is not very easy to satirize either, and like Shelley, with whom his affinities were deep, Crane goes on burying his critical undertakers. Whitman and Dickinson, Frost and Stevens all had enough, but Crane, perhaps more gifted than any of them, was finished at an age when they had begun weakly or not at all. A Gnosis of man as a stupendous antagonism, Orphic and Promethean, needs time to work itself through, but time, reviled by all Gnostics with a particular vehemence, had its literal triumph over Crane. As with Shelley and Keats, we have a truncated canon, and yet, as with them, what we have is overwhelming. And what is overwhelms, amidst much else, is any privileging of understanding as an epistemological event, prior to being the catastrophe creation of an aesthetic and spiritual value.

I am concerned here with Crane's "religion" *as a poet* (not as a man, since that seems an inchoate mixture of a Christian Science background, an immersion in Ouspensky, and an all but Catholic yearning). But by poetic "religion" I mean American Orphism, the Emersonian or national religion of out poetry, which Crane inherited, quite directly, from his prime precursor Whitman. True precursors are always composite and imaginary—the son's changeling-fantasy of the father that his own poetry reinvents—and there is usually a near-contemporary agon, as well as an antagonist. And sharper for Crane was certainly Eliot, whose anti-Romantic polemic provoked in Crane an answering fury of High Romanticism, absurdly undervalued by Crane's critical contemporaries, but returning to its mainstream status in the generation that receives the recent abundance of poetic maturation in Ashbery, Merrill, Ammons, Hollander and others.

The governing deities of American Orphism, as of the ancient sort, are Eros or Phanes, Dionysus or Bacchus, and Ananke, the Necessity who appears as the maternal ocean in Whitman and Crane, most overly, but clearly and obsessively enough in Stevens also. Not so clear, though just as obsessive, must be our judgment upon Melville's representations of an Orphic Ananke in the great shroud of the sea. Melville's "that man should be a thing for immortal souls to sieve through!" is the apt epigraph of a crucial chapter on Greek Shamanism in E.R. Dodds' great book *The Greeks and the Irrational.* Dodds traced to Scythia the new Orphic religious pattern that credited man with an occult self of divine origin. This self was not the *psyche*, but the *daemon*; as Dodds says, "the function of the daemon is to be the carrier of man's potential divinity and actual guilt." Crane's daemon or occult self, like Whitman's, is the actual hero and victim of his own poetry. Crane as American Orpheus is an inevitable image, exploited already by writers as diverse as Yvor Winters in his elegy for Crane, and Tennessee Williams in *Suddenly Last Summer.* The best of the Orphic hymns to Crane is the astonishing poem *Fish Food* of John Brooks Wheelwright, except that Crane wrote his own best Orphic elegy in "Atlantis," his close equivalent of Shelley's *Adonais.* But I narrow my subject here of Crane's "Orphism" down to its visionary epistemology or Gnosis. Crane's Eros, his Dionysus, above all his Whitmanian Ananke, remain to be explored, but in these remarks I concern myself only with Crane as "daemon," a potential divinity knowing simultaneously its achievement and its guilt.

The assumption of that daemon, or what the poets of Sensibility called "the incarnation of the Poetic Character," is the inner plot of many of the lyrics in *White Buildings.* The *kenosis* or ebbing-away of the daemon is the plot of the *Voyages* sequence, where the other Orphic deities reduce Crane to a "derelict and blinded guest" of his own vision, and where the "ocean rivers" churn up the Orphic heritage as a "splintered garland for the seer." Certainly the most ambitious of the daemonic incarnations is the sequence *For the Marriage of Faustus and Helen*, which is Crane at his most triumphantly Marlovian, but so much else is at play there that I turn two lesser but perfect hymns of Orphic incarnation, *Repose of Rivers* and *Passage*.

Crane is a great master of transumptive allusion, of achieving poetic closure by a final trope that reverses or sometimes even transcends both his own lyric's dominant figurations and the poetic tradition's previous exploitations of these images. So, *Repose of Rivers* concludes:

> ... There, beyond the dykes
> I heard wind flaking sapphire, like this summer,
> and willows could not hold more steady sound.

The poem's opening stanza gives a more complex version of that "steady sound" because the synaesthetic seeing/hearing of "that seething, steady leveling of the marches" is both an irony and an oxymoron:

> The willows carried a slow sound,
> A sarabande the wind mowed on the mead.
> I could never remember
> That seething, steady leveling of the marches
> Till age had brought me to the sea.

Crane is recalling his version of a Primal Scene of Instruction, a moment renewing itself discontinuously at scattered intervals, yet always for him a moment relating the inevitability of sexual orientation to the assumption of his poethood. The slow-and-steady dance of the wind on the marshes became a repressed memory until "age" as maturation brought the poet to the sea, central image of necessity in his poetry, and a wounding synecdoche here for an acceptance of one's particular fate as a poet. The repressed reveals itself as a grotesque sublimity, with the second stanza alluding to Melville's imagery in his story *The Encantadas*:

> Flags, weeds. And remembrance of steep alcoves
> Where cypresses shared the noon's
> Tyranny; they drew me into hades almost.
> And mammoth turtles climbing sulphur dreams

Yielded, while sun-silt rippled them
Asunder...

The seething, steady leveling of the mammoth turtles, their infernal love-death, is a kind of sarabande also. In climbing on another they climb dreams of self-immolation, where "yielded" means at once surrender to death and to one another. The terrible slowness of their love-making yields the frightening trope: "sun-silt rippled them / Asunder," where "asunder" is both the post-coition parting and the individual turtle death. Crane and D.H. Lawrence had in common as poets only their mutual devotion to Whitman, and its is instructive to contrast this stanza of *Repose of Rivers* with the Tortoise-series of Lawrence in *Birds, Beasts, and Flowers*. Lawrence's tortoises are crucified *into* sex, like Lawrence himself. Crane's Melvillean turtles are crucified *by* sex. But Crane tells a different story about himself: crucified *into* poetry and *by* poetry. The turtles are drawn into sexual Hades; Crane is *almost* drawn, with the phrase "hades almost" playing against "steep alcove." Embowered by steep alcoves of cypresses intensifying the dominant noon sun, Crane nearly yields to the sexual phantasmagoria of "flags, weeds," and the sound play alcoves/almost intensifies the narrowness of the escape from a primary sexuality, presumably an incestuous heterosexuality. This is the highly oblique burden of the extraordinary third stanza:

How much I would have bartered! the black gorge
And all the singular nestings in the hills
Where beavers learn stitch and tooth.
The pond I entered once and quickly fled—
I remember now its singing willow rim.

What he would have bartered, indeed did barter, was nature for poetry. Where the second stanza was a *kenosis*, an emptying-out, of the Orphic self, this stanza is fresh influx, and what returns from repression is poetic apperception: "I remember now its singing willow rim," a line that reverberates greatly against the first and last lines of the entire poem. The surrendered Sublime here is a progressive triad of entities: the Wordsworthian Abyss of birth of "the black gorge"; "the singular nestings," instructive of work and of aggression; most memorably the pond, rimmed by singing willows, whose entrance actually marks the momentary daring of the representation of Oedipal trespass, or perhaps for Crane one should say "Orphic trespass."

If everything heretofore in *Repose of Rivers* has been bettered for the antithetical gift of Orpheus, what remains is to represent the actual passage into sexuality, and after that the poetic maturation that follows homosexual self-acceptance. Whether the vision here is of an actual city, or of a New Orleans of the mind, as at the end of the "River" section of *The Bridge*, the balance of pleasure and of pain is left ambiguous:

> And finally, in that memory all things nurse;
> After the city that I finally passed
> With scalding unguents spread and smoking darts
> The monsoon cut across the delta
> At gulf gates ... There, beyond the dykes
>
> I heard wind flaking sapphire, like this summer,
> And willows could not hold more steady sound.

The third line of the stanza refers both to the pathos of the city and to Crane's own sexual initiation. But since "all things nurse" this memory, the emphasis must be upon breakthrough, upon the contrast between monsoon and the long-obliterated memory of sarabande-wind. "Like this summer," the fictive moments of the lyric's composition, the monsoon of final sexual alignment gave the gift of an achieved poethood, to hear wind synaesthetically, flaking sapphire, breaking up yet also distributing the Shelleyan azure of vision. In such a context, the final line massively gathers an Orphic confidence.

Yet every close reader of Crane learns to listen to the wind for evidences of *sparagmos*, of the Orphic breakup, as prevalent in Crane's winds as in Shelley's, or in Whitman's. I turn to *Passage*, *White Buildings*'s particular poem of Orphic disincarnation, where the rite of passage, the movement back to unfindable and fictive origins, is celebrated more memorably in the opening quatrain than anywhere else even in Crane, who is clearly the great modern poet of *thresholds*, in the sense definitively expounded in Angus Fletcher's forthcoming book of that title.

> Where the cedar leaf divides the sky
> I heard the sea.
> In sapphire arenas of the hills
> I was promised an improved infancy.

The Fletcherian *threshold* is a daemonic crossing or textual "image of voice," to use Wordsworth's crucial term. Such a chiasmus tends to hover where tropes collide in an epistemological wilderness. Is there a more outrageously American, Emersonian concept and phrase than "an improved infancy"? Crane presumably was not aware that *Passage* centered itself so directly at the Wordsworthian heart of the crisis poem, in direct competition with *Tintern Abbey* and the *Intimations of Immortality* ode. But the American version as established in the *Seadrift* poems of Whitman was model enough. Crane, inland far though he finds himself, hears the sea. The soft inland murmur promised Wordsworth so improved an infancy that it became an actual initiation of a more-than-poetic immortality. But for Whitman the secret of the murmuring he envied had to be listened or at the water-line. Crane quests for the same emblem that rewarded *Repose of Rivers*, but here the wind does not flake sapphire in the arenas of these inland hills, where the agon with the daemon, Whitman's dusky lemon and brother, is to take place.

In Whitman's great elegy of Orphic disincarnation, *As I Ebb'd with The Ocean of Life*, the daemon comes to the poet in the shape of a sardonic phantom, "the real Me," and confronts Whitman, who may hold his book, *Leaves of Grass*, in hand, since the phantom is able to point to it:

> But that before all my arrogant poems the real Me stands yet
>     untouch'd, untold, altogether unreach'd,
> Withdrawn far, mocking me with mock-congratulatory signs
>     and bows,
> With peals of distant ironical laughter at every word I have
>     written,
> Pointing in silence to these songs, and then to the sand
>     beneath.
> I perceive I have never really understood anything, not a single
>     object, and that no man ever can,
> Nature here in sight of the sea taking advantage of me to dart
>     upon me and sting me,
> Because I have dared to open my mouth at all.

In Crane's *Passage* the sulking poet, denied his promise, abandons memory in a ravine, and tries to identify himself with the wind; but it dies, and he is turned back and around to confront his mocking daemon:

> Touching an opening laurel, I found
> A thief beneath, my stolen book in hand.

It is deliberately ambiguous whether the real Me has stolen the book, or whether the book of Hart Crane itself is stolen property. Unlike the abashed Whitman, Crane is aggressive, and his phantom is lost in wonderment:

> "Why are you back here—smiling an iron coffin?"
> "To argue with the laurel," I replied:
> "Am justified in transience, fleeing
> Under the constant wonder of your eyes—."

But nature here, suddenly in sight of the sea, does take advantage of Crane to dart upon him and sting him, because he has dared to open his mouth to sing at all:

> He closed the book. And from the Ptolemies
> Sand troughed us in a glittering abyss.
> A serpent swam a vertex to the sun
> —Oh unpaced beaches learned its tongue and drummed.
> What fountains did I hear? what icy speeches?
> Memory, committed to the page, had broke.

The Ptolemies, alluded to here as though they were a galaxy rather than a dynasty, help establish the pyramid image for the serpent who touches its apex in the sun. The glittering abyss belongs both to time and the sun, and the serpent, drumming its tongue upon the beach where no Whitmanian bard paces, is weirdly prophetic of the imagery of Stevens's *The Auroras of Autumn*. The penultimate line glances obliquely at Coleridge's *Kubla Khan*, and the poem ends appropriately with the broken enchantment of memory, broken in the act of writing the poem. It is as though, point for point, *Passage* had undone *Repose of Rivers*.

### The Bridge

*The Bridge* can be read as the same daemonic vision subsequently undone by an ebbing-out of poethood. That reading, though traditional, seems to me a weak misreading, inadequate to *The Bridge*'s strong misreadings of its precursors. Nietzsche and Pater, both of whom Crane had pondered, taught a subtler *askesis*, and *The Bridge* advances upon *White Buildings* (except for *Voyages*), by mounting a powerful scheme of transumption, of what Nietzsche called the poetic will's revenge against time and particularly against time's proclamation of belatedness: "It was." Crane shrewdly wrote, in 1918: "one may envy Nietzsche a little; think of being so elusive,—so mercurial, as to be first swallowed whole, then coughed up, and still remain a mystery!" But veteran readers of Crane learn to observe something like that when confronted by the majesty of *The Bridge* at its finest, as here in the final quatrains of the "Poem":

> Again the traffic lights that skim thy swift
> Unfractioned idiom, immaculate sigh of stars,
> Beading thy path—condense eternity:
> And we have seen night lifted in thine arms.
>
> Under thy shadow by the piers I waited;
> Only in darkness is thy shadow clear.
> The City's fiery parcels all undone,
> Already snow submerges an iron year ...
>
> O Sleepless as the river under thee,
> Vaulting the sea, the prairies' dreaming sod,
> Unto us lowliest sometime sweep, descend
> And of the curveship lend a myth to God.

Crane in *White Buildings* is wholly Orphic, in that his concern is his relation, as poet, *to* his own vision, rather than *with* the content of poetic vision, to utilize a general distinction inaugurated by Northrop Frye; following after Ruskin. The peculiar power of *The Bridge* at its strongest is that Crane succeeds in becoming what Pater and Nietzsche urged the future poet to be: an ascetic of the spirit, which is an accurate definition of a purified Gnosis. Directly before these three final quatrains of "To Brooklyn Bridge," Crane had saluted the bridge first as Orphic emblem, both harp and alter, but then as the threshold of the full triad of the Orphic destiny: Dionysus or prophet's pledge, Ananke or prayer of pariah, and Eros, the lover's cry. It is after the range of relations to his own vision has been acknowledged and accepted that a stronger Crane achieves the Gnosis of those three last quatrains. There the poet remains present, but only as a knowing Abyss, contemplating the content of that knowing, which is a fullness or presence he can invoke but scarcely share. He sees "night lifted in thine arm"; he waits, for a shadow to clarify in the darkness; he knows, yet what he knows is a vaulting, a sweep, a descent, above all curveship, a realization of an angle of vision not yet his own.

This peculiarly effective stance has a precursor in Shelley's visionary skepticism, particularly in his final phase of *Adonais* and *The Triumph of Life*. Crane's achievement of this stance is the still-unexplored origin of *The Bridge*, but the textual evolution of "Atlantis," the first section of the visionary epic to be composed, is the probable area that should be considered. Lacking space here, I point instead to the achieved stance of *Voyages VI* as the earliest full instance of Crane's mature Orphism, after which I will conclude with a reading of "Atlantis" and a brief glance at Crane's testament, *The Broken Tower*.

The governing deities of the *Voyages* sequence are Eros and Ananke, or Emil Oppfer and the Caribbean as Whitmanian fierce old mother moaning for her castaways. But the Orphic Dionysus, rent apart by Titanic forces, dominates the sixth lyric, which like Stevens's *The Paltry Nude Stares upon a Spring Journey* partly derives from Pater's description of Botticelli's Venus in *The Renaissance*. Pater's sadomasochistic maternal love-goddess, with her eyes smiling "unsearchable repose," becomes Crane's overtly destructive muse, whose seer is no longer at home in his own vision:

My eyes pressed black against the prow,
—Thy derelict and blinded guest

Waiting afire, what name, unspoken,
I cannot claim: let thy waves rear

More savage than the death of kings,
Some splintered garland for the seer.

The unspoken, unclaimed name is that of Orpheus, in his terrible final phase of "floating singer." Crane's highly deliberate echo of Shakespeare's Richard II at his most self-destructively masochistic is assimilated to the poetic equivalent, which is the splintering of the garland of the laurel. Yet the final stanza returns to the central image of poetic incarnation in Crane, *Repose of Rivers* and its "hushed willows":

The imagined Word, it is, that holds
Hushed willows anchored in its glow.
It is the unbetrayable reply
Whose accent no farewell can know.

This is the achieved and curiously firm balance of a visionary skepticism, or the Orphic stance of *The Bridge*. It can be contrasted to Lawrence again, in the "Orphic farewell" of *Medlars and Sorb Apples* in *Birds, Beasts and Flowers*. For Lawrence, Orphic assurance is the solipsism of an "intoxication of perfect loneliness." Crane crosses that intoxication by transuming his own and tradition's trope of the hushed willows as signifying an end to solitary mourning, and a renewal of poetic deviation. *Voyages VI* turns its "imaged Word" against Eliot's neo-orthodox Word, or Christ, and Whitman's Word out of the Sea, or death, death that is the Oedipal merging back into the mother. Crane ends upon "know" because knowledge, and not faith, is his religious mode, a Gnosis that is more fully developed in *The Bridge*.

The dozen octaves of the final version of "Atlantis" show Crane in his mastery of the traditional Sublime, and are wholly comparable to the final seventeen stanzas of Shelly's *Adonais*. Crane's absolute music, like Plato's, "is then the knowledge of that which relates to the love in harmony and system," but Crane's love is rather more like Shelly's desperate and skeptical outleaping than it is like Diotima's vision. For six stanzas, Crane drives upward, in a hyperbolic arc whose burden is agnostic, struggling to break beyond every achieved Sublime in the language. This agon belongs to the Sublime, and perhaps in America it *is* the Sublime. But such an agon requires particular contestants, and "Atlantis" finds them in *The Waste Land* and, yet more repressedly, in Whitman's *Crossing Brooklyn Ferry*, the great addition to the second, 1856, *Leaves of Grass*, and Thoreau's favorite poem by Whitman.

Much of Crane's struggle with Eliot was revised out of the final "Atlantis," but only as overt textual traces; the deep inwardness of the battle is recoverable. Two modes of phantasmagoria clash:

> Through the bound cable strands, the arching path
> Upward, veering with light, the flight of strings,—
> Taut miles of shuttling moonlight syncopate
> The whispered rush, telepathy of wires.
> Up the index of night, granite and steel—
> Transparent meshes—fleckless the gleaming staves—
> Sibylline voices flicker, waveringly stream
> As though a god were issue of the strings....
>
> A Woman drew her long black hair out tight
> And fiddled whisper music on those strings
> And bats with baby faces in the violet light
> Whistled, and beat their wings
> And crawled head downward down a blackened wall
> And upside down in air were towers
> Tolling reminiscent bells, that kept the hours
> And voices singing out of empty cisterns and exhausted wells.

The latter hallucination might be called an amalgam of *Dracula* and the Gospels, as rendered in the high style of Tennyson's *Idylls of the King*, and obvious is in no sense a source or cause of Crane's transcendental opening octave. Nevertheless, no clearer contrast could be afforded, for Crane's lines answer Eliot's, in every meaning of "answer." "Music is then the knowledge of that which relates to love in harmony and system," and one knowledge answers another in these competing and marvelous musics of poetry, and of visionary history. Crane's bridge is to Atlantis, in fulfillment of the Platonic quest of Crane's Columbus. Eliot's bridge is to the Inferno, in fulfillment of the neo-Christian condemnation of Romantic, Transcendentalists, Gnostic quest. Crane's Sibylline voices stream upward; his night-illuminated bridge becomes a transparent musical score, until Orpheus is born out of the flight of strings. Eliot's Sibyl wishes to die; her counterpart plays a vampiric score upon her own hair, until instead of an Orphic birth upwards we have an impotent triumph of time.

This contrast, and others equally sharp, constitute the context of Crane's aspiration in "Atlantis." But this aspiration, which is for knowledge, in the particular sense of Gnosis, yields to Eliot, as it must, much of the world of things-as-they-are. The closing images of "The Tunnel," the section of *The Bridge* preceding "Atlantis," combine *The Waste Land*'s accounts of loss with Whitman's darker visions of those losses in *Crossing Brooklyn Ferry*:

> And this thy harbor, O my City, I have driven under,
> Tossed from the coil of ticking towers.... Tomorrow,
> And to be.... Here by the River that is East—
> Here at the waters' edge the hands drop memory;
> Shadowless in that abyss they unaccounting lie.
> How far away the star has pooled the sea—
> Or shall the hands be drawn away, to die?
>
> Kiss of our agony Thou gatherest,
>      O Hand of Fire
>      gatherest—

Emerson's was a Gnosis without Gnosticism; Crane's religion, at its darkest, shades from Orphism into Gnosticism, in a negative transcendence even of the Whitman who proclaimed: "It is not upon you alone the dark patches fall, / The dark threw its patches upon me also." The negative transcendence of "Atlantis" surmounts the world, history and even precursors as knowing, in their rival ways, as Eliot and Whitman. Crane condenses the upward intensities of his first six octaves by a deliberate recall of his own Columbus triumphantly but delusively chanting: "I bring you back Cathay!" But Crane's Columbus invoked the Demiurge under Emily Dickinson's name for him, "Inquisitor! incognizable Word / Of Eden." This beautiful pathos of defeat, in "Ave Maria," was consonant with Whitman's *Prayer of Columbus*, where the battered, wrecked old mariner denied all knowledge: "I know not even my own word past or present." Crane's American burden, in the second half of "Atlantis," is to start again where Dickinson and Whitman ended, and where Eliot had sought to show no fresh start was possible. Knowledge in precisely the Gnostic sense—a knowing that knows the knower and is, *in itself*, the form of salvation—becomes Crane's formidable hymn addressed directly to itself, to poem and to bridge, until they become momentarily "One Song, one Bridge of Fire!" But is this persuasively different from the "Hand of Fire" that gathers the kiss of agony"?

The dialectic of Gnosticism is a triad of negation, evasion, and extravagance. Lurianic Kabbalah renders these as contradiction, breaking-of-the-vessels, and restitution. Fate, freedom, power is the Emersonian or American equivalent. All of these triads translate aesthetically into a dialectic of limitation, substitution and representation, as I have shown in several critical books starting with *A Map of Misreading*. Crane's negation or limitation, his contraction into Fate, is scarcely different from Eliot's, but then such rival negative theologies as Valentinian Gnosticism and Johannine Christianity are difficult to distinguish in their accounts of how to express divinity. Gnostic evasion, like Crane's notorious freedom and range in troping, is clearly more inventive than authorized Christian modes of substitution, just as Gnostic extravagance, again like Crane's hyperbolical Sublime, easily surpasses orthodox expressions of power.

Crane's elaborate evasiveness is crucial in the seventh stanza of "Atlantis," where the upward movement of the tropology has ended, and a westward lateral sweep of vision is substituted, with the bridge no longer confronted and addressed, but seen now as binding the continent:

> We left the haven hanging in the night—
> Sheened harbor lanterns backward fled the keel.
> Pacific here at time's end, bearing corn,—
> Eyes stammer through the pangs of dust and steel.
> And still the circular, indubitable frieze
> Of heaven's meditation, yoking wave
> To kneeling wave, one song devoutly binds—
> The vernal strophe chimes from deathless strings!

The third line implies not merely a circuit of the earth, but an achieved peace at the end of days, a millennial harvest. When the bridge returns in this stanza's last four lines, it has become heaven's own meditation, the known knowing human knower. And such a knowing leads Crane on to the single most central stanza of his life and work:

> O thou steeled Cognizance whose leap commits
> The agile precincts of the lark's return;
> Within whose lariat sweep encinctured sing
> In single chrysalis the many twain,—
> Of stars Thou art the stich and stallion glow
> And like an organ, Thou, with sound of doom—
> Sight, sound and flesh Thou leadest from time's realm
> As love strikes clear direction for the helm.

Contrast the Precise Shelleyan equivalent:

> The One remains, the many change and pass;
> Heaven's light forever shines, Earth's shadows fly;
> Life, like a dome of many-colored glass,
> Stains the white radiance of Eternity,
> Until Death tramples it to fragments.—Die
> If thou wouldst be with that which thou dost seek!
> Follow where all is fled!—Rome's azure sky,
> Flowers, ruins, statues, music, words, are weak
> The glory they transfuse with fitting truth to speak.

Superficially, the two stanzas are much at variance with Crane's tone apparently triumphal, Shelly's apparently despairing. But the pragmatic or merely natural burden of both stanzas is quite suicidal. The bridge, as "steeled Cognizance," resolves the many into One, but this music of unity is a "sound of doom" for all flesh and its senses living in time's realm. Love's "clear direction," as in Shelley's climactic stanza, is towards death. But Shelley is very much involved in his own relation, as poet, to his own vision. Crane's role, as known to the bridge's knower, forsakes that relation, and a terrifyingly free concentration on the content of poetic vision is the reward. "Of stars Thou art the stich and stallion glow" Marlowe himself would have envied, but since both terms of the trope, bridge and stars, exclude human, Crane is impelled onwards to extraordinary achievements in hyperbole. When the bridge is "iridescently upborne / Through the bright drench and fabric of our veins," then the human price of Gnosticism begins to mount also. Crane insists that all this is "to our joy," but that joy is as dialectical as Shelly's despair. And Crane, supremely intelligent, counts the cost, foreknowing all criticism:

> Migrations that must needs void memory,
> Inventions that cobblestone the heart,—
> Unspeakable Thou Bridge to Thee, O Love.
> Thy pardon for this history, whitest Flower,
> O Answer of all,—Anemone,—
> Now while thy petals spend the suns about us, hold—
> (O Thou whose radiance doth inherit me)
> Atlantis,—hold thy floating singer late!

Would it make a difference if this read: "Cathay,—hold thy floating singer late!" so that the prayer of pariah would belong to Columbus and not to Orpheus? Yes, for the final stanza then would have the Orphic strings leap and converge to a question clearly different:

> —One Song, one Bridge of Fire! Is it Atlantis,
> Now pity steeps the grass and rainbows ring
> The serpent with the eagle in the leaves ...?

Crane's revision of the Orphic stance of *White Buildings*, of lyrics like *Repose of Rivers* and *Passage*, here allows him a difference that is a triumph. His serpent and eagle are likelier to be Shelly's than Nietzsche's, for they remain at strife *within* their border of covenant, the ring of rainbows. Atlantis is urged to hold its Orpheus late, as a kind of newly fused Platonic myth of reconcilement to a higher world of forms, a myth of which Gnosticism was a direct heir. "Is it Cathay?," repeating the noble delusion of Columbus, is not a question of hinting defeat, but foreboding victory. Yet Orphic victories are dialectical, as Crane well knew. Knowledge indeed is the kernel, for Crane astutely shows awareness of what the greatest poets always know, which is that their figurations intend the will's limits, in the bewilderments of the Abyss of troping and of tropes.

The coda to Crane's poetry, and his life, is *The Broken Tower*, where the transumption of the Orphic quest does allow a final triumph:

> And so it was I entered the broken world
> To trace the visionary company of love, its voice
> An instant in the wind (I know not wither hurled)
> But not for long to hold each desperate choice.

Crane mentions reading other books by Pater, but not the unfinished novel *Gaston de Latour*. Its first few chapters, at least, would have fascinated him, and perhaps he did look into the opening pages, where the young Gaston undergoes a ceremony bridging the spirit and nature:

> Gaston alone, with all his mystic preoccupations, by the privilege of youth, seemed to belong to both, and link the visionary company about him to the external scene.

The "privilege of youth" was still Crane's when he died, and *The Broken Tower* remains as one of those links. Such a link, finally, is not to be judged as what Freud called "a false connection" or as another irony to be ironically recognized, but rather as a noble synecdoche, self-mutilating perhaps as is a steeled Cognizance, but by its very turning against the self, endlessly reconstituting the American poetic self, the *pneuma* or spark of an American Gnosis.

# Further Reading

Auty, Robert and A.T. Hatto. *Traditions of Heroic and Epic Poetry*. London: Modern Humanities Research Assocation, 1989.

Bakker, Egbert J., and Ahuvia Kahane, ed. *Written Voices, Spoken Signs: Tradition, Performance, and the Epic Text*. Cambridge, Mass.: Harvard University Press, 1997.

Bernstein, Michael. *The Tale of the Tribe: Ezra Pound and the Modern Verse Epic*. Princeton: Princeton University Press, 1980.

Bowra, C.M. *From Virgil to Milton*. London: Macmillan, 1945.

Burrow, Colin. *Epic Romance: Homer to Milton*. Oxford: Oxford University Press, 1993.

Clark, John. *History of Epic Poetry*. New York: Haskell House, 1973.

Cook, Patrick J. *Milton, Spenser and the Epic Tradition*. Brookfield, VT: Scolar Press, 1996.

Downes, Jeremy M. *Recursive Desire: Rereading Epic Tradition*. Tuscaloosa: University of Alabama Press, 1997.

Dubois, Page. *History, Rhetorical Description and the Epic: From Homer to Spenser*. Cambridge: D.S. Brewer, 1983.

Feeney, D.C. *The Gods in Epic: Poets and Critics of the Classical Tradition*. New York: Oxford UP, 1991.

Fichter, Andrew. *Poets Historical: Dynastic Epic in the Renaissance*. New Haven: Yale University Press, 1982.

Foley, John Miles. *Companion to Ancient Epic*. Malden: Blackwell, 2005.

Giamatti, A. Bartlett. *Earthly Paradise and the Renaissance Epic*. New York: W.W. Norton, 1989.

Hainsworth, J.B. *The Idea of Epic*. Berkley: University of California Press, 1991.

Highet, G. *The Classical Tradition*. Oxford: Clarendon Press, 1949.

Kates, Judith A. *Tasso and Milton: The Problem of Christian Epic*. Lewisburg: Bucknell University Press, 1983.

Levy, Gertrude Rachel. *The Sword from the Rock: An Investigation into the Origins of Epic Literature and the Development of the Hero*. Westport: Greenwood Press, 1976.

Lord, Albert B., edited by Mitchell and Nagy. *The Singer of Tales* 2nd ed. Cambridge, Mass.: Harvard University Press, 2000.

MacDonald, Ronald R. *The Burial-Places of Memory: Epic Underworlds in Vergil, Dante, and Milton.* Amherst: University of Massachusetts Press, 1987.

Martindale, Charles. *John Milton and the Transformation of Ancient Epic.* Totowa: Barnes & Nobel Books, 1986.

McWilliams, John P., Jr. *The American Epic: Transforming a Genre, 1770-1860.* New York: Cambridge University Press, 1989.

Mori, Masaki. *Epic Grandeur: Toward a Comparative Poetics of the Epic.* Albany: SUNY Press, 1997.

Murrin, Michael. *The Allegorical Epic: Essays in Its Rise and Decline.* Chicago: University of Chicago Press, 1980.

Newman, John Kevin. *The Classical Epic Tradition.* Madison: The University of Wisconsin Press, 2003.

Oberhelman, Steven M., Van Kelly, and Richard J. Golsan, eds. *Epic and Epoch: Essays on the Interpretation and History of a Genre.* Lubbock: Texas Tech University Press, 1994.

Pope, Nancy. *National History in the Heroic Poem: A Comparison of the Aeneid and the Faerie Queene.* Taylor & Francis, 1990.

Quint, David. *Epic and Empire: Politics and Generic Form from Virgil to Milton.* Princeton: Princeton University Press, 1993.

Suzuki, Mihoko. *Metamorphoses of Helen: Authority, Difference, and the Epic.* Ithaca: Cornell University Press, 1989.

Tasso, Torquato. *Discourses on the Heroic Poem.* Oxford: Clarendon Press, 1973.

Treip, Mindele Anne. *Allegorical Poetics & the Epic: The Renaissance Tradition to Paradise Lost.* Lexington, KY: University Press of Kentucky, 1994.

Van Nortwick, Charles. *Somewhere I Have Never Travelled: The Second Self and the Hero's Journey in Ancient Epic.* New York: Oxford University Press, 1992.

Vries, Jan de, B.J. Timmer (trans.) *Heroic Song and Heroic Legend.* New York: Arno Press, 1978.

Walker, Jeffrey. *Bardic Ethos and the American Epic Poem: Whitman, Pound, Crane, Williams, Olson.* Baton Rouge: Louisiana State University Press, 1989.

Webber, Joan. *Milton and His Epic Tradition.* Seattle: University of Washington Press, 1979.

Wilkie, Brian. *Romantic Poets and Epic Tradition*. Madison: The University of Wisconsin Press, 1965.

Wofford, Susanne Lindgren. *The Choice of Achilles: The Ideology og Figure in the Epic*. Stanford: Stanford University Press, 1992.

Wolff, Hope Nash. *A Study in the Narrative Structure of Three Epic Poems: Gilgamesh, the Odyssey, Beowulf*. Taylor & Francis, 1987.

Yu, Anthony C., ed. *Parnassus Revisited: Modern Critical Essays on the Epic Tradition*. Chicago: American Library Association, 1973.

Zlatar, Zdenko. *The Epic Circle: Allegoresis and the Western Epic Tradition from Homer to Tasso*. Lewiston, NY: E. Mellen Press, 1997.

# Index

# About the Author

HAROLD BLOOM is Sterling Professor of the Humanities at Yale University. He is the author of over 20 books, including *Shelley's Mythmaking* (1959), *The Visionary Company* (1961), *Blake's Apocalypse* (1963), *Yeats* (1970), *A Map of Misreading* (1975), *Kabbalah and Criticism* (1975), *Agon: Toward a Theory of Revisionism* (1982), *The American Religion* (1992), *The Western Canon* (1994), and *Omens of Millennium: The Gnosis of Angels, Dreams, and Resurrection* (1996). *The Anxiety of Influence* (1973) sets forth Professor Bloom's provocative theory of the literary relationships between the great writers and their predecessors. His most recent books include *Shakespeare: The Invention of the Human* (1998), a 1998 National Book Award finalist, *How to Read and Why* (2000), *Genius: A Mosaic of One Hundred Exemplary Creative Minds* (2002), *Hamlet: Poem Unlimited* (2003), and *Where Shall Wisdom be Found* (2004). In 1999, Professor Bloom received the prestigious American Academy of Arts and Letters Gold Medal for Criticism, and in 2002 he received the Catalonia International Prize.